NINE FACES OF GOD

PETER HANNAN SJ

Nine Faces of God

A JOURNEY OF FAITH

THE COLUMBA PRESS
1992

First edition, 1992, published by
THE COLUMBA PRESS
93 The Rise, Mount Merrion, Blackrock, Co Dublin
Reprinted 1993

Cover by Bill Bolger
Origination by The Columba Press
Printed in Ireland by
The Leinster Leader, Naas
ISBN 1 85607 059 X

The author and publisher gratefully acknowledge the permission of the following to use their copyright material: *In Memory of My Mother* by Patrick Kavanagh is copyright Peter Kavanagh, New York and The Goldsmith Press, Newbridge, Co Kildare, 1984; Evangeline Patterson for *And that will be heaven*; Transworld Publrs Ltd for the quotation from *The Velveteen Rabbit* by Margery Williams.

If we have inadvertantly used other copyright material we invite the copyright-holders to contact the publishers so that appropriate changes can be made in future editions.

Unattributed poems are by the author.

Author's Note:
I wish to acknowledge my gratitude to Philip Harnett SJ for his encouragement during the years I have been working on this book. I owe an immense debt of gratitude to Genevieve Tobin who has been over every line of this book many times. She has been my most challenging critic as well as a constant source of inspiration and encouragement.

Biblical Quotations
Quotations from scripture are taken from the RSV, © Division of Christian Education of the National Council of Churches in the United States of America. Occasional alternatives marked [P] are from *The New Testament in Modern English* by J B Philips (Geoffrey Blew, London, 1960), and those marked [JB] are from *The Jerusalem Bible* (DLT, London).

Contents

I dedicate this book to the people,
like my parents, my family and my friends,
who have given me an impression
of what these nine faces of God are like.
Their love has inspired this book
and kept me going during the writing of it.

PART I

Believe the Good News

CHAPTER 1

Why Nine Faces?

Over twenty-five years of reading the Bible every day, I became fascinated by the range of aspects of the love of God which I found presented there. I began to collect passages which revealed these different aspects of love, and, in time, I found that nine separate aspects or 'faces of God' had emerged clearly and distinctly.

Some time later, I became interested in the Enneagram. This is a very perceptive body of traditional wisdom, based on the theory that there are nine kinds of people. It holds that we are made in God's image, and that each one of us reflects one of nine aspects or 'faces' of God.

I was intrigued by the fact that these nine faces correspond in a very enlightening way with those I had found in the Bible. I say this was enlightening because the Enneagram's description of the nine kinds of people helped me to draw a detailed picture of the nine faces of the one in whose image we are made.

Here is a brief description of each of the Faces:

1) God is intent on our being fully alive, and brings this about through accepting and affirming, rather than by correcting us. God gives Good News, rather than 'good advice'.

2) The love of God, which brings us alive, is called loving kindness in the Bible. It is symbolised by the male and female arms that embrace the prodigal son. It has all the affection of a mother's love, as well as of a father's.

3) God's is a provident or practical love, which works ceaselessly to bring to full flower his plan that we would live life fully.

4) God's love is very personal, calling the unique person in each of us by name, along a road peculiar to each one of us.

5) God reveals himself completely as love for each of us. The intimate knowledge of being loved in this way is the ultimate wisdom.

6) God's is a faithful love that makes an everlasting covenant with us, no matter how unfaithful we may be to him.

7) God is supremely happy and wants to share this happiness with us in his plan for our peace.

8) God loves us wholeheartedly, with the passion of one in love, and wants to be loved by us in the same way.

9) God loves us as friends with whom he wishes to share not only all he has, but himself. To do this he initiates and maintains a dialogue in which he speaks with each person 'face to face as with a friend'.

Appendix I (page 301) gives a more detailed account of the Divine Ideas in the Enneagram. Even though these Divine Ideas have provided valuable information for depicting the features of these faces, the word of God is their main source.

CHAPTER 2

Why the Nine Faces are important

The basic reason why the Nine Faces are important is that they draw out the meaning of the Good News in an attractive way. It is belief in this Good News that opens up the fullness of life which Jesus comes to give us. The many features of these Nine Faces of God reveal the rich variety of ways in which we are loved by God. It is this love that is the most creative force in our lives. It is what makes and sustains us.

It is Care that makes and sustains us
Care was crossing a river one day when she took some soft mud and shaped it into a human being. She wanted to give what she had made her own name but Earth also laid claim to this right because it was of her that the human being was formed. Care then asked Jupiter, who was passing by, to give her creation a spirit. This he gladly agreed to do but then he too wanted it called after him.

They decided to ask Saturn to be arbiter and he gave the following decision which seemed a wise one. Jupiter had given it spirit, so he would receive that back when death came. Since it was of earth or humus that it was formed, it would be called a human being. However, since Care had formed this human being, it would remain in her keeping to continue to form and sustain it.

If we are to accept the truth which this story illustrates, we will have to face a revolutionary change. Whereas most of us were taught that *being loving* is the essential of Christian living, the emphasis in the Bible is on our *being loved*. The image of God in us is primarily a potential to take in the love of God. It is from taking in love that the energy to give out love must come.

> God is all bounty while we are all need.
> (St Augustine)

This focusing of our attention on being loved, rather than on being loving, will be revolutionary for most people. Tony de Mello said that when he was leaving his noviceship, his Novice Master said to him, 'Tony, remember that the revolution will take place in your life when you realise that it is not so much your love for God that matters as the fact that God loves you.'

Our ability to accept fully the love of God, which formed us and sustains us, is very tied up with our own image of ourselves. We are easily dominated by the voice of our own insignificance. This is the tragic illusion that results when a small, dark fraction of our lives becomes the whole picture we see of ourselves. Seeing things in this way makes it very difficult for us to accept a vision of God as love and of ourselves as lovable in his eyes. As a result, our acceptance of the essential invitation of Christ, to believe the Good News of God's love and providence, is very limited.

> Cyrano de Bergerac was a man with an unusually large nose and this became the dominant feature of the way he saw himself. So he could not accept the love of Roxane, that he craved, because of this slight physical defect of an otherwise very noble person. At the end of the story, when Roxane has developed a profound love for him, one feels like saying, 'Would you forget about your nose and accept her love, and all the life and happiness that will bring you.' Sadly, he cannot believe in her love and so he dies, a very lonely and unhappy man.

This story poses the vital question about who we believe. Do we believe the people like Roxane in our life, or do we find the other voice Cyrano listened to more credible?

The emergence of a true self-image

Those who, like Roxane, believe in us, are what we might call significant people. They are the people, like our parents, friends and especially God, who play a very creative role in our lives. They do this by accepting our weakness and waywardness, seeing beyond these to all the good in us. This good they affirm by appreciating all that we are and encouraging all that we may become. They ask us to believe in their love for us and to believe in ourselves as loved and lovable. So significant people reflect back to us who we are and all that we mean to them. They put us in touch with a very positive image of ourselves and in this way make and sustain us in life.

There is a conviction among psychologists about the creative power of love. The modern philosopher Heidegger says:

People are constituted by care and maintained by her.

This conviction is central to the Bible and is expressed by Jesus in a variety of ways. For example, he says that what makes us fully alive is our belief in the Good News that we are loved by God and are the constant objects of his care. (Jn 5:24)

As well as making us fully alive, love is, in the view of the Bible, what makes us happy. In chapter 15 of John's gospel, after Jesus has told us that he loves us in exactly the same way as the Father has loved him, he goes on to say:

I have told you these things that my joy may be in you and that your happiness may be complete. (Jn 15:11)

It is our capacity to blind ourselves to this good news, and to the fullness of life and happiness it can generate in us, that caused Jesus to weep when he saw how this basic human tragedy affected people:

As he drew near and saw the city, he wept over it, saying, 'If you only knew the things that are for your peace. But now they are hid from your eyes.' (Lk 19:41-42)

The emergence of a false self-image

As well as the positive image of ourselves, which we pick up from the people in our lives who believe in us, there is also a false image, reflected back to us by others around us. This they do by loving us conditionally or even by failing to affirm us. By people saying to us, in effect, 'I love you if you do the right thing,' we are given to believe that our being lovable is dependent on our meeting the expectations of others. The love we receive becomes dependent on what we do and not on who we are. We can easily slip into the belief that all love must be earned and that it is not a gift.

However, the worth which we can earn is, in fact, very limited and very fragile. We can experience a lot of negative feelings when people fail to appreciate our attempts to earn this worth. These negative feelings can capture our attention and become pervasive. Then the 5% of ourselves that is bad becomes the 95% of what we see and creates a poor self image. This in turn limits or excludes our positive experience, the Good News that God asks us to accept. When this illusory vision becomes ingrained and dominant, as it tends to do, the tragedy of Cyrano becomes ours.

The way this tragedy develops is one way of understanding how we can be led down that road to 'destruction' that Jesus speaks about so graphically in his Parable of the Two Ways:

> Enter by the narrow gate, for broad is the way that leads to destruction, and many travel that way. The narrow gate and the hard way lead out into life, and only a few find it. (Mt 7:13-14)

CHAPTER 3

Believe the Good News

The story of Rapunzel has always intrigued me in the way it draws out the implications of the Parable of the Two Ways.

Rapunzel

There was a little girl called Rapunzel who was very beautiful. She was captured by a witch, who knew that if she wanted to hold on to the little girl, she had to convince her that she was ugly. If she knew she was beautiful, she would go off with one of the many young men who came to consult the witch. If on the other hand, she knew she was ugly, she would be afraid of being seen by them, and would therefore hide when they were around. So the witch gradually convinced Rapunzel that she was ugly and she hid for fear of being seen when anyone came to the witch's house.

One day when she was combing her hair in her room, she became conscious of someone looking at her through the window. Instinctively she looked up. It was then that she saw, in the eyes of the young man gazing at her through the window, that she was beautiful. Gradually, as she learned to believe this, her fear was replaced by joy. She set off on the long journey of freeing herself from the deadening influence of the witch in order to accept the life and happiness which the young man's love made available to her.

There are two voices influencing Rapunzel here, in the sense that they are reflecting back to her two visions of herself. These in turn cause two kinds of feeling. On the one hand, the witch gives her an impression of herself as ugly, so she feels fearful and as a result she hides when anyone comes to the house. The young man, on the other hand, reflects back to her the fact that she is beautiful. This vision of herself makes her feel happy and so she sets off on the journey into the new life which the young man's love opens up for her.

This story illustrates what Jesus is saying in the parable of the two ways. It puts in very forceful terms the need of being aware of who is leading us and what road we are being led along.

What is emphasised by the Rapunzel story is the central influence of the vision or image we have of ourselves. Being on the way to life, therefore, means basically believing in the image of ourselves which Jesus reflects back to us. Believing the witch's vision, on the other hand, is what leads to 'destruction'.

The way that leads to destruction

Certain questions arise from the Rapunzel story. For example, who plays the role of the witch in your life? How much of what the witch says to you do you accept as true, and how do you feel as a result? Is it, as it was for Rapunzel, an illusion, a distorted vision or false image of yourself that you live with?

It is strange how dominant this illusion can be – how, as the Book of Wisdom says, 'the consciousness of evil can throw good things into the shade.' (Wis 4:12)

> #### The Black Spot
> You might notice how a small black spot on a sheet of white paper can capture your eye. Even though it may occupy only 5% or less of the page, it can still dominate your attention.

Does an illustration like this help account for the poor self image most people have of themselves? Does the consciousness of having got angry during the day throw the 95% that was really good into the shade? If this view of ourselves gains a hold on us, is it not an example of how the witch's illusion makes us prisoners of the dark?

The solution to the problem is not to try and bury the dark side of life, but to seek freedom from its dominance. We can do this by seeing our life in perspective, by seeing the 5% that is bad against the background of the 95% that is good. We need to build up our sense of the white sheet of paper that symbolises all the ways we are loved, gifted and graced by God. Losing touch with this is disastrous. It is this lack of awareness of how deeply we are loved, that is truly 'the way that leads to destruction'.

What is essential for our peace and happiness is the sense of our worth which we find in Christ's eyes. He is the one symbolised by the young man in Rapunzel's life, reflecting back to us who we are for him. He makes visible the 'good news' of the Father's love, and our lovableness.

> Philip said, 'Lord, let us see the Father and then we shall be satisfied.' 'Have I been with you all this time, Philip,' said Jesus to him, 'and you still do not know me? To have seen me is to have seen the Father.' (Jn 14:8-9)

The basic invitation of Jesus in the gospel is that we would accept his vision of God, and of ourselves.

> It was after John's arrest that Jesus came into Galilee, proclaiming the gospel of God, saying, 'The time has come at last, the kingdom of God has arrived. You must change your hearts and minds and believe the good news.' (Mk 1:14-15)

These are the first words of Jesus in Mark's gospel. In his final discourse in John's gospel, he sees his revelation of this Good News of God's love as the main thrust of what he has been doing and what he will continue to do:

> I have made your name known to them and I will continue to make it known, so that the love you have for me may be in them and that I too may be in them. (Jn 17:26)

As is implied in the words, 'I will continue to make it known', it is the Spirit who will help us to know the full extent and depth of Jesus' love. Like a teacher he will lead us into it.

> The Holy Spirit whom the Father will send in my name, will be your teacher and will bring to your mind all I have said to you. (Jn 14:26)

This vision of God which Jesus and his Spirit reveal to us, like the one Rapunzel saw in the young man's eyes, is what makes us feel alive and happy.

> These things I have spoken to you, that my joy may be in you, and that your joy may be complete. (Jn 15:11)

Repent and believe the gospel

The vocation of the Christian to 'repent and believe the gospel' can be seen clearly in the light of the Rapunzel story. In its terms, we are being asked to let go of the witch's illusion and to accept the way God sees us. This Good News we are called to believe in, is that God is loving and that we are loved, in a rich variety of ways.

The 'repentance' or the change of mind and heart that this belief calls for, is no easy task. The illusions we need to let go of are so ingrained that we find it very difficult to part with them. They are like the crab's shell, and we have to 'repent of' or shed them if we are to grow:

The Crab's Shell

There is a certain kind of crab which lives in a shell, but not the same shell for life. As the crab grows it must discard the old shell which it has outgrown or it will die. Changing shells is not easy, for the crab becomes very vulnerable until the new one has grown. When the crab's shell becomes too thick, too tough to crack open, the crab cannot grow any more. That is when it dies.

Our shells are not as visible as the crab's, but they are as real. Ours are formed by years of habit, shells developed to protect us against others, shells that are shaped by the roles we play as parents or children, as employer or employee. Life is all the time inviting us to change our shell, to risk being vulnerable when, in order to grow, we have to shed one. The alternative is that we hold on to our shell until it becomes so thick that we cannot crack it or grow within it. We may be dead long before we die.

The crab-shells which we must shed are the false ideas about love, about God and about ourselves that we owe to the witch's influence. These ideas have deep roots in us and are very real for us. If God reveals something about himself or ourselves that is different from these ingrained ideas, we are likely to resist or reject it.

CHAPTER 4

The Journey of Faith

A way of understanding this basic call to 'repent and believe' is in terms of a journey. This is like the Exodus in which God's people were called out of Egypt, the land of slavery, to travel across the desert to the Promised Land. There they were to find the life and peace God planned for them. So, we will look at our journey of faith in terms of our call to 'repent' or to leave the land of slavery to illusion, in order to discover the life and happiness that belief in God's love opens up for us.

The journey we are looking at here centers on God's desire to reveal himself to us, and the power he gives us to know him. This makes possible an intimacy or union with God which is the object of God's self-disclosure and of all our journeying.

> Father, may they be one in us, as you are in me and I in you … may they be completely one that the world will realise that it was you who sent me and that I have loved them as much as you loved me. (Jn 17:21-23)

What we need for the journey

Spiritual writers from earliest times have insisted that the key requirement for this journey is *prayer* – an ability to listen and to respond honestly to what God reveals to us of his love. The central role of this dialogue in our journey is confirmed by the conviction of psychologists that any relationship will be as intimate or as good as the quality of the communication within it.

What you will be listening to in prayer is your *personal experience*, confirmed and expanded by both the *universal experience* which traditional wisdom makes available to us, and by the experience which we find in the *Bible*. You learn what to select from this vast store of experience by developing your capacity for *reflection*. This is a means of discerning who is leading you and where you are being led, whether along the way to life or along the way to destruction. All of these requirements for the journey presuppose, of course, that you develop a capacity to *make space*, in a very busy world, to reflect and pray.

We will now look at each of these requirements for the journey in more detail. However, you may like to get started with what is essential for the journey before delving any deeper into the theory. If so, you will find a simple outline in the last two pages of the book. You may use this to get you started and then refer back to this chapter for more information as you require it.

1) Making space for God

The first requirement for your journey is to make space in your life to 'know the gift of God.' (Jn 4:10) This may sound reasonably simple, but I know from experience that it may prove for many the most difficult stage of the journey.

We live in an atmosphere where the spiritual is seen as unreal or irrelevant. So, making time and space in these circumstances is a difficult task, but on it depends everything else that follows. You will need to establish prime time for solitude in your day and be able to hold on to this in a flexible way. A lot will have to do with getting others to accept that there is a time when you are not on call. You will first have to convince yourself, and then others, of the importance for you of this time alone.

> *Mother needs time apart*
> I remember hearing a lovely story of two young sons whose mother was beginning to make time to pray. They had spotted the difference her time apart had made to her good humour. So when they noticed her getting into bad form they would begin to suggest that she get together what they saw was part of the ritual of getting her back into good form. They had seen the effect of her time apart and felt that it was in everybody's best interest.

The atmosphere you set up in that place apart will be important. Such things as posture, whether you sit, kneel or walk, may seem trivial, but they are a vital part of involving the body as well as the spirit in prayer. It is important to engage your senses with things that are conducive to your central concern or you will easily

---

become distracted. You may be helped, for example, by an icon, a candle or music, as a point of focus.

When you have set up an atmosphere that is conducive to being apart, you then have to quieten and centre yourself. You can do this by focusing on something like the sounds you hear around you. This is an important exercise in its own right, for you need to take time to find the stillness and solitude essential for prayer.

When you have quietened yourself, become aware of the one for whom you have prepared this space. This is best done by choosing an image of God that appeals to you in your present circumstances. For example, you might be attracted by the verse, 'Be still and know that I am God.' You may find it helpful to stay with this image of God, inviting you into solitude, by means of a mantra. This is an important way of praying in its own right, quite apart from it being an essential preparation for the rest of your journey. When you are under stress, disturbed or very distracted it might occupy most of your time apart.

Two books that have helped me with this kind of time apart are *The Relaxation Response* by Dr Herbert Benson and *Sadhana* by Anthony de Mello. In the former, the importance for the whole of our lives of this kind of prayer is powerfully demonstrated. How we might go about quietening and centring ourselves is presented in the first fourteen exercises of de Mello's book.

2) *Exploring our own experience*

We tend to make use of a very small fraction of the rich treasury of experience that is available to each of us. This is very impoverishing. The insightful Carl Jung used the image of a small island in the middle of a great ocean to describe this impoverishment. For him, the island symbolises the very small amount of our experience we are aware of; the rest, represented by the ocean, stands for a vast range of experience that lies dormant in our subconscious. To live our whole life on this tiny island, unaware of the richness of our ocean, is a tragedy.

As you begin to look at any one of the Faces of God, you will need to spend time exploring your fund of experience connected with it. This is particularly true of two areas of this experience:

a) You need to attend to your experience of each of the kinds of love we are dealing with in these Nine Faces of God.

b) When you have looked at this kind of love and walked around in your experience of it, you will need to notice the resistance that it arouses. These resistances tend to hinder or prevent you seeing the Face of God you are contemplating. For example, if one of your parents was inclined to overwhelm or smother you with affection, it is a short step to transfer this experience on to God. When he tells you that he 'is constant in his affection for you,' you might not find this very attractive.

Each of the Nine Faces will be prefaced by a section entitled 'Getting in touch with your experience'. In it you will find three headings:

1) Under *The Key Experience*, there is a description of the kind of love peculiar to the Face you are looking at.

2) Under *Resistance*, there are suggestions as to various ways you might find yourself resisting this love.

3) Under *Arousing Dormant Experience*, there are a number of exercises you might do to bring the above two areas of your experience to the surface. It is presupposed that you have a lot of experience, but that much of this lies dormant and needs awakening.

After you have gone through this opening section of each of the Faces, it will be important to keep what you have learned in mind. Each time you pray you should return to the part of your experience that is most meaningful to you. Unless we let the Word of God speak to our experience when we pray, there is a danger that God will become irrelevant to our daily lives and the Good News unreal. If God's revelation of himself is to become real or relevant, it must become what we might call *felt* experience. There is a great danger that we settle for an abstract, intellectual knowledge and leave it at that. This will appeal to your head but will leave the rest of you untouched. It is essential that you be wholly and deeply touched, if you are to attain the intimacy with God that is the object of your journey. Nobody ever became drunk on an intellectual understanding of wine!

To make your own of God's love, you need to take the abstract idea of this love into your own personal experience of it. When you have aroused your felt experience, and walked around in it for a while, it will take on a lot of colour and feeling. You will know what the kind of love which you are contemplating tastes like. God needs to become flesh in this way if he is to win your whole heart and soul, your whole mind and strength. In the Anima Christi, it always startles me when I hear myself praying, 'Blood of Christ, inebriate me'; to pray to be so deeply moved seems so at odds with the intellectual way I was educated.

3) Universal experience: Traditional wisdom

Besides our personal experience there is another kind that is the common possession of the people. This is what is called *universal experience*. It is like a stream of traditional wisdom that runs through each person's life but has its source in the culture in which we grow up. The quiet flow of these deep waters does not catch our attention, with the result that we may live much of our lives out of touch with this stream of inner wisdom.

Each of us has to get in touch with this underground stream, and let the wisdom we find there influence the meaning and direction of our lives.

Most of us prefer to express what we think and feel by means of ideas. A much more basic way, which we learned to use when we were young, is through symbols. It is through symbols, such as stories, poetry, pictures and so on, that we get in touch with the traditional wisdom of the community in which we live. These stories, and other forms of symbolic expression, will give our personal experience colour and will get us more involved at an imaginative and emotional level. They will broaden and deepen our own personal experience.

At the beginning of each of these nine Faces there is a Main Symbol, often in the form of a story, which is central to appreciating the Face of God that we are contemplating. We should allow time to let this symbol speak to our personal experience.

When we begin contemplating these Faces of God, we may come with the belief that stories are an escape from reality. As such they may be okay for children, but not for adults who should be facing reality. It may take time, therefore, to really appreciate the wisdom embodied in them, the ways they comment profoundly on our everyday experience. It is worthwhile allowing time to let the stories fill out and enrich our experience.

We may notice in time that an image in a story or a line of a poem may speak volumes for us. The truth of the saying that a picture or a symbol is worth a thousand words may then come home to us. So, give stories, and the other forms of symbolic expression you find in these Faces of God, time to take root. Read them over and over, giving them a chance to express your own wisdom in a much broader and more colourful way. Learn to trust symbols as much as you do ideas.

4) The Biblical experience

Think of the way Jesus dealt with the two people on the road to Emmaus (Lk 24). Notice that he does not apply the Word to their situation immediately. Far from by-passing their experience, he draws their attention to it. He gets them to articulate their experience while sharing it with him. It is only then that Jesus, 'beginning with Moses and all the prophets, interpreted to them, in all the scriptures, the things concerning himself.' (Lk 24:27)

In brief, what Jesus is doing is challenging us to interpret all our experience in the light of the love which he expresses towards each of us. It is against the background of his love of us that we are invited to find the meaning of all our experience. This love is expressed in his word, and especially in its climax, the eucharist, in which he 'showed us the depth of his love.' (The Fourth Eucharistic Prayer)

The following parable symbolises the role Jesus wishes to play as the embodiment of the Word of God:

The Parable of the Good News

A woman was orphaned when she was very young. She spent her formative years in the care of people who gave her little attention or affection. As a defence against what she came to believe was a hostile world, she built a wall around herself.

When she went to school, and later into a job, people were attracted to her as she was very beautiful. They noticed, however, that they never got very close to her and so left her inside the fortress she had put up around herself.

There was one young man in her life, however, who refused to let her remain closed off. He persisted in trying to gain an entrance to her life. In time she gradually began to be influenced by his persistent love and by the resulting belief that it was safe for her to take down the wall behind which she hid. She began to dismantle this, brick by brick. At times she would become insecure and would stop taking down the wall or even begin to build it up again. In the end, however, his persistent attempts to win her affection won through. She began to accept that he believed in her and what this said to her about her worth and beauty. She opened up like a sunflower to the sun, she was set free and given new life through the influence of his love.

Piet Fransen, who wrote this story as an introduction to a book on Sanctifying Grace, comments that the young man may appear unreal in our harsh and hostile world. But he adds that with the advent of Christ the story becomes true for each of us. It is the story of our redemption.

In practical terms, what the Word will help you do is:

1) 'Change your mind and heart ...'

On the road to Emmaus, Jesus confronts the two people with how far from reality is their way of seeing their experience. He says, 'O foolish men and slow of heart to believe all that the prophets have spoken.'(Lk 24:25) The basic reality we are all confronted with is God's all-pervasive love and providence.

We have to be aware that we tend to confine God within the limits of our own weak, human love. It is as if we have a small box into which all our experience must fit, or be excluded.

> In the beginning God made us in his image,
> and ever since we have been making him in ours.

The Word will confront us with 'repenting' or changing our minds and hearts. We will be invited to let go of the wrong ways we have of seeing God and the negative feelings that result. This will involve letting the very confined area of our little box be remoulded according to the dimensions of God's everlasting and unlimited love. If we surrender to him in this way, he will be able to renew our minds and hearts as he wants to.

Don't let the world around you confine you to its own mould, but let God transform your minds. (Rom 12:2)

2) '... And believe the Good News.'

While all our human experience is of a kind of love that is limited, yet we have in it a very valuable opening to the love God has for us.

As an example of how human love is the best avenue to the divine, we might take the passage in Jeremiah 31:3. There God says, 'I have loved you with an everlasting love and my affection for you endures.' Now, we can come to this cold or warm. If we come cold, we approach it without drawing on our human experience of a love that is affectionate. If, however, we come to it with our rich experience of someone who has shown us deep affection, we will know in our bones what God is saying to us.

We need to keep letting each piece of God's word address our experience. In practice we have to read the Word, pausing where something strikes us, not to think about it or to work out its implications, but to listen to its revelation of God and to let this expand and deepen our experience of human love.

5) Prayer: Listening

When some word or phrase of Scripture strikes us we should pause and listen to it. We should treat what God draws our attention to, as a fact about his love to be absorbed, rather than as an idea to be thought about. A way of doing this is to repeat the word or phrase, mantra-like, to let what it says about God sink in. By staying with what God opens up for us in this way, we will be able to let it move down from our heads into our hearts. We can thus let it influence, not just the way we see God, but also the way we feel about him. In this way we answer Jesus' call to repentance – to change our minds and hearts in order to believe his revelation of himself.

We have a tendency to think about scripture, working out its meaning and implications. Instead of listening to God's revelation of himself, we can easily gravitate towards thinking about ourselves and what we should or should not be doing. It is important to ask ourselves what we end up with when we are praying with the Word, to see whether it is Good News or 'good advice'.

For example, when we hear God saying to us, in Jeremiah 31, that he is constant in his affection for us, what do we do? We can easily turn our attention to how fragile our own affection is, or how undeserving we are of this kind of love. It is easy to move from a sense of how far we fall below standard to thinking about how we might improve. So we end up getting 'good advice'. The Good News we should be listening to is the revelation of his love which God wishes to make to each of us.

Is God speaking to me or to us?

We will probably notice how we prefer God's love to be said, as it is in the Prophets, to the people of God, rather than to each of us personally.

In the Bible story there is a growth in the way people see God. This reflects the stages each person must pass through in coming to know God 'face to face as a friend.'(Ex 33:11)

1) We may see him as a rewarder and a punisher, giving us advice and warning us of the consequences of not following it.

2) God may also be seen as one who loves his people, but relates with each of us as part of a crowd. Relating with us face to face, is contrary to how transcendent he is.

3) From the announcement of the New Covenant in Jeremiah, it is clear that God wants to make himself known 'to the least no less than the greatest.'(Jr 31:34) Each of us is now in the position Moses was in when God spoke to him 'face to face as a person does with a friend.' (Ex 33:11)

We have to move towards letting his love be revealed to us personally as this is clearly God's wish. To help bring this about, we might use the device of inserting our own name into every piece of scripture we pray with. However we manage it, we must let God speak to us face to face, as to a friend.

Tasting a little

If we really want to digest what God reveals to us when we are listening in prayer, we have to be willing to linger with it. Repeating a little, in order to let it sink in, will have to become a feature of the way we pray. The quest for novelty and the fear of being bored may make it difficult for us to remain in the one place for long.

God will open up areas of light, attraction and desire, and it is important that we dwell with these, giving him a chance to expand and deepen them. So if some aspect of a piece of scripture is opened up for you, stay there and mine it. Muddy waters left stand, become clear.

> It is not a multiplicity of ideas that will satisfy the spirit but to taste a little interiorly. (St Ignatius Loyola)

6) Prayer: Responding honestly

If we give ourselves time to accept anyone's love, it is going to stir up a lot of strong feeling in us. Try to remember something loving that was said or done to you, and then notice the feelings that the memory arouses. You will probably have difficulty doing this, as you may not be used to dwelling with the feelings it will arouse. You may have been given the impression that feelings don't count, and so they may lie dormant, not noticed, named or shared. This impoverishes any relationship, but especially that which the dialogue of prayer seeks to build up.

Positive and negative feelings

When someone says, 'I love you' or 'I think you are doing a marvellous job,' we have two reactions. We will find very positive feelings saying something like, 'I love to hear what you are telling me, so keep it coming.' We may also notice that we resist what is said, or reject it as unreal, as too good to be true. It is important that we be honest with God about how we feel. This is the price of intimacy. In prayer, therefore, we have to:

- notice how we react when we listen to God revealing his love,
- put words on our positive as well as our negative reactions,
- share these with God.

In our effort to share our feelings with God, it is not necessary to express them in any but the simplest of ways. When we have strong feeling we want to express to someone, we often rehearse carefully how we will say it; we may not get another chance. We feel the need to word it well and maybe in a variety of ways. What we say to God should have none of this complexity. It would benefit from being said over and over again in the simplest of ways. So, while it is important to notice our feelings and to put words on them in order to share with God how we really feel, the simpler and the more often we say them to him the better.

Our positive reaction

We tend to be evasive when strong love or appreciation comes our way. We ought to welcome it. John Powell says somewhere that we should react to praise with words like, 'Would you like to say that again?' There is something in our upbringing that finds this a strange thing to say, whereas it expresses a very healthy reaction. We need all the affirmation we can get to sustain us on the way.

Sharing our positive reaction to the love which God reveals for us is an essential part of praying. Through it we intensify the experience of what he says and deepen very healthy feelings. Through noticing, naming and sharing positive feelings, we also deepen them, worship God and share ourselves with him

Our negative reactions

A large part of us will resist God's love and appreciation for a variety of reasons. Maybe we don't feel we have earned such love, and that in this world we don't get what we have not earned. We may also think that when we approach God he will demand changes in our lives, so we may feel anxious or fearful.

If we are not to be dominated by these feelings, we have to express them. By doing this, we gain a certain freedom from our relationship being ruled by them. In order to share them, however, we have to become aware of, and put words on them.

If we don't seek freedom from being dominated by our negative feelings, what resists God's love will remain in place and cause unbelief. This resistance cuts down, like a filter, the light of God's life-giving love. It is an essential part of prayer to notice negative feelings as resisting God's love, and then to put words on them in order to share them with God.

The Emmaus Road Walk

When you find strong negative feelings persisting in your experience you need to go on an Emmaus road walk with Jesus.

First of all, quieten yourself and enter the presence of one who walks with you as a friend: 'I have called you friends.' (Jn 15:15) Jesus asks you to share with him what is troubling you. He wants to share your passion, just as you share his. So in response to this invitation, you tell him about the way you see what is happening to you and how you feel. It would help this a lot if, before you began this exercise, you had already spent time becoming aware of, and putting words on what is troubling you.

You next ask Jesus how he feels about you. In reply, let him accept you where you are. He will remind you that 'he is familiar with all your weakness as he has been tempted in every way that you have been.' (Heb 4:15) Let him say to you, 'I know exactly how you feel, for I have been down that road myself.' He may ask you whether you accept his acceptance and whether you can forgive yourself.

A difficult final stage of this walk will also be the most healing one. This is to let Jesus tell you some of the things he appreciates about you, especially in the area of your life where you now find yourself weak. Let him tell you that he loves you most where you love yourself least. He might say, 'If someone did for you half of what you have done for me, would you not appreciate it? Would you let me have a bigger heart than you have?'

In brief, the stages of this exercise are:

> You meet Jesus as a friend.
> He invites you to share what troubles you.
> You ask him how he feels about you, and accept his acceptance.
> You let him appreciate how good you are in this area of your life where you feel weak.

7) Reflection on our experience

The purpose of reflection is to find God, his love and providence in all our experience. Through it we seek to become sensitive and responsive to the ways God is unfolding his plan for our peace. (Jer 29:11) By means of reflection we may hope to re-establish an awareness of God's presence in every area of life, to find God in all things. What this comes down to in practice, is that we become skilled at doing three things, first of all with prayer, and then with our daily experience:

a) The first of these is to notice the signs of God's guidance in the way he enlightens and attracts you, even in the most ordinary circumstances. God will be always opening up circles of light and desire or inviting you to extend or deepen ones he has already opened up. So when you have finished prayer, get into the habit of noting down in a prayer log what struck you, or where you were drawn to spend time.

b) The second step is to discern or understand the meaning of what you have noticed – the significance of these signs of God's guidance. This is the central task of reflection and one which people find very difficult. Its aim is to become more conscious of how God is present, revealing his love and providence in the most ordinary places. So, after you have noticed something that has moved you in your prayer, try to see God as enlightening and attracting you in this way to 'feel God's finger and find him.'(Hopkins) If you do not do this, you may continue to think of prayer as something you do for God, rather than what God is doing in you. God must be allowed to be the main agent in your prayer.

c) What you have done so far calls for the third step. Here you seek to respond by making your own of what God has revealed to you. God will unfold his love for you bit by bit, provided you work at making your own of what he reveals. Therefore, make sure to stay with and repeat what God has opened up for you in a period of prayer, in order to assimilate it.

Let one period of prayer direct the next. Take what God has opened up for you in one period of prayer into the next, in order to extend and deepen your experience of it. Don't be in any hurry to move on, for God can reveal his love for you only if you are willing to listen and make your own of what he reveals to you.

If you are faithful in regularly following these three steps of reflection, a body of interior knowledge and of desire will build up in you. If, through reflection, you listen and respond to this interior knowledge, God will be able to unfold to you a vision of his love. He will also be able to lead you to live consistently with this vision, in the decisions you make and in the way you act on them.

'In Fire by night'

Besides listening to God guiding us 'by day', reflection also helps us to become aware of the influence of dark forces on us, and of how God guides us with 'the pillar of fire by night'. We are most likely to notice the influence of these dark forces in times of hardship. Such hard times can become either constructive or destructive, times of invitation or frustration.

Two men looked out through prison bars;
one saw only mud, the other the stars.

Life's hardships can be constructive, as they can refine our faith in God's love. When, for example, you experience times in prayer when nothing seems to be happening, you are questioned by this experience about what is going on. You are asked whether you believe that God is really with you in spite of appearances. Thus your faith can be refined or deepened by this experience. The shadow side of life can become 90% gold, as Carl Jung believed it could.

Life's hardships can also become destructive. This happens, when God's apparent absence from your prayer leads you to doubt his love and providence. These doubts can erode your faith and hope in his love, and your belief in yourself as loved and lovable. This is a very painful experience and causes a whole range of negative feelings such as anxiety, fear, guilt or anger.

So when you go through a dark patch in prayer or in your daily experience, you need to watch where it takes you, whether along the road to 'life', or along the road to 'destruction'. The intimate connection between how you see dark times and how you feel about them is very important for discerning who is leading you and where you are being led. Therefore, focus on how you feel, as this will tell you whether you are being guided by God or by the witch.

When you 'travel through the valley of darkness', the role of reflection is to:

1) Notice how you are feeling – whether you are content or discontent, whether you are inclined to light a candle or curse the darkness.

2) Try to discern what your feelings are saying about how you see things. Feeling bad about the situation will indicate that you don't see what is happening as constructive. So in difficult times in prayer, you might ask yourself if you are being invited to face the reality of your own poverty in not being in complete control when you pray. Your feelings might be saying that you see the situation as a frustration of your plans for this period of prayer.

3) Respond by spending time sharing how you feel in the way

described above. You could use the model of the Emmaus Road Walk.

Conclusion

In conclusion, then, we have been reflecting on the journey we are invited on, to answer Jesus' call to repent and believe the gospel. We have examined what we require for our journey of faith, and we have seen how God is constantly leading us on this journey by enlightening and attracting us.

How effective God is going to be will depend on our willingness to be sensitive and responsive to his 'still small voice' constantly guiding us at each stage of our journey. The effectiveness of God's guidance will also depend on our willingness to become aware of, and master, what in us is blocking this revelation. This awareness will help to free us from what resists God's love.

The journey of faith is a long and difficult one, but each step along it will mean a growth in that fullness of life and happiness for which God has made us and into which he will be constantly guiding us.

> Do not be in dread or afraid of them. The Lord your God who goes before you will himself fight for you, just as he did for you in Egypt before your eyes, and in the wilderness, where you have seen how the Lord your God bore you, as a man bears his son, in all the ways that you went until you came to this place. Yet in spite of this word you did not believe the Lord your God, who went before you in the way to seek you out a place to pitch your tent, in fire by night, to show you by what way you should go, and in the cloud by day. (Dt 1:29-33)

PART II

The Nine Faces of God

Approaching the Nine Faces

The outline of each Face

The way we will approach contemplating these Nine Faces can be compared to painting a portrait. We sketch an outline of the face first of all, trying to capture the main impression we form of the subject's face. It is only when we are satisfied with this that we move ahead to concentrate on the main features, filling them in one by one. We have to contemplate each feature until we have captured what is distinctive about it in the face we wish to portray.

We will begin contemplating each of these Nine Faces of God's love by drawing our initial sketch. For this, we will call on our personal experience of the kind of love that is distinctive of each Face. To this we will add what the main symbol of the Face has to say to our experience.

Filling in the Features

Against the background of this initial sketch, we will begin to paint in the features one by one. You will notice that the rest of the material on each face is laid out as a series of features of the kind of love distinctive of the particular Face. Each of these features will be looked at mainly in the light of our biblical experience, the Word of God. A lot of pieces of scripture are offered since different pieces will appeal to different people's needs and tastes.

Even though the Word of God will be what reveals each feature most clearly, we will be adding in fresh personal experience and broadening this out with stories, poems, etc. We will, therefore, be looking at each feature in the light of an accumulation of experience which we bring to it, and we will constantly be adding to this as we go along.

To help sharpen our focus on each feature, there will be a short summary of it and some questions for reflection at the end of each.

A personal revelation

Running parallel to our efforts to arouse the full extent of our experience will be prayer and reflection. Through these we will be trying to appropriate what is central to our experience as we go along.

We will make our own of our experience by *listening* to God as he reveals himself to us personally. We will then have to overcome the *resistance* which his self-disclosure to us is bound to arouse. It is through reflection that we become aware of what God wants us to *listen and respond* to in prayer.

THE FIRST FACE OF GOD

A life-giving God

The Key Experience:
Affirmation
Resistance:
A demanding, critical God, lacking affection
The Main Symbol:
The Master Craftsman

What is distinctive about the love of this first Face of God is that it is so creative, so life-giving. It manifests God's concern that we would have the fullness of life. We see in this Face the serenity of one who accepts us where we are. God can weave into his tapestry of grace all our weaknesses and waywardness and even make these a feature of the work of art which we are. What is most life-giving about this Face is its capacity to make and sustain us through affirmation. In this way all the good that is in us is fully appreciated and all our initiatives to realise our deepest dreams are encouraged. Because of God's desire to remould us, to make us ever anew, he is compared to the potter. He is also compared to a refiner and a teacher because of his creative efforts to bring the best out of us.

THE FIRST FACE OF GOD 39

1. The tapestry is his work of art, not our achievement
Who we are is God's gift, not our achievement. If this gift, grace, or good news is really appreciated and owned, it brings us life and happiness.

2. Realising our inbuilt dream of being fully alive
The dream built into us, like that in the acorn, seeks maturity, or to realise its full potential. In this sense we are called to be holy or perfect. We need to stress the fact that God sees much of this already realised in us.

3. Accepting and affirming to help us to grow
God helps us grow to maturity by accepting and affirming us. He accepts the weak and wayward side of each of us with serenity, as well as appreciating the great good that is already there. This is very different from the critical or demanding God we might find ourselves living with, if we were perfectly honest with ourselves.

4. The tapestry of grace as the fruit of his life-giving love
Being accepted and affirmed by God is what gives us life. This is especially the effect of the love that is 'lifted up' on the Cross. This love alone has the power to draw our scattered lives into the tapestry of grace which God has planned.

5. The potter, remoudling our minds and hearts
The price we have to pay for God's life-giving love to be effective, is that we would accept it. This involves 'repenting' or letting go of our illusions, the ways we make God in our own image. It also

involves a lot of hard work trying to let the true image of God, the vision of himself which he puts before us in his Word, influence us. This work of 'repenting and believing' is one which God seeks to facilitate as the potter and the refiner.

6. *The teacher seeking to realise our dream*
God guides us, like a teacher, to realise the rich potential of the deep dream he has built into each of us. He does this by enlightening and attracting us, not just in the peak times but also in the valley periods.

7. *Living in the love he has for Jesus*
We see in this Face of God one who leads us into the life he shares with Jesus and their Spirit. We are each the focus of the love he has for Jesus and are invited into the intimacy they delight in.

There is a principle I learned as a teacher which is true of people at any stage of life. It is that praise or affirmation enlivens pupils and that too much correction deadens them. Unfortunately, the way we have thought to promote growth in people has been largely through pointing out where they might improve. This has had a profound effect on the way we see God and ourselves; God becomes the Critical Eye and we experience ourselves as always falling below his standards. We tend to hear not so much good news as good advice.

Resistance

The resistances that we are likely to notice here, may be influenced by an experience of demanding parents. They may, with the best of intentions, have been critical of us if we did not meet their high expectations or standards; never quite satisfied with us as we were. Again, those who have given us our strongest impression of who God is, may have been lacking in affection. We may have therefore grown up with an image of God who was lacking in affection or was cold and remote.

Arousing dormant experience

Getting in touch with some of the following experiences may help you to see more clearly this Face of God and also to discover what is blocking you seeing it clearly:

1) Begin by entering your inner room and there quieten and centre yourself. Then become aware of God present 'in that secret place.'(Mt 6:6)

2) While sitting quietly in your inner room, become aware of all that is represented of your story by the pictures around its walls.

Then turn your attention to the tapestry of your life that occupies the centre of the room. Become aware of and admire the marvellous range of colours of which it is woven, the bright ones, as well as the darker shades. Notice how these dark colours act as a foil for the veins of silver and gold that reflect the richness of your story. After you have dwelt with this, say what it arouses in you, and then listen to what God says to you in reply.

3) You might feel that you want to point out to God that the tapestry does not seem to reflect all the mistakes you have made in your life. In reply God invites you to believe that 'he works all things together onto good' for you.(Rom 8:28)

The Main Symbol:
The Master Craftsman

The tapestry maker weaves his artwork on a piece of gauze stretched across the centre of a room. He is on one side of this while on the other are a number of small boys, each with his own colour of thread from which the tapestry is woven. The tapestry maker indicates where he requires the particular colour he wants to be pushed through the gauze, and the little boy with that colour follows his instruction. But from time to time one of the boys loses concentration and pushes through the wrong colour or not at the place indicated. It is very difficult to undo this mistake but the master craftsman, being so skilled, can incorporate it into his plan and even make it a feature of the tapestry.

*

Because of our good Lord's tender love to all those who will be saved, he quickly comforts them saying. 'The cause of all this pain is sin. But all shall be well, and all shall be well, and all manner of things shall be well.' These words were said so kindly and without a hint of blame to me or to any who shall be saved. So how unjust it would be for me to blame God for allowing my sin when he does not blame me for falling into it. (Julian of Norwich)

FEATURE 1

The tapestry is God's work of art, not our achievement

Most of us have been brought up to believe that the way to bring the best out of people is to set them certain standards of perfection or excellence. We tend as a result to believe that growth is largely the result of our own effort or striving. This may be true with regard to the job we do each day, where we are very much in control. In the area of the spirit, however, we have not the same kind of control, because growth here is not so much something we bring about, as what God effects in us. It is less what we do for God than what he does in us – a tapestry he is weaving in our lives.

The belief that the Christian life consists in a gift of God rather than something we achieve, is one that Paul finds it necessary to constantly return to in his letters:

> For by grace you have been saved through faith; and this is not your own doing; it is the gift of God, not because of works, lest any man should boast. For we are his workman-ship. [We are God's work of art.(JB)] (Eph 2:8-10)

> ... for God is at work in you, both to will and to work for his good pleasure.' (Phil 2:13)

God's work of art

The tapestry God weaves out of all the circumstances of our lives is designed according to a plan he has for our welfare. This plan, which is also called his will, is that we would have a full life and all that we need to be happy.

> For I know the plans I have for you, says the Lord, plans for welfare and not for evil, to give you a future and a hope. Then you will call upon me and come and pray to me, and I will hear you. You will seek me and find me; when you seek me with all your heart, I will be found by you, says the Lord. (Jer 29:11-14)

The full life God wants for us is not something he tells us to achieve. It is what is called 'grace' or a gift of God that is already ours and that he invites us to come to know, appreciate and make our own of.

> If you only knew the gift of God and who it is that is saying to you, 'Give me a drink,' you would have asked him and he would have given you living water.' (Jn 4:10)

The more we accept this gift of God, the more we will experience the effect it had on the Samaritan woman. This gift of God is the reality we are asked to accept when Jesus calls us to change our minds and hearts and believe the Good News (the gospel).

> The time has come at last, the kingdom of God has arrived. You must change your minds and hearts and believe the good news. (Mk 1:15)

We are being asked to make our own of the fact that we are loved just as we are, warts and all. There is nothing that can make us more alive and happy.

The Prayer
Come, for I need thy love,
More than the flower the dew or grass the rain;
Come, gently as thy holy dove;
And let me in thy sight rejoice to live again.

Yes, thou wilt visit me;
Nor plant nor tree thine eye delights so well,
And, when from sin set free,
My spirit loves with thine in peace to dwell.
(Jones Very)

Summary

Who we are is God's gift, not our achievement. If this gift, grace, or Good News is really appreciated and owned, it brings us life and happiness.

Questions for reflection

1) Is the Christian life largely something you are doing for God, or is it more something God is doing in you?
2) Do you see God as one whose main interest is that you would be fully alive and happy?

Realising our in-built dream of being fully alive

We are on a journey to the fullness of life which God has in mind for us. Like an oak tree, for example, we are all the time moving on towards being fully grown, towards a realisation of all the potential in us. This urge to mature is like a dream built into the tree that keeps moving on towards fulfilment. We too want to fulfil the dream which God has for us that we should be fully alive – to fulfil the will of God that we should be holy or perfect.

> You shall be holy; for I the Lord your God am holy. (Lev 19:2)

> You, therefore, must be perfect, as your heavenly Father is perfect. (Mt 5:48)

It is helpful to see this perfection or holiness in terms of a dream which God has built into us, and whose potential he calls us to realise.

At any stage of life's journey, there is a certain amount of this perfection, or the realisation of our dream, which we have already arrived at. There is always, however, further to go. We have to keep a delicate balance between enjoying what we are and, at the same time, moving on towards what we may be. If we concentrate just on what is already achieved, we may fail to grow. If, on the other hand, we give all our attention to what we should be, we may cease to enjoy life as we ought to and become very restless and tense.

Jesus highlights these two aspects of being fully alive or perfect, in a very striking way, when he says that the least in the kingdom of God is greater than John the Baptist. Jesus also says that we have to battle our way into the fullness of this life which he wants for us.

> Believe me, among those born of woman there has risen no one greater than John the Baptist; yet he who is least in the kingdom of heaven is greater than he. From the days of John the Baptist until now, the kingdom of heaven has suffered violence, and men of violence take it by force. (Mt 11:11-12)

The tree that leans to one side needs to be tied in the opposite direction for some time, if it is to grow straight. Similarly we need to stress the way God delights in what we already are, in order to remedy our excessive emphasis on what we may become. The God who calls us to be perfect, calls us to realise that he has clothed us with his own splendour. His perfection is already ours, though its fullness has always to be striven for.

> Consider the lilies how they grow; they neither toil nor spin; yet I tell you, even Solomon in all his glory was not arrayed like one of these. But if God so clothes the grass which is alive in the field today and tomorrow is thrown into the oven, how much more will he clothe you, O people of little faith! (Lk 12:27-28)

It is easy for this call to perfection to belittle us, making us feel that we have fallen far short of the ideal set us. In fact it is mainly a call to become aware of 'the gift of God' that is already ours, to believe that the least in the kingdom of God is greater than John the Baptist.

> There is a great man who makes every man feel small.
> But the really great man is the one
> who makes every man feel great.
> (Chesterton)

God is the really great person who makes everyone feel great rather than one who belittles them with huge expectations.

Summary

The dream built into us, like that in the acorn, seeks maturity, or to realise its full potential. In this sense we are called to be holy or perfect. We need to stress the fact that God sees much of this already realised in us.

Questions for reflection

1) What comes to mind, when you reflect on your call to be holy or perfect? Is it an ideal you would own, or is it for other people to aim at this? What image do you have of God, who calls you to be perfect as he is?
2) Do you find that you stress perfection as something already realised in your life, or is it mainly something yet to be achieved? Which does God stress?

God gives us life by accepting and affirming us

If we hear in this call to be holy and perfect something very unrealistic, we may be living with a false image of God.

> *Up, Shep!*
> A man was collecting sheep from the side of a mountain with his dog. He kept urging it to go higher in search of the sheep. Every so often, the dog, finding the going hard, would stop and look back, but each time the man would urge it on to fresh heights and shout, 'Up, Shep!'

The image of God as one who uses correction, rather than affirmation, as a way of getting us to grow, can be a great block to coming close to him. If every time we come near God, we feel we are falling below standard, we will not really want to come closer to him. Due to the influence of this image of God as the 'critical eye,' part of us may feel uneasy when we read lines like these in the psalms:

> O Lord you have searched me and you know me...
> you discern my thoughts from afar...
> you are acquainted with all my ways...
> Whither shall I go from your Spirit?
> Or whither shall I flee from your presence?
> (Ps 139:17)

Even though we may know in our head that God does not look on us with a critical eye, we may still experience the effects of this image in the way we feel about him and in our instinctive reaction to his searching glance. There is a lifetime of conversion needed if we are to really let go of our 'false gods' and not make God in our image, or squeeze him into the mould of our all-too-human experience.

> Do not let the world mould your mind but let God transform you from within. (Rom 12:2)

We need to keep in touch with the principle that God is at least as good as the best of our friends.

A friend is one to whom one may pour out all the contents of one's heart, chaff and grain together, knowing that the gentlest of hands will take and sift it, keep what is worth keeping and, with a breath of kindness, blow the rest away.

It is when we recognise that God is a 'lover of life' that we can be corrected 'little by little' in a life-giving way.

For you love all things that exist, and loath nothing of all you have made, for you would not have made anything if you had hated it. How could anything have endured if you had not willed it? Or how could anything not called forth by you have been preserved? You spare all things, for they are yours, O Lord, lover of life. For your immortal spirit is in all things. Therefore, you correct little by little those who trespass, and you remind them of the things wherein they sin, that they may be freed from wickedness and put their trust in you, O Lord.' (Wis 11:24, 12:2)

Gazing more deeply into Wisdom's face
We may discover the mystery of love
An intimate knowledge born of love
Seen in eyes loving us wholly and deeply.
Perceptive of all that is good
And accepting of all that is weak;
A deep appreciation inspired by deep love
That relishes all we are and may become.

Gently loving

lovely-felicitous Providence
Finger of a tender of, O of a feathery delicacy.
(G M Hopkins)

The Father is one who accepts us as we are, as a mixture of good and bad. Like the tapestry maker, he works serenely with our mistakes and can weave them 'with a feathery delicacy' into the pattern of our tapestry.

Jesus portrays this face of his Father in the parable of the weeds and wheat where we are invited to see him as a God who lives serenely with the concoction of good and bad that we are:

The servants said to him, 'Then, do you want us to go and

gather them?' But he said, 'No, lest in gathering the weeds you root up the wheat along with them. Let them both grow together until the harvest.' (Mt 13:28-30)

The Lord is gracious and merciful,
slow to anger and abounding in steadfast love.
The Lord is good to all,
and his compassion is over all that he has made. (Ps 145:8-9)

God hates the sin and its destructiveness but loves the sinner. He is like a mother who has a special concern, a 'weakness' for her wayward son, even when he has given her every cause to abandon him.

But Zion said, 'The Lord has forsaken me, my Lord has forgotten me.' Can a woman forget her sucking child, that she should have no compassion on the son of her womb? Even these may forget, but I will not forget you. Behold, I have graven you on the palms of my hands. (Is 49:14-16)

A passage of Scripture like this makes us realise how strange are the ways in which God establishes his kingdom in our inconstant hearts.

It is no pushing of your authority, then
That makes you King of our inconstant hearts,
But a love we will always be struggling to tell.

... Even 'enemies'

We have a strong tendency to cut people out of our lives if they continually let us down. It is thus hard to believe that God continues to befriend the very imperfect or messy side of each of us and of our world. This sinful person is the 'enemy' inside and outside ourselves which God invites us to love in the accepting and tolerant way he does.

You have heard that it was said, 'You shall love your neighbour and hate your enemy.' But I say to you, Love your enemies and pray for those who persecute you, so that you may be the sons of your Father who is in heaven, for he makes his sun to rise on the evil and on the good, and sends his rain on the just and on the unjust ... You, therefore, must be perfect just as your heavenly Father is perfect. (Mt 5:43-48)

We see this gentle love of God, even towards enemies, being acted out in the story of Israel's infidelity to God, in chapter 9 of the book of Nehemiah.

> But our fathers grew proud ... they refused to obey and were not mindful of the wonders which you performed among them; ... But you are a God ready to forgive, gracious and merciful, slow to anger and abounding in steadfast love and you did not forsake them ... but so gently loving, you did not forsake them in the wilderness; the pillar of cloud which led them in the way did not depart from them by day, nor the pillar of fire by night which lighted for them the way by which they should go. You gave your good Spirit to instruct them and did not withhold your manna from them and gave them water for their thirst. (Neh 9:16-20)

The demanding God

Another false image that we often associate with this Face of God is that he demands perfection now. Far from being 'gently loving', I grew up with an image of a God who was pushy and demanding. I still find it hard not to read this into the words:

> You must love the Lord your God with your whole heart and soul, with your whole mind and strength. (Dt 6:5)

Tony de Mello, at one of his workshops, told us to keep an eye out for a demand which we felt God was making on us, and then, in prayer, to tell God that he could not have it. This was strong medicine, but it has helped me to realise that ours is not a demanding God, he does not insist on having our whole heart now. Rather, he gently leads us into his acceptance of our weakness and the fact that he 'likes what he sees' in us.

> *I Like What I See*
> The Father knocks on my door
> Seeking a home for his Son.
> Rent is cheap, I say.
> I don't want to rent, I want to buy, says God.
> I'm not sure I want to sell,
> But you might come in to look around.
> I think I will, says God.
> I might let you have a room or two.

I like it, says God.
I'll take the two. You might decide to give me more some day. I can wait, says God.
I'd like to give you more, but it's a bit difficult.
I need some space for me.
I know, says God, but I'll wait; I like what I see.
Hmm. Maybe I can let you have another room.
I really don't need that much.
Thanks, says God. I'll take it. I like what I see.
I'd like to give you the whole house,
but I'm not sure.
Think on it, says God; I would not put you out.
Your house would be mine and my son would live in it.
You'd have more space than you've ever had before.
I don't understand at all.
I know, says God, but I can't tell you about that.
You have to discover it for yourself.
That can only happen if you let me have the whole house.
A bit risky, I say.
Yes, says God, but try me.
I'm not sure. I'll let you know.
I can wait, says God. I like what I see.

Nowhere is this total acceptance of God's love so explicit as in the parable of the prodigal son. This portrait of the Father's reaction to the labyrinthine paths of our waywardness is hard to believe. That God could be so serene and tolerant, so tender and compassionate, so uncritical and accepting of so much of our perversity, is very hard for us to accept. I often think that if I did something similar to my father, I would have been very happy if he had said, 'I will give you another chance but you will have to prove yourself by meeting the following demands ...' The father of the prodigal son is recklessly tolerant and undemanding by any human standard.

> And he arose and came to his father. But while he was yet at a distance, his father saw him and had compassion, and ran and embraced him and kissed him. And the son said to him, 'Father, I have sinned against heaven and before you; I am no longer worthy to be called your son.' But the father said to his servants, 'Bring quickly the best robe, and put it on him; and put a ring on his hand and shoes on his feet; and

bring the fatted calf and kill it, and let us eat and make merry; for this my son was dead and is alive again, he was lost and is found.' And they began to make merry.' (Lk 15:20-24)

But he (the elder son) was angry and refused to go in. His father came out and entreated him, but he answered his father, 'These many years I have served you and I never disobeyed your command.' ... And he said to him, 'Son, you are always with me and all that is mine is yours. It was fitting to make merry and be glad for this your brother was dead and is alive, he was lost and is found.' (Lk 15:28-33)

Surgeon or Midwife?

God focuses his attention on where life is emerging and not on our winter world.

New Life
Today I saw a snowdrop
The first of Spring,
And I wondered
How it dared break through
The cold, hard winter earth
With such startling delicacy.

There is hope here
That the refined beauty
Of true humanity
Will survive our winter world
If we have an eye
For where it is emerging.

Jack Dominion in his book, *Cycles of Affirmation*, uses the images of a surgeon and a midwife to symbolise two approaches to helping people to grow. If we see God as one who brings about growth by means of correction, the image of him as a surgeon cutting out unhealthy bits of us may be an apt one. If, however, we see God as bringing new life out of us, or drawing us towards maturity, through affirmation, then the model of midwife may be the more suitable.

The soul that sins will die ... Repent and turn from all your transgressions, lest iniquity be your ruin. Cast away from you all the transgressions which you have committed against me and get yourselves a new heart and a new spirit! Why should you die? For I take no pleasure in the death of any one, says the Lord God; so turn and live. (Ezek 20:30-32)

We long for a God who 'will take the gentler path'. We all have that suspicion of Charlie Brown that, though God speaks gently, he carries a big stick with which he will drive us if we will not be led.

Discipline
Throw away thy rod,
Throw away thy wrath:
O my God,
Take the gentle path.

For my heart's desire
Unto thine is bent:
I aspire
To a full consent.

Then let wrath remove;
Love will do the deed;
For with love
Stony hearts will bleed.
(George Herbert)

Summary

God helps us grow to maturity by accepting and affirming us. He accepts the weak and wayward side of each of us with serenity, as well as appreciating the great good that is already there. This is different from the critical or demanding God we might find ourselves living with, if we were perfectly honest with ourselves.

Questions for reflection

1) Do you find the notion that God accepts the weak and sinful side of you, clashes with the way you instinctively think about him? Does this view of God appear to you a bit soft or permissive?
2) Do you ever let God affirm you, i.e. appreciate all that you are and all that you have done for him and others? Does he encourage your initiatives much?
3) Does God make many demands on you? Do you find him critical, when you put your life before him? Does your head give one answer to these questions, and your heart another?

The tapestry of grace as fruit of this life-giving love

The image of the bronze serpent, as it was developed in the Bible, may help us to understand the way God draws life out of us, even when we may seem more dead than alive. This image first appears in the book of Numbers, where the people asked Moses to intercede with God, as many of them were dying of snake bite.

> The people came to Moses and said, 'We have sinned for we have spoken against the Lord and against you; pray to the Lord that he take away the serpents from us.' So Moses prayed for the people. And the Lord said to Moses, 'Make a fiery serpent and set it on a pole and every one who is bitten, when he sees it, shall live.' So Moses made a bronze serpent, set it on a pole; and if a serpent bit any man, he would look at the bronze serpent and live. (Num 21:7-9)

Jesus makes powerful use of the image of the bronze serpent as a symbol of the life-giving power of his Father's love. He says that the Father loves us so much, that he allowed Jesus to be lifted up before us on the cross, so that looking at this sign of his love with faith, we would have the fullness of life.

> And as Moses lifted up the serpent in the wilderness, so must the Son of man be lifted up, that whoever believes in him may have eternal life. For God so loved the world that he gave his only Son, that whoever believes in him should not perish but have eternal life. For God sent the Son into the world, not to condemn the world, but that the world might be saved through him. (Jn 3:14-17)

How much of this love we make our own depends on how much of it we are willing to believe in, how much we let this vision of faith influence us.

> If you accept the Gospel and become Christ's,
> you will stumble on wonder upon wonder,
> and every wonder true.
> (Brendan to King Brude)

The tapestry of grace inspired by this love

God not only loves us but manifests this in a plan which he has to share the fullness of his life with us. This plan is symbolised by the tapestry of grace which God is weaving out of all the circumstances of our lives. We have to become aware of the tapestry and make our own of its beautiful design and rich range of colours as these stand for the extent and depth of God's love, working 'all things together onto good' for us.

> We know that in everything God works for good with those who love him, who are called according to his purpose. For those whom he foreknew, he also predestined to be conformed to the image of his Son in order that he might be the firstborn among many brethren. And those whom he predestined he also called; and those whom he called he also justified and those whom he justified he also glorified.' (Rom 8:28-30)

Not to be able to notice and appreciate the inner eventfulness of our lives, was seen by the Greeks of old to be the great sin. Jesus confirms the tragic nature of this kind of blindness to the signs of God's love at work in our lives, when he so often says things like:

> Keep your eyes open ... Don't you understand or grasp what I say even yet? Are you like the people who having eyes, do not see, and having ears do not hear? (Mk 8:17-18)

The circumstances of our lives seem so ordinary that it is easy for us to miss the many-splendoured thing that God is working out, even in the most mundane areas of our experience.

The jewel at the heart of all

There was a certain king who held audience for his people each day and anyone could approach him with a petition or a gift. Each week a certain old man came and offered the king a slice of fruit. Not wanting to be offensive, and at the same time not wanting to eat the not very appetising piece of fruit, the king passed it to one of his attendants. He in turn disposed of it through a hole in the platform behind where the king was standing.

Then one day, as the king was receiving the old man's gift, a pet monkey grabbed the fruit out of the king's hand and began to eat it. As it did so, a precious jewel dropped out of the centre of the fruit.

The king wasted no time in getting his servants to see if there were jewels in any of the previous gifts of the old man. Sure enough, under the platform where the fruit had been thrown and rotted there was a heap of jewels.

The work of God in our lives is so gentle and gradual that we can easily miss the significance of what is happening:

The kingdom of God is as if a man should scatter seed upon the ground and should sleep and rise night and day, and the seed should sprout and grow, he knows not how. The earth produces of itself, first the blade, then the ear, then the full grain in the ear. But when the grain is ripe, at once he puts in the sickle, because the harvest is come. (Mk 4:26-29)

Summary

Being accepted and affirmed by God is what gives us life. This is especially the effect of the love that is 'lifted up' on the Cross. This love alone has the power to make of our scattered lives the tapestry of grace which God has planned.

Questions for reflection

1) Why was the bronze serpent such an important symbol for Jesus? Does his being 'lifted up' on the Cross remind you more of suffering, your sins, or of his love for you? Do you find the Cross life-giving, or does it make you gloomy?
2) What does the story, *The jewel at the heart of all*, mean to you?

God as the potter, remoulding our minds and hearts

God is the potter, we the clay
It is not you who shapes God, but God who shapes you.
If then you are the work of God,
await the hand of the artist
who does all things in due season.
Offer him your heart, soft and tractable,
and keep the form in which the artist has fashioned you.
Let your clay be moist, lest you grow hard
and lose the imprint of his fingers. (Iraneaus)

We grow up with two visions of ourselves. One is reflected back to us by those for whom we are not very significant. The other is the vision of those who tell us we are really worthwhile. When God invites us to accept the way he sees us, this involves a letting go of all that runs counter to this.

God speaks of himself as the potter – one who is always moulding us. If you ever watched a potter at work, you would notice his practice of breaking down what he has moulded out of the clay, when a defect occurs. The potter has to undo what has gone wrong to make it afresh, but the breaking down will always be with a view to making it anew and better.

'Arise and go down to the potter's house, and there I will let you hear my words.' So I went down to the potter's house and there he was working at his wheel. And the vessel he was making of clay was spoiled in the potter's hand, and he re-worked it into another vessel, as it seemed good to the potter to do. Then the word of the Lord came to me: 'House of Israel, can I not do with you as this potter has done?' says the Lord. 'Behold, like the clay in the potter's hand, so are you in my hand.' (Jer 18:2-6)

O Lord, you are our Father; we are the clay, and you are our potter; we are all the work of your hand. (Is 64: 8)

The image of *The Crab's Shell*, on page 18, is very relevant here and may be worth reading again.

To live is to change,
and to mature is to have changed often. (J. H. Newman)

The way God helps us break open the very confining shell of a poor self image will vary from person to person. Some, God will mould 'with fire' forging his will. With others he will use, like he did with St Augustine, 'a lingering out sweet skill'. It will always, however, be in a way that is just right for each person.

> With an anvil ding
> And with fire in him forge thy will
> Or rather, rather then, stealing as Spring
> Through him, melt him but master him still:
> Whether at once, as once at a crash Paul,
> Or as Austin, a lingering out sweet skill,
> Make mercy in all of us, out of us all
> Mastery, but be adored, but be adored King. (G M Hopkins)

Let God remould your minds

God as the potter seeks to mould anew our minds and hearts, our vision and values, the way we see and feel about him, ourselves and others. Taking on this vision of faith involves 'repenting' or a change of mind and heart, to make room for the 'Good News' of who God is and who we are in his eyes.

> ... you have put on the new nature which is being renewed in knowledge after the image of its creator. (Col 3:10)

> Do not be moulded by this world but let God remould your mind. (Rom 12:2)

There is always a mysterious or hidden quality in the way God, like the potter, remoulds us.

> And what I beheld again
> What is, and no man understands;
> And out of darkness came the hands
> That reach through nature, moulding man.
> (Alfred Lord Tennyson)

Refining them like gold

Another image God uses of himself is that of the refiner who is intent on bringing out the best in us. This involves purifying us of all that is alien to the image of himself which he reveals to us.

I remember once being taken on a tour of a copper mining plant in Zambia and being very impressed with the way copper is refined. What struck me most was the immense labour involved at one stage when it was put into huge furnaces and became bright liquid. At another stage there was a very quiet and ingenious way of refining it with acid. The whole experience reflected in some measure the way we are refined by life's intense experiences, as well as by coping with those 'years without event'.

> For he is like the refiner's fire and like the fullers' soap; he will sit as a refiner of silver and he will purify the sons of Levi and refine them like gold and silver, till they present right offerings to the Lord.' (Mal 3:23)

> I will smelt away your dross in the furnace and remove all your alloy. (Is 1:25)

I find in myself a tendency to tune in to a side of these images of God that stirs up resistance in me to what he is doing. It may be because I fear to hear from him what Charlie Brown hears from Linus:

> Charlie Brown feels unhappy so he asks Linus why this is so. When he is advised to see what way he should improve he says to himself, 'I hate that answer'.

Summary

The price we have to pay for God's life-giving love to be effective, is that we would accept it. This involves 'repenting' or letting go of our illusions, the ways we make God in our own image. It also involves a lot of hard work trying to let the true image of God, the vision of himself which he puts before us in his Word, influence us. This work of 'repenting and believing' is one which God seeks to facilitate as the potter and the refiner.

Questions for reflection

1) What do the images of the potter and the refiner reveal to you about this Face of God?
2) What way do you resist what this feature of God reveals to you?

THE FIRST FACE OF GOD

The teacher seeking to realise our dream

A teacher draws out of people their latent potential, leading them to discover and own their rich resources. As our teacher, God is concerned to open up for us the fullness of life for which he has made us. He does this by inviting us to discover his life-giving vision of ourselves which he asks us to accept. What he invites us to do, as our teacher, is to go on a voyage of discovery with him.

> Sail forth – steer for the deep waters only.
> Reckless O Soul, exploring, I with thee, and thou with me,
> For we are bound where mariner has not yet dared to go,
> And we will risk the ship, ourselves and all.
> O my brave soul! O farther, farther sail!
> O daring joy, but safe! are they not all the seas of God!
> O farther, farther, farther sail!
> (Walt Whitman)

God is always leading or guiding us, so that we might realise the potential he has planted in our inmost hearts.

> I am the Lord your God who teaches you to profit, who leads you in the way you should go. O that you had harkened to my word! Then your peace would have been like a river.
> (Is 48:17-18)

> If I take the wings of the morning,
> and dwell in the furthest parts of the sea,
> even there your hand shall lead me,
> and your right hand shall hold me. (Ps 139:9-10)

> Help me know your ways, O Lord;
> teach me your paths.
> Lead me in the way of your truth and teach me,
> for you are God my saviour. (Ps 25:4)

> Remember how Yahweh led you for forty years in the desert to humble you, to test and know your inmost heart ... Learn

from this that Yahweh your God is training you as a man trains his child. (Deut 8:2,5)

As our teacher, God is always with us on our way, leading us with the pillar of cloud by day and with the pillar of fire by night.

> ... you have seen how the Lord your God bore you as a man bears his son, in all the way that you went until you came to this place. Yet in spite of this word you did not believe the Lord your God who went before you in the way to seek out a place to pitch your tents, in the fire by night, to show you by what way you should go and in the cloud by day.' (Deut 1:31-33)

... in the cloud by day

In any relationship there are times of light and times of darkness, times when we are together and times when we are apart; both are important for growth.

When God leads us 'by day' he will open up areas of light and attraction for us in our daily experience. If we take the pains to notice and make our own of these, we will be led by God who says, 'This is the way, walk in it.'

> Therefore the Lord waits to be gracious to you; ... He will surely be gracious to you at the sound of your cry; when he hears it he will answer you. And though the Lord give you the bread of adversity and the water of affliction, yet your teacher will not hide himself any more, but your eyes shall see your teacher, and your ears shall hear a word behind you, saying, 'This is the way, walk in it', when you turn to the right or when you turn to the left.' (Is 30:18-21)

... in the fire by night

God is also leading us 'by night' or in times of darkness or dryness when nothing much seems to be happening and he appears to be far away.

> As for me, I said in my prosperity,
> 'I shall never be moved'...
> You hid your face and I was thrown into confusion.
> (Ps 30:6-7)

These times may challenge us to grow even more than the times of light, for they question us about what we really believe. They ask us, 'Do you believe that God is loving and provident now that you do not feel it?'

> Though I walk in the midst of trouble,
> you preserve my life.
> The Lord will fulfil his purpose for me;
> your steadfast love endures for ever.
> Do not forsake the work of your hands.
> (Ps 138:7-8)

We all have a preference for what is tangible, so that when our experience is felt, we conclude that it is real. But when love, for instance, is not felt, we are inclined to judge that it is not real. It is often in hard times that we learn most effectively to 'judge not the Lord by feeble sense but to trust him for his grace.'

> *Light shining out of darkness*
> God moves in a mysterious way
> His wonders to perform;
> He plants his footsteps in the sea,
> And rides upon the storm.
>
> Deep in unfathomable mines
> Of never failing skill
> He treasures up his bright designs,
> And works his sovereign will.
>
> Judge not the Lord by feeble sense,
> But trust him for his grace;
> Behind a frowning providence
> He hides a smiling face.
>
> His purposes will ripen fast
> Unfolding every hour;
> The bud may have a bitter taste,
> But sweet will be the flower.
>
> Blind unbelief is sure to err,
> And scan his work in vain;
> God is his own interpreter,
> And he will make it plain.
> (William Cowper)

Life's hardships can deepen our conviction that God is loving and provident, that he works all things together onto good. (Rom 8:28) This was Job's conviction that had been fashioned in the fire of his own dark night:

> I know that you can do all things and that no purpose of yours can be thwarted ... Therefore I have uttered what I did not understand, things too wonderful for me, which I did not know. ... I had heard of you by the hearing of the ear, but now my eye sees you.' (Job 42:2-5)

Summary

God guides us, like a teacher, to realise the rich potential of the deep dream he has built into each of us. He does this by enlightening and attracting us, not just in the peak times but also in the valley periods.

Questions for reflection

1) What has God got in common with a teacher?
2) What is the meaning of God leading you by the pillar of fire by night and by the pillar of cloud by day?
3) Is there a sense in which God can teach you more by night than by day?

Living in the love he has for Jesus

'Now my eye sees you'

What Job is expressing in these words is an experience to which
God led him, through the light and the darkness of his life. It was
a mysterious experience of seeing God in an entirely new way.
This experience is now available to all who are willing to be led
into it by the Father.

> Behold, the days are coming says the Lord, when I will make
> a new covenant with the house of Israel ... not like the cove-
> nant which I made with their fathers ... which they broke,
> though I was their husband, says the Lord ... I will put my
> law within them and I will write it upon their hearts; and I
> will be their God and they shall be my people. And no long-
> er shall each man teach his neighbour and each his brother,
> saying, 'Know the Lord,' for they shall all know me, from
> the least of them to the greatest, says the Lord.' (Jer 31:31-34)

The word 'know' describes the abundance of life God wishes to
share with us. (Jn 17:3) It is compared in the Bible to the intimacy of
a marriage and is an experience of being deeply known and loved
by God and all that this calls out of us. It is through this realisation
of his love that the potter will make of us 'a new creation'.

> How long will you waver, O faithless daughter? For the
> Lord has created a new thing on the earth; a woman will
> seek her husband again. (Jer 31:22)

> I have loved you with an everlasting love; therefore I have
> continued my faithfulness to you [I am constant in my affec-
> tion for you]. Again I will build you, and you shall be built, O
> virgin Israel!' (Jer 31:34)

> So if anyone is in Christ, there is a new creation: everything
> old has passed away: see, everything has become new.
> (2 Cor 5:17)

> The Lord your God is in your midst, a warrior who gives vict-

ory; he will rejoice over you with gladness, he will renew you in his love; he will exult over you with loud singing as on a day of festival.' (Zeph 3:17)

... Just as the Father knows me

How radically new what God is now creating is, can be guaged from the fact that it will make us capable of knowing God as Jesus does (Jn 10:14-15) This means that we are loved by God in the same way as Jesus is and that we share the intimacy which they enjoy.

> The glory that you have given me I have given them, so that they may be one as we are one, I in them and thou in me, that they may become completely one, so that the world may know that you have sent me and have loved them even as you have loved me. (Jn 17:22-23)

The life that the Father enjoys with Jesus and the Spirit, and which they wish to share with each of us, is beautifully portrayed in the Rublev Icon. It expresses all the serenity of this face of God and also the invitation that we would join the Trinity at their banquet of life in which they 'know' each other intimately.

> For see, I create a new heaven and a new earth; and the former things will not be remembered or come to mind. But be glad and rejoice for ever in that which I create; for see, I create Jerusalem to be joy and my people to be gladness. I will rejoice in Jerusalem and be glad in my people; no more will be heard in it the sound of weeping and the cry of distress.' (Is 65:17-19)

Summary

We see in this Face of God one who leads us into the life he shares with Jesus and their Spirit. We are each the focus of the love he has for Jesus and are invited into the intimacy they delight in.

Questions for reflection

1) What is the meaning of the saying, 'We see ourselves in others' eyes?'
2) In the light of this saying, what is the most important reality about ourselves, that we see in the Father's eyes?

The affection of God

The Key Experience:
Affection
Resistance:
Memories of domineering or insensitive love
The Main Symbol:
The two hands around the Prodigal

The Second Face manifests God's affection, 'the loving kindness of the heart of our God.' (Lk 1:78) This affection is illustrated by the two hands that embrace the prodigal son.' There is, in other words, a male as well as a female quality to this affection. We are struck by the perfect balance between a love that is sensitive to how we feel and one that is concerned to meet our every need in a practical way. The two hands also symbolise the kinds of affection that are proper to God being our mother as well as our father. In this Face we see, therefore, a rich variety of affection that is sensitive, tender and compassionate, as well as non-possessive, practical and challenging.

1. One who shows a woman's as well as a man's affection

The woman's hand around the prodigal son symbolises the sensitive and compassionate love, the warm affection and the affirming quality of God as a woman. The man's hand represents the respect for our freedom and the practical nature of God's love as a man, as well as its challenging and generous nature.

2. One whose affection makes and sustains us

Some features of this face of God will be resisted by us as unreal. The love of God, symbolised by his two hands, makes and sustains us, if we overcome this resistance and accept his affection.

3. A practical, non-possessive, challenging affection

God as Father expresses his love by making us, sustaining us, teaching us, respecting our freedom and challenging us to take responsibility for our lives.

4. A warm, tender, all-pervasive affection

God as Mother is portrayed as one who centers her concern on us, a concern that is constant and all-pervasive. God is sensitive to our needs and feelings, in the way a woman can be. There is an intensity and depth in her affection for all, but especially for the weak and the wayward. There is an unconditional quality in her love.

5. A balanced affection of mind and heart

There is a balance between the mind and heart of love. To be able to recognise these two features of this face of God, we have to build up our appreciation of them from our human experience.

The love which we experience in our family forms the basis of what we find in this Face of God. It includes all the sorts of affection which make and sustain us as we grow up.

Our mother may open our heart to a love that is sensitive to our moods and needs, as well as being warm and tender. The love of our father, on the other hand, may be caring in a less tender but no less real way; while providing security, this may be challenging in getting us to stand on our own two feet. The love of our sisters and brothers provides a strong bond of loyalty as well as an atmosphere in which we are free to be honest and to be ourselves.

Resistance

A lot of our resistances to being loved are also picked up within the family. We may have learned, for example, that love can smother our creativeness and not leave us room to make our own decisions. Love may have a very domineering side to it that will always treat us as children. It may also have a strong element in it that suffocates us with feeling and makes us want to run away so that we can be free. It may also appear hard and insensitive to how we feel or what we need.

Arousing dormant experience

To become aware of your experience of the kind of love you are focusing on in this Face of God, you may be helped by some of the following reflections:

1) What is the most striking thing you have learned about love from each of your parents and from your brothers and sisters? What is peculiar to their love, compared to the love you experience from friends?

2) What shortcomings has their love? Do these defects dominate the good things you remember? You may notice how these deficiencies tend to colour unduly the overall experience of the rich variety of love in your family.

3) What qualities are most important for you in a mother, a father, in brothers and in sisters? It may help to think of parents you admire, and see what it is you admire most in them.

4) Are there ways of loving that are peculiar to a woman compared to a man?

The Main Symbol:
The two hands around the Prodigal

Around 1668 Rembrandt painted his fourth picture on the parable of the prodigal son, The Return of the Prodigal Son. Attention is focused on the father's hands which express his love for his son despite his sorry state. One of these hands is a woman's and the other a man's. These two hands image two sides of the God in whose likeness we are made, and even though they are two, they are made to be 'one flesh' or one person. In this way they represent a whole tradition about the mind and heart of love and about two kinds of love that reflect the male and female in each of us.

In our sinful state, it is difficult for us to prevent one hand becoming too dominant at the expense of the other. The emphasis on God being male has often led to a lack of appreciation of the female elements in God's loving kindness.

> Then God said, 'Let us make humankind in our image, according to our likeness ...' So God created humankind in his image, in the image of God he created them; male and female he created them. (Gen 1:26-27)

Clearly, if we are made in God's image and we are male and female, then God is as much female as male. Because of a cultural bias, many of us will be out of sympathy with some of the qualities of God as mother and of God as woman.

A lot of this difficulty arises if we have not taken responsibility for getting in touch with our own 'invisible partner'. This is the other half of ourselves which is male if we are women and female if we are men. A lot of our development as human beings depends on what kind of relationship we have with our invisible partner.

One who shows a woman's, as well as a man's, affection

The loving kindness of God is most profoundly symbolised in the father of the prodigal son. (Lk 15:11-33) This is Jesus' portrait of the 'loving kindness'* of the heart of our God' (Lk 1:78) and is reflected in the significance of the two hands embracing the son in Rembrandt's painting.

The woman's hand

The woman's hand symbolises the sensitivity of the father seeing the son while he was still a long way off, as if he kept scanning the horizon in the hope of his son's return.

> But while he was yet at a distance, his father saw him and had compassion. (Lk:15:20)

God has what we might call a 'weakness' for the sinner that is obvious in the scene. We may hear echoes in ourselves of the elder brother's complaint that the father is being too soft on his errant son.

> But when this son of yours came, who has devoured your living with harlots, you killed for him the fatted calf.
> (Lk 15:30)

There is also a tenderness, a warm affection about this scene that is an expression of the feminine hand of God.

> ... he ran and embraced him and kissed him. (Lk 15:20)

Again, the woman's hand affirms the son and makes him aware that it is very good that he is back. His return is like finding again something precious that was lost. It is a cause for celebration. This belief in us, no matter what wrong we have done, is very distinctive of a woman's love.

> ... and let us eat and make merry for this my son was dead and is alive again; he was lost and is found. And they began to make merry. (Lk 15:23-24)

* *'Loving kindness' is a translation of the Hebrew word 'hesed' which is the most basic quality of God's love in the Old Testament.*

NINE FACES OF GOD

Central to these feminine features of this Face of God is courtesy, that refinement of manners which is based on sensitivity and tact but above all on kindness.

This Courteous Lord

His loving Lord, now tenderly looking upon his servant, regards him in two ways. First, outwardly, very lovingly and gently, with great compassion and pity ... Then, secondly ... I saw the Lord greatly rejoicing in the thought of the deserved rest and high honour he will surely bestow on his servant by his bounteous grace ... It was as though this courteous Lord had said, 'See my beloved servant here, what hurt and distress he has endured in service for love of me and of his goodwill. Is it not fitting that I should reward him for his fright and fear, his pain and his wounds, and all his grief? ... I saw that it must indeed be by virtue of his Lord's great worth and goodness that his beloved servant, whom he loves so dearly, should be truly and happily rewarded, beyond all that would have been if he had not fallen. Yes, and yet more, that his falling and his grief which he has taken upon himself, should be turned into surpassing glory and endless joy. (Julian of Norwich)

The man's hand

The man's hand symbolises his willingness to let his son go and then to take him back. There is a sense of the father giving his son freedom to make mistakes, and resisting the temptation to rescue him from the consequences of these.

Father, I have sinned against heaven and before you, I am no longer worthy to be called your son. But the father said to his servants, 'Bring quickly the best robe ...' (Lk 15:21-22)

There is a sense of the practical love of a man of action who runs out to meet his son.

... he ran to the boy, clasped him in his arms. (Lk 15:20)

The father is 'weak' enough to plead with his elder son to come to the banquet and yet 'strong' enough to confront him about his reasons for not coming in.

He was angry and refused to go in, and his father came out to plead with him. (Lk 15:28)

Son, you are always with me and all that is mine is yours. It was fitting to make merry and be glad, for this your brother was dead, and is alive, he was lost and is found.
(Lk 15:31-32)

This is a hand that is outstretched, giving gifts, and to such an extent that God seems to be the one that is 'prodigal'. He plans and provides generously for both his sons.

Son, you are always with me and all that is mine is yours.
(Lk 15:31)

Summary

The woman's hand around the prodigal son symbolises the sensitive and compassionate love, the warm affection and the affirming quality of God as a woman. The man's hand represents the respect for our freedom and the practical nature of God's love as a man, as well as its challenging and generous nature.

Questions for reflection

1) What are the qualities of God, symbolised by the two hands around the Prodigal Son, that stand out for you?
2) Are there other qualities, not mentioned, that you would like to include?

One whose affection makes and sustains us

There is a lot of resistance in us to accepting the portrait which Jesus paints of his Father in the parable of the prodigal son. We need to become aware of the ways we resist being held in these two arms of God, and then share this with 'The Divine Lover'.

The Divine Lover
Me, Lord? Canst thou mis-spend
One word, misplace one look on me?
Call'st me thy Love, thy Friend?
Can this poor soul the object be
Of these love-glances, those life-kindling eyes?
What? I the centre of thy arms' embraces?
Of all thy labour I the prize?
Love never mocks, Truth never lies.
Oh how I quake: Hope fear, fear hope displaces:
I would, but cannot hope: such wondrous love amazes.
(Phineas Fletcher)

God being this sensitive and compassionate may seem unreal and remain an abstract idea only – not felt at the heart's core. If we do not overcome our resistance to God's deep affection for us, his love will not 'make us real', or it may do so only in a limited way.

Reality
'What is real?' asked the rabbit one day when they were lying side by side near the nursery fender, before Nana came in to tidy the room. 'Does it mean having things that buzz inside you and a stick out handle?' 'Real isn't how you are made,' said the Skin Horse. 'It's a thing that happens to you. When a child loves you for a long, long time, not just to play with, but *really* loves you, then you become *real*.' 'Does it hurt?' asked the rabbit. 'Sometimes,' said the Skin Horse, for he was always truthful. 'When you are real you don't mind being hurt.' 'Does it happen all at once, like being wound up?' he asked, 'or bit by bit?' 'It doesn't happen all at once,' said the Skin Horse. 'You become. It takes a long time. That's

why it doesn't often happen to people who break easily, or have sharp edges, or who have to be carefully kept. Generally, by the time you are Real, most of your hair has been loved off, and your eyes drop out and you get loose in the joints and very shabby. But these things don't matter at all, because once you are Real you can't be ugly, except to people who don't understand.' 'I suppose you are Real?' said the rabbit. And then he wished he had not said it, for he thought the Skin Horse might be sensitive. But the Skin Horse only smiled. 'The boy's uncle made me Real,' he said. 'That was a great many years ago, but once you are real you can't become unreal again. It lasts for always.'

(*The Velveteen Rabbit* by Margery Williams)

Read again the story about Care on page 11 and compare its impact on you with that of the extract from the *Velveteen Rabbit*. Both symbolise something fundamental about human nature which the philosopher Heideggar expressed in the words:

We are constituted by care and maintained by her.

There are parts of us that resist being formed by these two hands of God. This is especially true of the female side of men and the male side of women. It is, therefore, as important for a woman to accept and appreciate a God who confronts her, as it is for a man to find God warm and affectionate. This appreciation brings to life the male side of women and the female side of men that otherwise lies dormant. This balance is needed if we are to appreciate the richness of a God who makes us male and female in his own image.

So God created man in his own image, in the image of God he created him; male and female he created them. (Gen 1:27)

This balance of the male and female sides of God is reflected in the conclusion people came to at the end of the Exodus. In this central event of the Old Testament, they found God to be non-aggressive, kind and gracious, yet he is one who confronts their waywardness.

... a God merciful and gracious, slow to anger and abounding in steadfast love ... but he will by no means clear the guilty, visiting the iniquity of the fathers upon the children and the children's children to the third and the fourth generation. (Ex 34:6-7)

These male and female aspects of God are reflected in what Micah says about what God wants from us above all:

> He has told you, O mortal, what is good; and what does the Lord require of you but to do justice, and to love kindness, and to walk humbly with your God? (Mic 6:8)

Each of us has some idea of the ideal balance between male and female affection, from the way our parents loved us and thus 'made us real'. We know as well the way we would like to combine the two in our experience of being parents or of being generative of others' lives. We can thus appreciate that for God to 'make us real' he must challenge us to take responsibility for the way we live.

> I call heaven and earth to witness against you today that I have set before you life and death, blessings and curses. Choose life so that you and your descendants may live, loving the Lord your God, obeying him, and holding fast to him; for that means life to you and length of days, so that you may live in the land that the Lord swore to give to your ancestors, to Abraham, to Isaac, and to Jacob. (Deut 30:19-20)

We know too that God is as sensitive to how we feel and as compassionate towards us in our frailty as his Son is:

> Here is my servant, whom I have chosen, my beloved, with whom my soul is well pleased. I will put my Spirit upon him, and he will proclaim justice to the gentiles. He will not wrangle or cry aloud, nor will anyone hear his voice in the streets. He will not break a bruised reed or quench a smoldering wick until he brings justice to victory. And in his name the gentiles will hope. (Mt 12:18-21)

Summary

Some features of this face of God will be resisted by us as unreal. The love of God, symbolised by his two hands, makes and sustains us, if we overcome this resistance and accept his affection.

Questions for reflection

1) Do some qualities, symbolised by the two hands of God, seem unreal to you? What ones does the writer of The Divine Lover resist most?
2) What do *Reality* and *Care* say to you about God? In what sense does Care make and sustain us?

A practical, non-possessive, challenging affection

What the word father calls up for each of us will have a big influence on the way we see and feel about God. For many people the word brings to mind an image of one who is the breadwinner and who has the ultimate authority in the home. In the Bible, however, the image is of one who knows, loves, cares for each one and thus gives life.

> *Beyond Mind's Ken*
> We are born of Love,
> Of a love that
> Touches, caresses and affirms,
> Of mother's love
> That listens and is compassionate:
> And of a father's
> Worldly-wise providence.
>
> It is in another's affection
> That if we are to be,
> We are born ever anew and nourished
> With the basic food of the heart.
>
> The extent of our being touched
> Forms the horizon
> Of our being touched by Him
> Who took on flesh and blood
> To make love tangible.
>
> This love is beyond the mind's reach
> And cannot be taught.
> It is caught in another's love,
> It touches and is touched
> By what is beyond mind's ken
> The Heart of Him.

Care moulding us

God, as father, is one who plans and creates, fashions and moulds us.

Is not he your father who created you, who made you and established you? (Dt 32:6)

For you formed my inward parts, you knit me together in my mother's womb. I praise you for you are fearful and wonderful [I thank you for the wonder of my being JB] Wonderful are your works! You know me right well; my frame was not hidden from you [my body held no secret from you JB] when I was being made in secret, intricately wrought in the depths of the earth. (Ps 139:13-15)

A continuing creation

God as father also sustains, protects and guards what is very precious to him. He is like one leading a small child by the hand through a dark wood at night, conscious of how threatening this can be for the child. God's love is one that is protective and makes us secure.

… fear not for I am with you [I am holding you by the right hand JB], be not dismayed for I am your God; I will strengthen you, I will help you, I will uphold you with my victorious right hand. (Is 41:10)

He found him in a desert land, and in the howling waste of the wilderness; he encircled him, he cared for him, he kept him as the apple of his eye. (Deut 32:10)

This sustaining love of God is not just maintaining us where we are, but is like a continuing creation in which God is always leading us on into new areas of his dream for us. There is always a certain area of ourselves that is ripe for change. It is here that God is at work with our desire, in order to realise his plan for our welfare and for a future full of hope.

For I know the plans I have for you, says the Lord, plans for welfare and not for evil, to give you a future and a hope. Then you will call upon me and come and pray to me, and I will hear you. You will seek me and find me; when you seek me with all your heart. I will be found by you, says the Lord. (Jer 29:11-14)

In this sense, God is seen to be a teacher. He trains or educates the vast potential in us, challenging our resources. He leads us, step by step, into what we are ready to become, provided we are willing to be taught, or to seek the 'future full of hope' he plans for us.

> O God, from my youth you have taught me,
> and yet your wonders stretch out beyond me still.
> (Ps 71:17)

> He has been taught this discipline by his God who instructs him. (Is 28:26)

God respects our freedom, stands back and lets us choose, inviting us to take responsibility for our choices. He is always putting life and destruction before us, challenging us to choose life, but leaving the decision to us.

> The soul that sins will die. ... Repent and turn from all your transgressions, lest iniquity be your ruin. Cast away from you all the transgressions which you have committed against me and get yourselves a new heart and a new spirit! Why should you die? For I take no pleasure in the death of any one, says the Lord God; so turn and live. (Ezek 20:30-32)

God as father does not 'rescue' us, in the way a mother might, from the consequences of our bad choices. It is like the way the father of the Prodigal does not go into the far country, to bring his son back. We see this love, which invites us to take responsibility for our mistakes, in the way God deals with Cain.

> The Lord said to Cain, 'Why are you angry, and why has your countenance fallen? If you do well, will you not be accepted? And if you do not do well, sin is couching at the door; its desire is for you, but you must master it. (Gen 4:6-7)

Part of this training, and perhaps the place where God has most to teach us, takes place in our difficult or dark periods when God seems far away and we feel as if we are in life's wilderness.

> He will surely be gracious to you at the sound of your cry; when he hears it, he will answer you. And though the Lord give you the bread of adversity and the water of affliction, yet your Teacher will not hide himself any more, but your ears will see your Teacher. And your ears will hear a word behind you, saying, 'This is the way, walk in it' when you turn to the right or when you turn to the left. (Is 30:19-21)

What God most wishes to guide us into is the Good News. This

Good News is not a message. In this Face of God it is the accumulated experience of the affection we have received throughout our lives. Much of this is a dormant memory which we need to arouse and keep alive.

Living out of the memory of being loved

Rollo May, in his book *Love and Will*, tells of a practice that has been a source of inspiration for him. From the time he was a student he learned to nourish himself on the rich memory of those who believed in him. He found that by returning to these experiences, especially when he felt low, he was uplifted and enlivened again. It was as if he had a rich store of inner wisdom in the memory of those people who believed in him. This he could draw on at any time he wished to, and be strengthened by it.

Jack Dominian, in his book *Cycles of Affirmation*, describes the source of these memories of being loved and how they are gradually built up. He believes in the importance of what he calls the 'significant people' in our lives. These are people like our parents, our friends and God. They are significant because they have affirmed us – they have expressed their appreciation of all that we are. They have also encouraged our initiative so that we might realise all our potential.

By far the most significant person in our lives is God and the most loving memory is the fact that he 'gave up his Son' that we might have the fullness of life. Jesus invites us to keep alive the memory of this supreme demonstration of God's loving kindness when he tells us to celebrate it in the eucharist. 'Do this in memory of me.'

Summary

God as Father expresses his love by making us, sustaining us, teaching us, respecting our freedom and challenging us to take responsibility for our lives.

Questions for reflection

1) What picture of God as Father emerges for you from the above? What two or three qualities appeal to you most?
2) How would the above portrait of the Father differ from your own? What features of it do you find yourself resisting most?

A warm, tender, all-pervasive affection

> Love for a man is a thing apart;
> 'tis a woman's whole existence.

We are not used today to seeing God portrayed as anything else than masculine, yet there is a very strong stream of Christian tradition that thinks of God as feminine. This is especially true of the Holy Spirit, whose feminine aspect is emphasised by the fact that one of the most common names that is used for her is the feminine version in Greek of 'Holy Wisdom'.

Much of our imagery connected with God's affection for us will inevitably come out of the experience of our mothers and the feminine side of life.

> *In Memory Of My Mother*
> You will have the road gate open, the front door ajar
> The kettle boiling and a table set
> By the window looking out at the sycamores
> And your loving heart lying in wait
>
> For me coming up among the poplar trees.
> You'll know my breathing and my walk
> And it will be a summer evening on those roads
> Lonely with leaves of thought.
>
> We will be choked with the grief of things growing,
> The silence of dark green air
> Life too rich, the nettles, docks and thistles
> All answering the prodigal's prayer.
>
> You will know I am coming though I send no word
> For you were lover who could tell
> A man's thoughts, my thoughts, though I hid them.
> Through you I knew Woman and did not fear her spell.
> (Patrick Kavanagh)

The enduring and all-pervasive quality of the mother's love in this poem is but a pale reflection of what God says she feels.

But Zion said, 'The Lord has forsaken me, my Lord has forgotten me.' Can a woman forget her sucking child, that she should have no compassion on the son of her womb? Even these may forget, yet I will not forget you. Behold, I have graven you on the palms of my hands. (Is 49:14-16)

Familiar with all your ways

The sensitivity peculiar to a mother is a reflection of much that is said about God in scripture. Probably nobody will ever know her child as she does, for her intimate knowledge of all her child's ways, feelings and needs, is born of the immense sensitivity and concern of a mother's love.

> You know when I sit and when I rise;
> you know every detail of my conduct.
> If I take the wings of the morning,
> and dwell in the furthest parts of the sea,
> even there your hand shall lead me,
> and your right hand shall hold me.
> For you formed my inmost parts;
> you knit me together in my mother's womb.
> For all these wonders I thank you,
> for the wonder of myself and all your works.
> You know me through and through;
> my frame was not hidden from you,
> when I was being made in secret,
> intricately put together in the depths of the earth.
> (Ps 139:2,9-10,13-15)

The perceptiveness of God is beautifully illustrated by the following incident which John Powell recounts:

A pair gave a party to celebrate the silver jubilee of their marriage. The wife was asked by one of the guests how her husband was after his recent illness. She said that he was not so well. This puzzled the guest as his host had appeared to him to be in the best of spirits when he greeted him on his arrival at the party. So when he got a chance, he asked him again about how he felt, only to be assured that even though he felt well when he first greeted him, he now felt unwell. Later the guest asked the hostess how she knew her husband was unwell and she smiled and said, 'I'm his wife.'

This sensitivity contrasts very sharply with the indifference of the male-dominated society we experience today, with its sin of indifference. George Bernard Shaw says somewhere that the worst sin against others springs not from hatred, but from indifference.

'I am constant in my affection for you'

A marked feature of a mother's love is the depth and intensity of her affection for her children, and she can show it in an explicit way that most fathers do not find easy.

> I have loved you with an everlasting love and am constant in my affection for you. (Jer 31:3)

> He will feed his flock like a shepherd, he will gather the lambs in his arms, he will carry them in his bosom and gently lead those that are with young. (Is 40:11)

This affection is so deep that it can absorb a lot of neglect and ingratitude, and retain a special compassion for the weak and wayward.

> Is Ephraim my dear son? Is he the child I delight in? As often as I speak against him, I still remember him. Therefore I am deeply moved for him; I will surely have mercy on him, says the Lord. (Jer 31:20)

There is a medieval legend which makes the point of the constancy of a mother's affection in a startling way:

> There was once a youth who fell in love with a young woman who demanded more of his heart than he should have given. But he was enthralled with her and so could refuse nothing she asked. She took advantage of his weakness and insisted that if he was to have her heart, he would have to give her the heart of his mother. So he went off and killed his mother. When he was bringing back her heart, he fell and hurt himself. It was then that he heard the spirit of his mother asking him, 'Son, have you hurt yourself?'

The story has always been a bridge for me to the steadfastness of God's affection.

> The Lord is merciful and gracious,
> slow to anger and abounding in steadfast love.

He does not deal with us according to our sins,
nor repay us according to our faults.
For as the heavens are high above the earth,
so great is his steadfast love
towards those who revere him.
As a father has compassion on his children,
so the Lord pities those who fear him.
For he knows of what we are made;
he remembers that we are dust.
(Ps 103:8-14)

Praise is well, compliment is well, but affection – that is the last and final and most precious reward that any man wins, whether by character or achievement. (Mark Twain)

Summary

God as Mother is portrayed as one who centers her concern on us, a concern that is constant and all-pervasive. God is sensitive to our needs and feelings, in the way a woman can be. There is an intensity and depth in her affection for all, but especially for the weak and the wayward. There is an unconditional quality in her love.

Questions for reflection

1) What are the qualities of God as Mother or as feminine, that you have seen above? Are there others that you would add?
2) Which of these do you like best? Which are the ones that you resist most?

A balanced affection of mind and heart

People have always found it very difficult to get the right balance between a father's way of loving and a mother's, between the mind and heart of love. The weakness of a love which is too much of the mind is that it is so devoted to doing things that it has little time to be with another person in any depth. The weakness of the heart of love is that it can smother with affection and helpfulness and not allow another freedom to be apart.

> There is a singlemindedness
> About the sea
> That moves in caressingly
> To take possession of the shore.
> But when the time comes
> For the tide to turn,
> It can let what seemed so much its own,
> Be its original self again.
>
> I watched a pair whose gaze
> Was held by their child
> Collecting sea shells
> Oblivious of the hold she had on them.
> I wondered would they be able,
> Like the sea, to relinquish their hold
> And let her be a sacrament
> Of their love and His.
>
> As I wandered on down the shore,
> I wondered where life would take her.
> For she was surely setting off
> Enlivened by their love.
> In the years to come I prayed
> That she might continue to be nourished
> By the rich memory of what
> They had so painstakingly given her.

The Bible does show a balance of the heart and mind of love, in that God is warm, compassionate and gracious but also confronts us with taking responsibility for our freedom and with the misuse we make of it when we sin.

> I myself will search for my sheep, and I will seek them out. As a shepherd seeks out his flock when some of his sheep have been scattered abroad ... and I will rescue them from all the places where they have been scattered on a day of clouds and thick darkness ... and I will feed them on the mountains of Israel ... I myself will be the shepherd of my sheep, and I will make them lie down, says the Lord God. I will seek the lost and I will bring back the strayed, and I will bind up the crippled and I will strengthen the weak, and the fat and the strong I will watch over, I will feed them in justice.

> ... I will save my flock, they shall no longer be a prey; and I will judge between sheep and sheep ... And I will make with them a covenant of peace ... and I will send down showers in due season, and they shall be showers of blessing ... and they shall be secure in their land ... when I break the bars of their yoke and deliver them from the hand of those who enslave them ... And you are my sheep, the sheep of my pasture, and I am your God says the Lord God. (Ezek 34:11-31)

This passage also brings out God's capacity to share with us not just the areas of our lives where we feel strong and joyful. He is also able to be with us, in a very compassionate way, in our weakness and times of sorrow.

> *On Another's Sorrow*
> Can I see another's woe,
> And not be in sorrow too?
> Can I see another's grief,
> And not seek for kind relief?

> Can a mother sit and hear
> An infant groan, an infant fear?
> No, no! never can it be!
> Never, never can it be!

> He doth give his joy to all;
> He becomes an infant small;

He becomes a man of woe;
He doth feel the sorrow too.

O! he gives to us his joy
That our grief he may destroy;
Till our grief is fled and gone
He doth sit by and moan.
(William Blake)

Rediscovering the heart of God

Many of the words connected with the affectionate side of God may have lost a lot of their meaning for us. The result is that they are no longer effective in calling up a love that sustains us. This is often because our ideas about God, and the love he is, are not rooted in our experience, but have become part of a spiritual world, separated from what is a felt and a real experience for us.

> But your sons were not conquered by the teeth of venomous serpents. For your mercy came to their help and healed them. To remind them of your oracles they were bitten and then were quickly healed, lest by falling into deep forgetfulness, they become unresponsive to your kindness [be cut off from your kindness JB]. For neither herb nor poultice cured them, but it is your work, O Lord which heals all people. (Wis 16:10-12)

We can remedy this forgetfulness by delving into our rich store of experience of people who took a special interest in us or who believed in us. Through getting in touch with the memory of some of these people, we might be able to reawaken experiences of being loved and loving that are now dormant.

For example, if we wish to appreciate more the compassion of God, we might take an experience we have had of compassion being shown us by someone in our own life and, if possible, relive that experience. This will help to bring the word compassion to life, and to enrich our application of it to God. In this way we continue the incarnation by putting the loving kindness of the heart of our God in human terms.

> No one has ever seen God; the only Son, who is in the bosom of the Father [who is closest to the Father's heart], he has made him known. (Jn 1:18)

The Two Brothers

There were two brothers who lived on adjoining farms. One was married and the other lived on his own. They were very concerned for each other: one for his brother who had to make ends meet for his family, and the other for his brother who was living alone.

At night they would each take some of their own grain and add it to the other's. One night they met and embraced with joy in each other's goodness. It was then they heard the words, 'Here at last is the place where I will build my temple. For where my brothers meet in love, there my presence will dwell.'

The people who have built up in us an appreciation of what love is about become the sacraments of that love for us. If we have experienced great respect from someone, we now know what respect feels like and can use this as a stepping-stone to experience the way God respects us. In this way the word becomes flesh or incarnate again for us. God's loving kindness becomes real for us.

And the Word became flesh and dwelt among us, full of grace and truth [i.e. full of loving, kind and faithful love]. (Jn 1:14)

The lack of appreciation of the feminine side of life, or of the heart of love, and the effect of this is symbolised by our final story:

The Selfish Giant

There was once a giant who owned a house surrounded by a beautiful garden, where children loved to play. Now the giant was very selfish so he forbade the children the use of his garden. With the children, however, went all the beauty of the garden; winter never left it. Then one day the giant heard the sweetest music he had ever listened to and, when he looked out the window to see where it came from, he was greeted by a strange sight.

The children had returned to the far end of his garden and everything there was beautiful again. When the giant ran out to greet the children all but one ran away. This was a tiny child trying to climb onto a branch of a tree but who was in tears because he could not; he was too small. So the giant bent down to help him and the little child threw his arms around him. After that day, the rest of the children returned to play in the garden but not the little child. The giant welcomed them but longed to see the little child once more because he had discovered his heart again through him.

One winter's day many years later, when the giant was now old and grey, he saw that the tree at the bottom of the garden was in blossom and the little child sitting under it. He ran to greet him but was shocked to see wounds in the child's hands and feet. The giant was angered and wanted to know who had done this, but the child smiled and said, 'These are the wounds of love.' Then the child said that he had come to take the giant home with him. The next day the children found the body of the giant under the tree covered in blossoms. (An adaptation of a story by Oscar Wilde)

As long as the giant refuses to relate with the children, to be sensitive and compassionate towards them, he remains in his winter wilderness. As soon, however, as he can reach out to the little child, spring comes to his heart and he is ready for the fullness of life, for heaven.

Summary

There is a balance between the mind and heart of love. To be able to recognise these two features of this face of God, we have to build up our appreciation of them from our human experience.

Questions for reflection

1) Do you notice, in your own experience, a lack of balance between the male and female features of this Face of God? It might manifest itself with the resistance you find when people speak of God as female or mother.
2) What features of this Face of God appeal to you most? What symbols of these have you found helpful?

The providence of God

The Key Experience:
The very practical concern of parents
Resistance:
We are smothered with well-intentioned kindness
The Main Symbol:
The dream in the acorn

This Face of God shows a love which is not abstract or remote but practical and deeply involved. In all the circumstances of each day, this loving providence is at work to bring our deepest dreams to full flower. Nothing that happens to us falls outside the very concrete concern of this love for us. God is a busy lover, ceaselessly at work to realise that portion of our dream for which we are at present ripe. As Jesus tells us, this work of God is to help us to believe the Good News. (Jn 6:29) God also works to heal the wounds caused by our unbelief, as well as to set us free from being dominated by false images of God and of ourselves.

1. One who has a practical plan to realise our dream

God reveals himself in a practical plan for our peace which he is
working out. This plan, like the dream in the acorn, is built into
us, and is not just an external 'will of God.' It springs from the image of God in us, which is an immense capacity to be loved and to
be loving.

2. One who works to bring our dream to be

God 'works' to realise his dream in us. This is that we would
'own' the new creation which we have become. This new life is
brought about by our belief in his love, or by coming to 'know the
one true God'.

3. One who is energetic – a busy lover

There are a lot of images used to describe the way God is working
out his dream for us. We are being moulded, shaped and transformed into the divine nature.

4. One who is deferential as well as assertive

We each have to realise our unique dream by listening and responding to it. God leaves us free to do this. Because so few respect our freedom, we cannot imagine God doing so. He invites
us to flow with the river.

5. One who works ceaselessly for our good

God is constant and consistent in guiding us to realise our dream.
There is a beautiful pattern in the way he weaves even the most
insignificant details of our lives into his grand design.

6. One who is not deterred by the poverty of our response

God is not limited by our limitations in his constant commitment to our happiness. God's providence is not blocked by our lack of fidelity.

7. One who works to heal the wounds of our waywardness

God heals the wounds of our unbelief by inviting us to look at how worthwhile we are in his eyes.

8. One who works to free us from our enslavement

God in his providence works to free us from the slavery of sin, so that we may enter the promised land of his life and peace. We are thus called to repent or to free ourselves from our illusions so that we can believe in God's life-giving way of seeing things.

9. One who works to bring us to full flower

God in his providence seeks to release the immense energy in us, like that in the oak tree, to reach maturity. The ordinariness of our lives resists the fact that God is so powerfully at work in us.

10. One who guides us in our peak and valley periods

There is a deference which respects our freedom, as well as an intimacy in the way God influences us. There is a vision of this face of God that we, like Job, can get only when God leads us through the valley of darkness.

The experience we will focus on here is the trouble our parents have taken in rearing us. When we look at the painstaking way that animals look after their young, it is a constant source of wonder as to what urges them to go to such rounds. Animals, however, are driven by instinct and the period of their concern is brief compared to the years of arduous effort that must back the decision of parents to express this very provident kind of love.

Even though I usually take it for granted, I am awe-struck when I do give thought to how much of herself my mother invested in me during my first six years. I recall in particular being very subject to a bad cough during those years and I still remember very clearly all the trouble she went to in order to prevent it lasting into later life. There was an endless round of hot drinks, vick rubs, and the constant attention that I loved most of all.

As we move through life we are warmed by glimpses of this kind of love when, for instance, we get a puncture on a dark rainy night and someone pulls off the road and asks if we are in need of help.

Resistance

Experiences of the excess or the neglect of this kind of love can dominate us and act as a block to our appreciating it. Such experiences can originate from overbearing parents who steamroll our initiatives, or who are so concerned with their own plans, that they are insensitive to ours. From this it is a short step to seeing God as being so insistent on his will that there is nothing for us to do but grin and bear it.

Arousing dormant experience

1) Recall some experiences of the ways your parents were con-

cerned for what was best for you and the trouble they took to help you get this. You might re-live one of these, going through all that was said and done. You may in this way gain an appreciation of the benefit of arousing the rich store of experience of this kind of love that lies dormant in you. It is with this kind of positive experience in mind that you can safely look at some of the excesses or deficiencies of this kind of provident love in your own life. In this way you might become freer of what is resisting God's efforts to reveal to you his provident love.

2) Notice the ways brothers or sisters, friends or strangers have surprised you with their helpfulness in times of difficulty. Notice your own desire to help them in similar circumstances and how that desire is tempered with deference for their freedom so that you do not push yourself on them.

3) Try to appreciate the creative ways you seek the best for those you love, the trouble you take with all the details that may be involved in this quest.

With all the experience that you revive in this way, it is worth while noticing whether God is at least as loving as you or your parents, friends and others are in these ways.

The Main Symbol:
The dream in the acorn

The dream in the acorn

It is awesome to think that an oak tree we might see in the park is the realisation of something that was in the acorn from which it grew. We might call what was in the acorn a plan or dream that was built into it and which directed its growth to become this unique oak tree. It did not grow at random, for even though it was influenced by circumstances such as storms, its main thrust came from its in-built dream. It is always being directed by this plan of God from within.

Our lives too are directed by a dream God has built into us, but we differ from the oak tree in that the fulfilment of our dream is not automatic. We have to get in touch with it and decide to take responsibility for its realisation. It is very easy for this 'still small voice' to be drowned out by other concerns so that love's providence is no longer listened to and this face of God is no longer seen.

Characteristics of the dream

1) The dream in each of us, like that in the acorn, is unique. This means that God will lead each of us along a very special way so that our story is different from that of anybody else. Each of us can say, 'There will never be another me.'

2) Just as the dream in the oak tree will be realised in a very constant way, so God guides us in a way consistent with our unique dream. If we can only take the trouble, we will notice recurring patterns of enlightenment and attraction that will be peculiar to each of us. Every step of the realisation of our dream grows very naturally out of what has gone before. God will not suddenly make a u-turn in our lives but will be always on the look-out for what is the next step that is just right for us.

3) Just as there is a record of the tree's growth, written in the rings of the tree, so there is a story of the way our dream unfolds. This is manifest in the unique recurring patterns of the experience peculiar to each of us.

4) There is an essential energy in all things that urges them on towards maturity. The Greeks gave this energy the name *eros*, which is one of their words for love. It is something that may strike us in the surge of life in a tree in spring, or in the energy we notice in people who fall in love.

5) This energy pushes on relentlessly towards maturity or wholeness. Just as the dream in the acorn never rests until it is realised in the fully grown oak tree, so the dream in us is restless till it rests in God.

6) We have to get in touch with our dream and be constantly taking responsibility for it. Many of the parables Jesus told focus on the critical nature of our decision to realise our God-given talents. If we do not listen to the Word of God and put it into practice, we will, as Jesus warned, be building our lives on sand.

N.B. I have chosen the notion of 'the in-built dream' as what love's providence seeks to realise, rather than the more traditional term, 'the will of God'. The notion of the dream helps us to focus on the inbuilt plan which God is working out for us. The term 'will of God', on the other hand, focuses our attention on something outside ourselves that we are meant to do for God. By looking at God's plan in terms of a dream which God has built into us, we may be better able to accept what St Paul constantly reminds us of – that the Christian life is more a matter of grace or gift than something we achieve by our fidelity to the law or to God's will.

One who has a practical plan to realise our dream

The love which we contemplate in this Face of God is practical love. When we are really concerned for others we want to do all that we can for them. So God not only loves us but this shows in the plan he has for our welfare.

> I know the plans I have in mind for you, says the Lord, plans for welfare (peace), not for evil, to give you a future and a hope ... When you seek me you shall find me, when you seek me with all your heart, you will be found by me.
> (Jer 29:11-14)

God has revealed himself more through his actions than by way of words. In the Old Testament, people learned most about God through what they called his 'wonderful works' and these were much more full of meaning for them than what he said: deeds do speak louder than words.

> You have multiplied, O Lord my God,
> Your wondrous deeds and designs for us;
> none can compare with you!
> Were I to proclaim and tell of them,
> they would be more than can be numbered. (Ps 40:5)

His plan as in-built dream

I grew up seeing God's main concern as that I should obey his will, even if it were contrary to all that I felt most deeply about. He was for me like parents who, in a distorted way of loving, impose their plans on their children, without much consideration for their children's wishes in the matter. God's aim is in fact what St Paul calls sanctification, or in our language, the fullness of life and happiness for which God has made us.

> This is the will of God, your sanctification ... For God has not called us for uncleanness, but in holiness. (1 Thess 4:3-7)

A very important aspect of God's plan for us, is that it is not outside us but rather something that is built into us. It is like the dream in the acorn that directs its growth throughout its life-span, urging it to realise all its potential to become a fully grown oak tree.

Our dream is the realisation of the fact that we are made in the image of God.

> Then God said, 'Let us make humankind in our image, according to our likeness ... So God created humankind in his image, in the image of God he created them; male and female he created them. (Gen 1:26-27)

God's image in us is our capacity to be loved by him. It is with the realisation of this capacity that the Great Commandment is concerned.

> You must love the Lord your God with all your heart and soul, with all your mind and strength ... Do this and life is yours. (Lk 10:27-28)

Whereas it may appear that the stress here is on our loving response, it is in fact secondary to and dependent on God first loving us.

> In this the love of God was made manifest among us, that God sent his only Son into the world, so that we might live through him. In this is love, not that we loved God but that he loved us and sent his Son to be the expiation for our sins. (1 Jn 4:9-10)

> We love, because he first loved us. (1 Jn 4:19)

It is this dream that Jesus longs for us to realise, when he says to the woman at the well, 'If you only knew the gift of God!' It is this gift of God or 'grace' that enables us to bring to full flower all the potential of our being made in his image.

Summary

God reveals himself in a practical plan for our welfare which he is working out. This plan, like the dream in the acorn, is built into us, and is not just an external 'will of God.' It springs from the image of God in us, which is basically an immense capacity to be loved.

Questions for reflection

1) Do you see the will of God as outside you, or as in-built, like the dream in the acorn? Is it something you are meant to be doing for God, or is it mainly something God is doing in you?

2) Are you at home with the fact that God's plan is primarily that you believe in yourself as loved? Is this the good news that Jesus asks you to believe in?

One who works to bring our dream to be

God is intent on not allowing the immense potential of his in-built dream in us to lie dormant. This is what Jesus calls the 'work' of his Father – that we should discover and make our own of the plan he has for us. This plan is that we would 'change our minds and hearts and believe the good news.'

> This is the work of God, that you believe in him whom he has sent. (Jn 6:29)

> Jesus came into Galilee, proclaiming the gospel of God, saying, 'The time is come at last, and the kingdom of God has arrived. You must change your minds and hearts and believe the good news.' (Mk 1:14-15)

It is in his God's that we learn to see our real worth, beneath what may appear to others' eyes as of doubtful value. The work of love's providence is to uncover all the potential of the image of God in us. This may be obscured by our apparent ordinariness.

The Old Violin
The old battered violin that was left with the auctioneer seemed hardly worth asking people to bid for. This was borne out when the bidding for it started; nobody appeared to be interested. Just before it was to be knocked down for a mere pittance, an old man walked from the back of the room, dusted it off and began to play. People stood in wonder at what the touch of the master's hand could draw from what seemed useless; how the treasure that lay in the instrument could be uncovered by him.

A new creation
What God wants to reveal to us, through Jesus, is so much beyond our wildest dreams that it is what the Bible calls a new creation. Each of us has become what Paul calls a `new person altogether.'

> So if anyone is in Christ, there is a new creation: everything old has passed away; see, everything has become new! (2 Cor 5:17)

THE THIRD FACE OF GOD

As this new creation, we can come to know that we are loved by the Father, just as Jesus is, and thus share their life and happiness.

> I know my own and my own know me as the Father knows me and I know the Father. (Jn 10:14-15)

This means that we are loved, and are as lovable in the Father's eyes, as Jesus. This is the essentially life-giving thing which Jesus has come to ask us to believe in. Fostering this belief is the essential 'work' God is doing in us. (Jn 6:29)

> And this is eternal life, that they know you the only true God, and Jesus Christ whom you have sent. (Jn 17:3)

The growing conviction that we are loved in this way is what makes us truly happy, and this, Jesus tells us, is the purpose of his revelation.

> I have told you these things that you might share my joy and that your happiness may be complete. (Jn 15:11)

> The supreme happiness in life
> is the conviction of being loved.
> (Victor Hugo)

> See, I am doing a new thing; now it springs forth, do you not perceive it? (Is 43:19)

Summary

God 'works' to realise his dream in us. This is that we would 'own' the new creation which we have become. This new life is brought about by our belief in his love, or by coming to 'know the one true God'.

Questions for reflection

1) In what sense is God at work in your life, judging from what Jesus says in Jn 6:29?
2) Is there a realistic way of seeing yourself as a new creation?
3) Does the story of The Old Violin say anything to you about your resistance to what God is helping you to become?

FEATURE 3

One who is energetic – a busy lover

God intends us to be gradually transformed, or 'transfigured' like Jesus was on Tabor, in 'ever-increasing splendour' into his image.

> We are transfigured in ever-increasing splendour into his own image and the transformation comes from the Lord who is the Spirit.[P] (2 Cor 3:18)

> God's gifts put man's best dreams to shame.
> (Browning)

Our human dreams are so limited that we find it hard to take in the revelation of what God has planned for us. In a note on our being made in God's image, the Jerusalem Bible says, 'This relationship ... involves a general similarity of nature, intellect, will, authority. It paves the way for a higher revelation, the human share in the divine nature by virtue of grace.' The dream which God built into us has been extended and deepened, through grace, beyond anything we could have hoped for.

> But it is written, 'What no eye has seen, nor ear heard, nor the heart of man conceived, what God has prepared for those who love him, God has revealed to us through the Spirit.' (1 Cor 2:9-10)

> Glory be to him whose power working within us can do infinitely more than we can ask or imagine. (Eph 3:20)

You are being transfigured

If we are so intent on seeing this new creation as something we can achieve, we may miss the reality that it is largely something God is doing in us.

God will be working with us to realise this dream, to 'transfigure us in ever-increasing splendour' into the likeness of Christ. A whole series of images are used in the Bible to describe how God is working with us to realise his dream for us. These include shaping, moulding, weaving, watching over with tender care, and planning our future. They bear out the truth of the Spanish proverb that God is a busy lover.

Your own hands shaped me, modelled me ... and wove me of bone and sinews ... watched every breath of mine with tender care. Yet all the while you had a secret plan. (Job 10:8-12)

It is not you who shapes God, but God who shapes you.
If then you are the work of God,
await the hand of the artist
who does all things in due season.
Offer him your heart, soft and tractable,
and keep the form in which the artist has fashioned you.
Let your clay be moist, lest you grow hard
and lose the imprint of his fingers.
(Iraneaus)

In all their affliction he was afflicted, and the angel of his presence saved them; in his love and in his pity he redeemed them; he lifted them up and carried them all the days of old. (Is 63:9)

How long will you waver, O faithless daughter? For the Lord has created a new thing on the earth; a woman will seek her husband again. (Jer 31:22)

The reality of all of this is so far beyond anything we are used to in our daily experience that it is difficult to believe that God is so active in us, that he is the main agent in our lives. To bring home the reality of this, a wise teacher used to ask the question, 'Who feeds the baby?' It is worthwhile pondering what answer you would give.

Summary
There are a lot of images used to describe the way God is working out his dream for us. We are being moulded, shaped and transformed into the divine nature.

Questions for reflection
1) Which of the images used to describe the way God is working out his dream for you do you like best?
2) What answer would you give to the question, 'Who feeds the baby?' Does it help you to realise your role, and God's, in working out his dream for you?

FEATURE 4

One who is deferential as well as assertive

> God who made us without our consent
> will not save us without our consent.
> (St Augustine)

The dream in the acorn directs its growth automatically. We, however, have (1) to get in touch with and (2) to take responsibility for 'seeking' ours. It is only if we seek God 'with all our hearts' that we will find him and satisfy the fundamental thirst which we are.

> I know the plans I have in mind for you – it is Yahweh who speaks – plans for peace, not disaster, reserving a future full of hope for you ... When you seek me you shall find me, when you seek me with all your heart, I will let you find me. (Jer 29:11-14)

Like the dream in the acorn, which will direct the oak tree to be different from any that has ever been or will be, so the dream God has built into each of us is also unique. This means that nobody can tell us our dream; we alone can become conscious of it, and give it full expression.

> Deep within you is written your own song;
> sing it with all your heart.

To be able to realise this dream, we must listen to God's word and respond to it. Not to do this is to build on the sand of our own superficial dreams and not on the rock of the dream which God has built into us. God challenges us to face this reality.

> Every one who comes to me, hears my words and does them, I will show you what he is like: he is like a man building a house, who dug deep, and laid the foundations on rock; and when a flood arose, the stream broke against that house and could not shake it, because it had been well built. But he who hears and does not do them is like a man who built a house on the ground without a foundation; against which the stream broke, and immediately it fell, and the ruin of that house was great. (Lk 6:46-49)

My mother and my brothers are those who hear the word of God and do it. (Lk 8:21)

One of the reasons why we may not be attracted to this face of God is that we imagine him to be like parents who, in a misguided way, push their plans for us aggressively. This may create resentment so that we resist their interference, and their not being sensitive to where we are and what we feel we need.

We must assume that God is at least as loving as good parents. They affirm their children, which means that they appreciate what they do as well as encourage their initiatives. To have to check everything out with an outer authority before we do it is a sign of immaturity. It means that we lose touch with our dream, with the unique way God is working out his plan for our peace. With Paul, we need to pray to have the eyes of our heart enlightened, to be able to discern for ourselves the gentle enlightenment and attraction of God from within.

I do not cease to give thanks for you, remembering you in my prayers, that the God of our Lord Jesus Christ, the Father of glory, may give you a spirit of wisdom and of revelation in the knowledge of him, having the eyes of your hearts enlightened, you may know what is the hope to which he has called you, what are the riches of his glorious inheritance in the saints. (Eph 1:17-18)

And it is my prayer that your love may abound more and more, with knowledge and all discernment, so that you may recognise what is excellent.(Phil 1:9-10)

We have a tendency to look outside ourselves for guidance, to get another to carry our soul for us. We need to let go of people's expectations and listen to, as well as follow, the dream which God has implanted in our hearts.

Flowing With The River
Some clinging creatures lived at the bottom of the river. To resist the rushing current, clinging was a way of life. One creature, however, decided to let the current take it where it would. Clinging, he would die of boredom, so he decided to let go. The others laughed at the idea and predicted disaster. When he did let go, he was buffeted by the current and then lifted free by it.

Some creatures downstream shouted, 'Messiah!' when they saw the one carried by the current but he answered that the river delighted to lift us free if only we dare to let go. He was convinced that our true work was this adventure, this voyage.

Rather than clinging to superficial dreams, we have to surrender ourselves to the essential one, to the river of God's care that encompasses us all the day long.

Of Benjamin he said, 'The beloved of the Lord, he dwells in safety by him; he encompasses him all the day long, and makes his dwelling between his shoulders. (Deut 33:12)

Summary

We each have to realise our unique dream by listening and responding to it. God leaves us free to do this. Because so few respect our freedom, we cannot imagine God doing so. He invites us to flow with the river.

Questions for reflection

1) In what way does God show his respect for your freedom?
2) What does the story, Flowing with the River, say to you?
3) Do you notice much resistance to this feature of God?

One who works ceaselessly for our good

God remains with us 'all along the way we have travelled on the road to this place.' The constancy of God's care stretches down all our years, imprinting itself on our past, pervading the present and going before us to prepare resting places, showing the way and even carrying us at times.

> The Lord your God who goes before you will himself fight for you, just as he did for you in Egypt before your eyes, and in the wilderness, where you have seen how the Lord your God bore you, as a man bears his son in all the ways that you went until you came to this place. Yet in spite of this word you did not believe the Lord your God, who went before you in the way to seek you out a place to pitch your tents, in fire by night, to show you by what way you should go, and in the cloud by day. (Deut 1:30-33)

It is an interesting feature of the dream in the acorn that it is real-ised in a very constant way. Even though the way it develops is unique – there will never be another like it – it will not suddenly change course in its growth path. Similarly, God leads us in a very constant and consistent way along our unique path.

> Listen to me, all ... who have been borne by me from your birth, carried from the womb; even to your old age I am he, and to grey hairs I will carry you. I have made, and I will bear; I will carry and will save. (Is 46:3-4)

The story of God's dealings with us in realising our in-built dream is written into our own life-stories. It is important that we come to know the unique and recurring patterns of events recorded there. From them we can gather a sense of the meaning of our lives and of direction for the future.

> The further you want to see ahead
> the further you should look back.

> I remember the days of old,
> I meditate on all that you have done;

I muse on what your hands have made.
I stretch out my hands to you;
as my soul thirsts for you like a parched land.
(Ps 143:5-8)

Sometimes when we are being directed by someone in our work over a number of years, we may feel that we are well understood and have got used to that person's style. If we are changed to another place, the new person's methods may be at odds with what we have been used to. From this example we might get some sense of how consistent is the plan God is working out in us, for he understands perfectly where we have come from and where we might move next.

There's a pattern in God's weaving

There is a way of weaving a design on to a piece of gauze with bits of woollen thread of various colours. What is distinctive about the finished product is that on one side there is a clearly defined picture that the weaver has worked out of the great variety of colours of thread. On the other side, however, there is a mass of threads with no discernible pattern.

We may be conscious of our lives as being like the wrong side of what is woven on to the gauze. We are, however, invited by God to discover in our story the rich design he is weaving out of all the circumstances of our lives. The pattern will be a record of his unique and constant way of working with us in shaping our lives. It is easy to be unaware of this because of our lack of reflection on the confusing mass of our experience.

No detail is too insignificant

There is a strong feeling in us that we should not expect God to concern himself with the details of our lives, especially the more insignificant ones. It is hard to credit that he concerns himself with every detail of our story.

Are not five sparrows sold for two pennies? And not one of them is forgotten before God. Why, even the hairs of your head are all numbered. Fear not, you are of more value than many sparrows. (Lk 12:6-7)

Consider the ravens, they neither sow nor reap, they have neither storehouse nor barn, and yet God feeds them. Of how much more value are you than the birds? ... But if God so clothes the grass which is alive in the field today and tomorrow is thrown into the oven, how much more will he clothe you, O men of little faith? And do not seek what you are to eat and what you are to drink, nor be of anxious mind. For all the nations of the world seek these things; and your Father knows you need them. (Lk 12:24-30)

A ceaseless effort for your good

It is in a mother's love that we may find our strongest image of one who is untiring in her efforts for our good.

> *Mother-Mine*
> I knew her full-well,
> For she was mother-mine;
> Her care the making of me.
> Respect too there always was
> for me being me,
> Sensitive to mood and need
> And endless helpfulness.

No matter how provident the mother of a large family is, she cannot be everywhere at once. She has to divide her time and be where she is most needed, even if that means neglecting some of her children at such times. She has to say in effect, 'You are not the only pebble on the beach.' It is hard for us, therefore, to accept that, for God, each of us is the only pebble on the beach. The sun heats all the pebbles on the beach and their numbers do not mean that any one gets less of the warmth of the sun. God's love is like that, for the full warmth of his caring is there for each of us always.

> For in everything, O Lord, you have exalted and glorified your people; and you have not neglected to help them at all times and in all places. (Wis 19:22)

> In that day: A pleasant vineyard, sing of it! I, the Lord, am its keeper; every moment I water it. Lest any one harm it, I guard it night and day. (Is 27:2-3)

To those who urged us to put God back into our lives the Master said, 'He is already there.' Our business is to recognise this.

> O God, from my youth you have taught me,
> and yet your wonders stretch out beyond me still.
> (Ps 71:17)

Summary

God is constant and consistent in guiding us to realise our dream. There is a beautiful pattern in the way he weaves even the most insignificant details of our lives into his grand design.

Questions for reflection

1) Do you notice much evidence in your life of your dream being unfolded in a constant and consistent way? Is there a pattern in it or is it all loose ends?

2) Do you find resistance to the belief that God is working out something really good in your life and that he can work all things that happen into this?

3) How does this feature of God's providence appear to you? What piece of Scripture illustrates it best for you?

One who is not deterred by the poverty of our response

In all things and at all times, God is intent on our happiness and has explicitly committed himself to this in an everlasting covenant of peace.

In the Bible, the word peace means the perfect happiness which Jesus as Messiah brings and this happiness is central to God's design for each person's life.

> I will make a covenant of peace with them; it shall be an everlasting covenant with them; and I will bless them ... and will set my sanctuary in the midst of them for evermore. My dwelling place shall be with them; and I will be their God and they shall be my people. (Ezek 37:26-27)

> I will make an everlasting covenant with them. I will not cease in my efforts for their good.JB (Jer 32:40)

It is hard to conceive how this dream that God has, this plan for our peace, is not blocked by our limitations, our mistakes or our sinfulness. Yet, no matter how adverse the circumstances, God can make all things work towards our good, and fit everything into his plan for us.

> We know that in everything God works for good [turns everything to their good JB] with those who love him, who are called according to his purpose. (Rom 8:28)

As we saw in the main symbol of the First Face (p 44), God can weave even the most adverse circumstances into the plan for our peace to which he has committed himself.

> God tempers the wind to the shorn lamb

> The Lord guides a person's steps
> and protects those in whom he delights;
> though he fall, he shall get up again,
> for the Lord is the stay of his hand. (Ps 37:23-24)

Summary

God is not limited by our limitations in his constant commitment to our happiness. God's providence is not blocked by our lack of fidelity.

Questions for reflection

1) In the light of your own reaction to people who let you down, do you find it strange that God is so committed to caring for you?
2) Are there other facts in this section that you find yourself resisting?

One who works to heal the wounds of our waywardness

The dream in the acorn is subject to accidents and may not be fully realised. A lot of things can happen along the way to its becoming an oak tree and these may slow down or prevent its proper growth.

There are many things, too, that may interfere with the realisation of our dream. Chief among these is a poor image of ourselves, due to our failure to accept fully God's way of seeing us. What he does to heal the painful wound caused by this illusion is to invite us to see ourselves as he sees us, to undergo the change of mind and heart involved in believing the good news about ourselves.

> ... change your minds and hearts and believe the good news. (Mk 1:14-15)

A symbol of God's desire to heal us is the bronze serpent. This is what God told Moses to lift up before the people so that those who had been bitten by snakes, on looking at it might be healed.

> So Moses made a bronze serpent and set it on a pole; and if a serpent bit any man, he would look at the bronze serpent and live. (Num 21:9)

The main source of our woundedness is the fact that we live with the destructive illusion of our own insignificance. We believe this rather than God's word, the good news of God's love and our own lovableness.

> But your sons were not conquered by the teeth of venomous serpents for your mercy came to their help and healed them. To remind them of your oracles they were bitten and then were quickly healed, lest by falling into deep forgetfulness they become unresponsive to your kindness [be cut off from your kindness JB]. For neither herb nor poultice cured them, but it is your word, O Lord, which heals all people. (Wis 16:10-12)

It is easy for us to 'get cut off from his kindness' because there is such resistance in us to his love. This comes mainly from our sense of utter unworthiness of it. There is a voice in each of us that says, 'Me, Lord? Canst thou mis-spend one word, misplace one look on me?' Read again *The Divine Lover* on page 77.

If it is God's love that heals, then there is nothing so healing as the most powerful sign of his love. This he showed us in giving up his only Son to be lifted up on the cross, like the Bronze Serpent, so that seeing this love of us 'to the end' we might be healed.

> And as Moses lifted up the serpent in the wilderness, so must the Son of man be lifted up, that whoever believes in him may have eternal life. For God so loved the world that he gave his only Son that whoever believes in him should not perish but have eternal life. (Jn 3:15-16)

> In this is the love of God made manifest among us, that God sent his only Son into the world, so that we might live through him. In this is love, not that we loved God, but that he loved us and sent his Son to be the expiation for our sins. (1 Jn 4:9-10)

We will probably find it hard to adjust our minds and hearts to this image of God's providence. We seem to identify more readily with an image of God as one who does not let human considerations get in his way when it comes to imposing his will on our lives. We have often heard this expressed in a statement like, 'We've got to grin and bear it.' This is a mentality that was expressed by an image from Greek philosophy: one of a little dog tied to its master's chariot – no matter how it feels about things it has to go along or it will be dragged.

Summary

God heals the wounds of our unbelief by inviting us to look at how worthwhile we are in his eyes.

Questions for reflection

1) What is the most deadly wound God wishes to heal? Why is it so deadly? If you accept that you are wounded in this way, how do you find yourself resisting God's efforts to heal your woundedness?

One who works to free us from our enslavement

One of the greatest signs of God's provident love is the Exodus. In this central event of the Old Testament, God freed the people from the land of sin and slavery, so that they might be free to enter the promised land. In the Book of Wisdom we too find ourselves described as 'captives of the dark' and needing to be freed from being 'exiles from eternal providence.'

> For when lawless people supposed they had the whole nation in their power, they themselves lay as captives of darkness and prisoners of the long night, shut in under their own roofs, exiles from eternal providence. (Wis 17:2)

Through the prophet Hosea, God expresses his desire to lure us into the desert, to speak to and win our hearts. He thus aims to free us from our tendency to become enslaved to false gods, so that we would be free to enter a new life of intimacy with him.

> That is why I am going to lure her and lead her out into the wilderness and speak to her heart ... There she will respond to me as she did when she was young, as she did when she came out of the land of Egypt ... I will betroth you to myself with faithfulness, and you will come to know Yahweh.[JB] (Hos 2:16-17,22)

> I have seen the affliction of my people who are in Egypt and have heard their cry ... I have come down to deliver them out of the hand of the Egyptians and to bring them up out of that land to a good and broad land, a land flowing with milk and honey. (Ex 3:7-8)

Jesus sees the work the Father sends him to do as to 'set at liberty those who are oppressed'.

> The Spirit of the Lord is upon me, because he has anointed me to preach good news to the poor. He has sent me to proclaim release to the captives and recovering of sight to the blind, to set at liberty those who are oppressed, to proclaim the acceptable year of the Lord. (Lk 4:18-19)

NINE FACES OF GOD

This then is the essential call of Jesus to 'repent' or change our minds and hearts in order to free ourselves from our illusions and false values. Thus we might be free to believe the good news of God's love and our lovableness.

> Jesus came into Galilee, proclaiming the gospel of God, saying, 'The time is come at last, and the kingdom of God has arrived. You must change your minds and hearts and believe the good news.' (Mk 1:14-15)

This freeing of ourselves from our ingrained illusions is like a dying to our false self in order that we might experience the life-giving effects of God's way of seeing things.

Summary

God in his providence works to free us from the slavery of sin, so that we may enter the promised land of his life and peace. We are thus called to repent or to free ourselves from our illusions so that we can believe in God's life-giving way of seeing things.

Questions for reflection

1) How do you see the work of God's providence as being concerned with our freedom?
2) Is Jesus' invitation to repent and believe, a call, like the Exodus was, to freedom?

One who works to bring us to full flower

Just as the dream in the acorn constantly pushes on towards the maturity of the fully grown oak tree, so there is a persistent voice in us urging us on to realise all the potential of our in-built dream.

In David's final prayer before he died, he expressed his conviction that God can bring all our desires and dreams to full flower.

> He who rules men with justice, who rules in the fear of God, is like morning light at sunrise (on a cloudless morning) making the grass of the earth sparkle after rain. Yes my house stands firm with God: he has made an everlasting covenant with me, all in order, well assured; does he not bring to full flower all that saves me, all I desire?[JB] (2 Sam 23:3-5)

There is an immense energy in all of nature, urging all things towards maturity. The acorn never rests, but pursues wholeness until it finds expression in the fully grown oak tree. Our dream must also find expression in the realisation of the rich potential of the image of God in us. God can, in spite of all our limitation and weakness, bring to full flower all that we desire.

> And I am sure that he who began a good work in you will bring it to completion (God will go on developing what he has begun in you JB) (Phil 1:6)

> We are transfigured in ever-increasing splendour into his own image, and the transformation comes from the Lord who is the Spirit. (2 Cor 3:18)

Paul here is comparing what God is working out in us now, through his Spirit, to what happened to Jesus on Tabor. It is an experience of God transforming us, through his Spirit, in 'ever-increasing splendour into his own image.' This can easily remain hidden from us unless we take the trouble to get in touch with it. One of life's greatest tragedies is that we are unaware of the inner eventfulness of our lives, that the glory of God dwells within each of us.

> I will be to her a wall of fire round about, says the Lord, and
> I will be the glory within her ... he who touches you touches
> the apple of my eye ... Sing and rejoice, O daughter of Zion;
> for I come and I will dwell in the midst of you, says the Lord.
> (Zech 2:5,8,10)

What seems to deny this dream is the ordinariness of our lives,
the fact that we live in a very small world. Yet God, even in these
circumstances, can 'crowd career with conquest' as Hopkins describes him doing, in his poem on St Alphonsus Rodriguez.

> Yet God (that hews mountain and continent,
> Earth, all, out; who, with trickling increment,
> Veins violets and tall trees makes more and more)
> Could crowd career with conquest while there went
> Those years and years of world without event
> That in Majorca Alfonso watched the door.

Summary

God in his providence seeks to release the immense energy in us,
like that in the oak tree, to reach maturity. The ordinariness of our
lives resists the fact that God is so powerfully at work in us.

Questions for reflection

1) What is the maturity, or the full flowering, that we seek? Why
do we not seek the realisation of our in-built dream with the same
energy as the oak tree does?
2) What does this feature of God's providence reveal to you?

One who guides us in our peak and valley periods

Hopkins wrote his most famous poem about the wreck of a ship at sea in which many lives were lost. In the following extract from it, he expresses his sense of the delicate designs God's love can weave out of such violent events. Hopkins experiences in himself a deep concern for the:

> Comfortless unconfessed of them
> No, not uncomforted; lovely felicitous Providence
> Finger of a tender of, O of a feathery delicacy,
> ... is shipwreck then a harvest
> does tempest carry the grain for thee?

The kind of loving seen in this Face of God is very deferential towards our freedom. It is sensitive to that portion of our dream for which we are ripe at any particular time in our lives.

We may find it hard to conceive how God, who knows where our happiness lies and is so intent on it, would not be more assertive or forceful with us. He is in fact, as Isaiah experienced him, 'gracious' to us, and when he does speak, it is with a 'still small voice' or 'a gentle whisper.'

> Therefore, the Lord waits to be gracious to you; therefore he will exalt himself to show mercy to you. For the Lord is a God of justice; blessed are all who wait for him. (Is 30:18)

> ... and after the earthquake a fire, but the Lord was not in the fire; and after the fire a still small voice {the gentle whisper} and when Elijah heard it he wrapped his face in his mantle ... (1 Kgs 19:12-13)

In speaking of the movement of God's providence in our lives as a 'still small voice', or as a 'gentle whisper', we stress the intimate or interior quality of it. In the early part of the Old Testament God spoke in very dramatic and tangible ways, as he did to Moses in the burning bush. From the time of Elijah, however, he speaks in a much more intimate way, with a 'still small voice.'

O to be satisfied
with that fleeting glimpse
of your face
and the gentle pace
of your grace growing.

Putting us in touch with our dream

God does not manifest his plan by issuing detailed instructions as
to how everything is to be done. That would not challenge us to
do what is more maturing, i.e. to `discern what is best.'

> My prayer for you is that you may have still more love, that
> your love may abound more and more in knowledge and
> depth of insight so that you may be able to discern what is
> best. (Phil 1:9)

God is like a good parent or leader who is always inviting us to do
what we think best and thus take responsibility for making our
own decisions. So if you ask God what is his will, or what you
should do in some complex situation, he will ask you to do what
you honestly think is best. Then he will draw the best out of what
you decide, even if you are mistaken in your decision. It is as if
God is saying, 'Accept my love and then do what you feel is the
loving thing.' He helps us work this out by 'enlightening the eyes
of our hearts' but he will not do it for us.

> I do not cease to give thanks for you, remembering you in
> my prayers, that the God of our Lord Jesus Christ, the Father
> of glory, may give you a spirit of wisdom and of revelation
> in the knowledge of him, having the eyes of your hearts en-
> lightened that you may know what is the hope to which he
> has called you, what are the riches of his glorious inheri-
> tance in the saints. (Eph 1:16-18)

Educating us through darkness

Times of hardship or darkness may do most to give us a deep appreciation of God's loving providence. At times like these he
leads us with 'fire by night'.

> ... in the wilderness where you have seen how the Lord
> your God bore you, as a man bears his son, in all the way

that you went until you came to this place. Yet in spite of this word you did not believe the Lord your God, who went before you in the way to seek you out a place to pitch your tent, in the fire by night, to show you by what way you should go, and in the cloud by day. (Deut 1:31-33)

Hardships have a way of questioning us as to what we really believe about God's loving providence. It is in wrestling with our answer that we learn a depth of personal belief; in dark times we have to cling to the promise made in the light.

Remember the word which Moses the servant of the Lord commanded you saying, 'The Lord your God is providing for you a place of rest, and will give you this land.' (Josh 1:13)

The poet Francis Thompson came to realise that life's hardships are the 'shade of his hand outstretched caressingly.'

Halts by me that footfall;
Is my gloom, after all
shade of his hand outstretched caressingly?
'Ah fondest, blindest, weakest,
I am He Whom thou seekest!
Thou drvest love from thee who drvest me.
(Francis Thompson)

… you shall weep no more. He will surely be gracious to you at the sound of your cry; when he hears it he will answer you. And though the Lord give you the bread of adversity and the water of affliction, yet your Teacher will not hide himself any more, but your eyes shall see your Teacher. And your ears will hear a word behind you, saying, 'This is the way, walk in it', when you turn to the right or when you turn to the left. (Is 30:18-21)

Like Job, we are often moved from what we see with our mind to what we feel with our heart through a period of darkness or suffering such as he underwent. Life's hardships have a way of questioning us about our belief in God's providence, whether our 'gloom', after all, is 'shade of his hand outstretched caressingly.'

I know that you are all-powerful: what you conceive, you can perform. I am the man who obscured your designs with my empty-headed words. I have been holding forth on matters I cannot understand, on marvels beyond me and my knowledge ... I knew you then only by hearsay; but now, having seen you with my own eyes, I retract all I have said, and in dust and ashes I repent. (Job 42:2-6)

So God works in mysterious ways his wonders to perform, even though we do not always understand what he is doing or the way he goes about it. We are sure, however, that he wants to bring us to full flower and that he will take the best way to bring this about for each person. As Hopkins says in the poem on page 60, this may be, as it was with Paul on the road to Damascus, brought about in a startling way. On the other hand, the work of God's providence in us may take the form it did with Augustine, of 'a lingering out sweet skill.' It may be 'with fire in us that he forges his will', or it may creep into our lives as gently as Spring. God tempers the wind to the shorn lamb.

Summary

There is a deference which respects our freedom, as well as an intimacy in the way God influences us. There is a vision of this face of God that we, like Job, can get only when God leads us through the valley of darkness.

Questions for reflection

1) When Scripture says that God speaks with 'a still small voice,' what does it mean? What does it reveal to you about this Face of God? Does God guide you from within, or without?
2) Most people would like God to declare his will for them very clearly. Why does he not do this, do you think? What impression does this give you of God?
3) When you recall times of hardship in your life, are there insights you got then that you could not see when all was going well?

A personal God

The Key Experience:
Being called by name
Resistance:
We resist this because the world is very impersonal
The Main Symbol:
The thread that runs through each person's life

This Face manifests one who loves us in a deeply personal and intimate way. God chooses us out of the crowd to know him face to face. We are called by a name that stands for the unique relationship which God has with each person. God compares the depth and intimacy of this relationship with that of a marriage and even with that which he enjoys with Jesus, his 'beloved' in whom he delights. In spite of our weakness and our waywardness we remain special, for nobody is common in God's eyes.

1. One who is personally involved with you

God wants an intensely personal relationship with us, in which we know him face to face. We screen ourselves from this awesome reality, allowing a wall to be built, to shield us from it.

2. One who chooses you out from the crowd

The personal quality of the way God relates with each person is emphasised by his choosing us. There is a sense of being personally chosen, 1) to be his own, 2) for our inner worth and not for our accomplishments, 3) because he knows us through and through, 4) to be extraordinarily honoured, and yet 5) having our freedom treated with deference.

3. One who calls you by your name

Your name calls up the whole unique relationship you have with God. This relationship is always changing so that there is a special name which God calls you by just now. God wants us to discover this very personal way he calls us.

4. One who constantly calls you along a unique way to life

The way God calls each person is constantly changing just as his or her relationship with God is. The call will always be adapted to the unique person that is constantly emerging in us. Each of us receives a personal vocation.

5. One who speaks to you face to face

Our calling is to know God intimately, as he reveals himself to each person in 'a still small voice'. The Old Testament uses the image of marriage to portray the intimacy of 'knowing' God. Jesus takes as his model, the friendship he enjoys with his Father and uses it to describe the intimacy God wants with us. This involves his complete self-revelation.

---

6. One for whom nothing about you is common

Our sense of insignificance makes it difficult for us to accept being loved by the Father as Jesus was. This love is for the least no less than the greatest and is revealed in the most mundane places. No one loved by God is common, but all are, by this love, made unique. We are confirmed in this belief by those who believe in us, but there is much in our world to deny it. We easily succumb to the illusion of insignificance.

7. One who convinces you of how special you are

We have to let God 're-teach us our loveliness' in the way the prodigal son learned, on his return home, a new appreciation of himself, from his father. God can see beyond our weakness to what is precious, and give this permanent expression. This he does by teaching us the full extent of his love and our lovableness, through his Spirit who is given equally to all. He has all the sensitivity of a mother to where we are and to how we feel.

.

We get an impression of this Face of God from people who call us by our name. Each of us is unique and travels through life along a road no one else follows. It is rare, however, that we are treated in this very personal way.

We live in a very impersonal world, which values conformity rather than recognising that deep within, we each have our own song to sing. We need to be encouraged to sing it with all our heart. We have, therefore, to get in touch with times in our lives when we felt called by name, chosen out of the crowd, or when we experienced what is very personal to our own story. In this way we may be led to recognise the very distinct style of being loved and loving that is ours and how good it is when others acknowledge and respect this.

Resistance

In a very impersonal world, people tend to feel uncomfortable with the personal or intimate details of our story. So we tend to hide this side of ourselves and to get embarrassed when attention is drawn to it. We may have learned to believe that God is more interested in our conformity to his will than in adapting his plan to the very special person each of us is. We are so often required to submerge our personal interests, and the ways we are different from others, that we can lose touch with our uniqueness. All this makes the intimate and personal relationship God wants with each of us unreal, as this intimacy is not our day-to-day experience.

Arousing dormant experience

1) Take some time to be quiet in your inner room, and then give your attention to the pictures around its walls that represent your life story.

2) Look at one of these pictures and remember the kind of person you were at that time. Notice how different you were from others who are in the picture and notice the ways your path diverged from theirs.

3) Now let yourself become aware of how God was in all of this, calling you by your name, along this unique way, to fulfill a very special dream God has for you.

There is a thread that runs through our lives and it is absolutely unique to each person. It emerges from God, runs through all our days and inevitably makes its way back to him. It begins with God choosing us and calling us by name into a deep personal relationship with him.

The way God calls us is like a path along which he leads us on our journey to him, a path which is special to each one and where we are sometimes with others, but often alone. We may not be conscious of it, but it is the way we follow in answering when God calls us by name.

This thread of our story is as unique to each of us as our fingerprints, as the way we see a sunrise or hear another's voice. We will be most content in life when we are in touch with this unique way in which God wants to be with each of us.

> Its secret is not heard
> By the curious ears of the mind
> But by those alert to wonder
> Listening childlike to the soul of things.

The symbol of the thread that runs through each person's life emphasises the unique and yet consistent way in which God leads us into a personal relationship with him.

> ... for you are his personal concern. (1 Pet 5:7)

One who is personally involved with you

God had always spoken to people, but his voice became more intimately personal with those, like Abraham and Moses, through whom he spoke to the people that he called his own. In time it became clear that God wanted this intimate relationship, not just with the leaders of his people, but with each person. The desire of God to relate with us in this way has been repeated so often in the Bible that we may miss the richness of it through over-familiarity. The overwhelming reality, however, is that God and each person are as two who belong to each other.

> I will be their God and they shall be my people. (Jer 31:33)

In the Song of Songs the intimate nature of this relationship is put more strikingly:

> My beloved is mine and I am his. (Song 2:16)

Jeremiah reveals to us that God wants to relate with each one of us in this way:

> And no longer shall each man teach his neighbor and each his brother saying, 'Know the Lord' for they shall all know me, from the least of them to the greatest, says the Lord. (Jer 31:34)

> This feature of God's face
> Is best glimpsed by the heart;
> Like the intuitive grasp of life
> That comes with the wisdom of years.
> Its concern is people and providence
> And is the intimate understanding
> Mirrored to us in the loving gaze
> Of the One who knows us through and through.

Screening ourselves from being face to face

This kind of personal intimacy has to be seen against the background of how awesome the holiness of God is in the Bible.

THE FOURTH FACE OF GOD

> Then God said, 'Do not come near; put off your shoes from your feet, for the place on which you are standing is holy ground.' And he said, 'I am the God of your father, the God of Abraham, the God of Isaac, and the God of Jacob.' And Moses hid his face for he was afraid to look at God. (Ex 3:5-6)

Alongside this awesome reverence, there developed a deeply personal relationship between God and Moses, one in which the two would speak 'face to face as a man speaks to his friend.'

> And when all of the people saw the pillar of cloud standing at the door of the tent they would rise up and worship, everyone at his own tent door. Thus the Lord used to speak to Moses face to face, as a man speaks to his friend. (Ex 33:11)

> There has not arisen a prophet since in Israel like Moses, whom the Lord knew face to face. (Deut 34:10)

This 'face to face' relationship was initially confined to Moses, as leader of Israel, and he would pass on to the people what God had said. They had no direct contact with God but would rely on Moses to tell them what God was like. To become so personally intimate with God, as Moses had, was too awesome and even fearsome, so they 'kept their distance while Moses approached the dark cloud where God was.' The people here reflect the feelings of most of us about God becoming so personal.

> ... and they kept their distance. 'Speak to us yourself,' they said to Moses, `and we shall listen, but do not let God speak to us or we shall die' ... So the people kept their distance while Moses approached the dark cloud where God was. (Ex 20:18-21)

St Paul, in his Second Letter to the Corinthians, notes how the Jews of his own day kept a veil between themselves and the intimacy God wanted:

> Yes, to this day whenever Moses is read a veil lies over their minds; but when a man turns to the Lord the veil is removed ... And we all, with unveiled face, seeing the glory of the Lord, are being changed into his likeness from one degree of glory to another. (2 Cor 3:15-18)

We too tend to screen ourselves from the intimacy God wants with us. We allow a wall to be erected between ourselves and God

Nine Faces of God

Peter Hannan SJ

WHAT YOU NEED FOR YOUR JOURNEY

This brief outline of what you need for your journey of faith will help as a reference for you as you begin to contemplate the Faces of God. More detailed background on each of the requirements is to be found in Chapter 4.

Making space for God

Always start by quietening yourself and then become aware of God's presence.

Exploring our own experience

The Key Experience which you find at the beginning of each Face is meant to help you to arouse areas of your experience that may lie dormant. This will make what you contemplate in each Face more tangible and real.

Take the time you need to make your own of the Key Experience, the ways you resist this and what is suggested to you in the exercises. Carry with you what you find helpful of this experience into your contemplation of the features of each Face. Keep adding to your experience what will make each Face of God more real for you.

Universal experience: traditional wisdom

The purpose of the Main Symbol, and of all the other symbolic material like stories and poems throughout these Faces, is to broaden out your own personal experience and get you more involved in it.

Read the story of the Main Symbol a few times in the light of the experience which you have so far surfaced. Ponder what it has to say to this experience. The story may take time to surrender its meaning, especially until you develop a facility for using stories to speak to your own experience.

Bible experience

What we have seen so far is an outline sketch of the Face of God which we are contemplating. We have now to fill in, one by one, each of the main features of this Face. The main place where God will reveal each of these features to you is in God's word. In order to bring what he reveals to life, it is vital that you contemplate it against the background of all the experience you have so far accumulated.

Read a passage of scripture in the light of the feature you are contemplating. Beware of the tendency to get side-tracked from the feature that is meant to be the focus of your attention. Pause when some word or phrase of scripture says something to you about this feature. Ponder this word or phrase in the light of your experience so far.

Prayer: a conversation with God

The purpose of prayer here is to absorb what God has opened up about himself and his love for you, in whatever feature of this love you are focusing on. This will involve listening to what has struck you most forcefully about God's love for you. It will also involve responding, as honestly as you can, to the love he has expressed for you.

Listen to any aspect of God's love for you that has captured your attention. Let God say this to you in some simple and personal way. After some time this will give rise to certain feelings in you. Some of these feelings will be positive, but others will signify that you have difficulty taking in what God is saying to you. Become aware of both positive and negative feelings and, after you have found words for them, share how you feel, in as frank a way as you can, with God.

Reflection on our experience

The purpose of reflection is to become aware of the fact that God reveals himself to you in prayer. It is also meant to help you to become familiar with how God goes about this, by enlightening your mind and attracting your heart.

At the end of any period of prayer, spend time becoming aware of what struck you and what you felt attracted to stay with during your prayer. Record this, however briefly. Begin your next prayer period by reading what you have written. This will give continuity and lead to a build-up of what is being revealed to you. From this, a true vision of who God is, and who you are for God, will take shape. In this way you will be answering the essential Christian call to repent and believe the Gospel. (Mk 1:15)

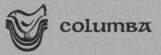 COLUMBA

in somewhat the same way as can happen in the most intimate human relationships. This comes about in a very subtle and gradual way unless we take the pains to foster intimacy.

The Wall

Some time, between their first child and their last, they allowed a wall to be erected between them. At the beginning it was little differences that were not sorted out but stored away. It then became too much of a risk to reveal their darker feelings as they emerged with time.

He hid his fear of failure, and she, her sadness at losing him. Each sought refuge in other places and persons rather than in each other. He escaped to his office while she channelled her energy into their children.

So there it stood between them, a wall so tall and thick that they could no longer touch each other. It was not the fruit of hostility or conflict so much as apathy and a failure to take the pains to work regularly at removing the obstacles to their communing.

If we really want to see this face of God we have to work at removing this wall, which symbolises our reserve when God approaches us in the intimately personal way he obviously wants to.

Summary

God wants an intensely personal relationship with us, in which we know him face to face. We screen ourselves from this awesome reality, allowing a wall to be built, to shield us from it.

Questions for reflection

1) What aspect of the personal way God wishes to relate with each of us appeals to you?

2) What way do you notice yourself building a wall to protect yourself from being face to face with God?

One who chooses you out from the crowd

From the beginning of the Bible, there was a deep sense of certain people being personally chosen by God. This was a sense of being selected by God for some work he had confidence they could do, despite their own lack of trust in themselves.

> But you, Israel, my servant, Jacob, whom I have chosen, the offspring of Abraham, my friend; you whom I took from the ends of the earth, and called from its farthest corners, saying to you, 'You are my servant, I have chosen you and not cast you off.' (Is 41:8-9)

When someone chooses us, it is so often because of our usefulness. It is, therefore, hard for us to get the feel of being chosen because God wants to be ours and we his.

> I will put this third into the fire, and refine them as one refines silver, and test them as gold is tested. They will call on my name, and I will answer them. I will say, 'They are my people' and they will say, 'The Lord is my God.' (Zech 13:9)

When God tells Jeremiah that he has chosen him from the womb, it means that he was chosen because God loved Jeremiah for himself, and not for anything he had or would accomplish.

> The Lord addressed me as follows: 'I knew you even before I formed you in your mother's womb, before you were born I set you apart, appointing you as a prophet to the nations.' I answered, 'Lord, I am not able to speak, I am too young.' God replied, 'Do not say that you are too young ... for I will be with you to protect you.' (Jer 1:4-8)

We have only to go back to an experience in our own lives of being chosen, to realise what it adds to the personal quality of a relationship. There is a sense of someone finding something special in us, and having confidence in the person we are. This can raise our whole relationship with them to a new level.

Being chosen beyond our apparent worth

When I was at school we used to play football in the yard at every available opportunity. Two lads would pick their teams and I would wonder just how soon I would be chosen. Your rating as a player would vary according to your form in the previous game. Sometimes I would be chosen much sooner than my performance had justified and I would know that it was due to something more personal than my rating had earned me. The result was a sense of being chosen as Peter, of privilege, and to justify their choice I would be willing to play my heart out.

The experience of being chosen and of being known personally through and through, is now a reality each of us has to own. We have difficulty with this because, even though people choose us for some reason, they rarely want to know us at any depth. The fact that God knows each person in depth is expressed beautifully in the words of Psalm 139:

> You know when I sit and when I rise;
> you know every detail of my conduct.
> If I take the wings of the morning,
> and dwell in the furthest parts of the sea,
> even there your hand shall lead me,
> and your right hand shall hold me.
> For you formed my inmost parts;
> you knit me together in my mother's womb.
> For all these wonders I thank you,
> for the wonder of myself and all your works.
> You know me through and through;
> my frame was not hidden from you,
> when I was being made in secret,
> intricately put together in the depths of the earth.
> (Ps 139:2,9-10,13-15)

We are chosen for an honour God wants to bestow on us, in spite of the fact that we have no claim to it.

> You have seen what I did with the Egyptians and how I bore you on eagles' wings and brought you to myself. Now therefore, if you will obey my voice and keep my covenant, you will be my own possession among all the peoples; for all the earth is mine, and you shall be to me a kingdom of priests and a holy nation. (Gen 19:4-6)

Paul has a deep sense of being personally chosen, to be honoured in an extraordinary way by God, and he sees this as true for each Christian.

> Then God, who had especially chosen me while I was still in my mother's womb, called me through his grace and chose to reveal his Son to me. [JB] (Gal 1:15-16)

> We know that by turning everything to their good God co-operates with those who love him, with all those he has called according to his purpose. They are the ones he chose especially long ago and intended to become true images of his Son. (Rom 8:28-29)

It is very hard to respect the freedom of those we love, especially when we know that they are making a bad decision. It is, therefore, awesome that God should so respect our freedom in what is a matter of life and death. He treats the freedom of each of us with such deference when we choose our individual destiny.

> He has set fire and water before you; put out your hand to whichever you prefer. People have life and death before them; whichever people like best will be given them.
> (Sir 15:17-18)

Experiences of being chosen, not for any use people can make of us, but for who we are and what we may be, have a profound effect on us.

Summary

The personal quality of the way God relates with each person is emphasised by his choosing us. There is a sense of being personally chosen, 1) to be his own, 2) for our inner worth and not for our accomplishments, 3) because he knows us through and through, 4) to be extraordinarily honoured, and yet, 5) having our freedom treated with deference.

Questions for reflection

1) Which aspects of being chosen by God appeal to you, or make you feel special? Which do you resist most?
2) Is there an experience like that in *Being Chosen Beyond our apparent Worth* that means a lot to you? How does recalling or re-living it make you feel?

FEATURE 3

One who calls you by your name

We are deadened by being treated impersonally, as if we had no name. On the other hand it means a lot to us if people remember our name and call us by it.

> Yet you have said, 'I know you by name' ... Is it not in your going with us that we are distinct, I and your people, from all other people on the face of the earth? (Ex 33:12-16)

A name has great significance in the Bible as it stands for a person's whole relationship with God. When God calls us by our name he is calling up all we are before him. This is what happened to Abraham. He was initially called Abram before God chose him for a very special role. When he was given this, and as a result his whole relationship with God was raised to a new level, he received the name Abraham.

> You shall no longer be called Abram; your name shall be Abraham, for I make you father of a multitude of nations ... I will make my covenant between myself and you ... to be your God and the God of your descendants. (Gen 17:5-7)

The name by which God calls us changes, because the relationship it stands for is something that is growing and has a past, a present and a future.

> Listen to me ... (you) who have been borne by me from your youth, carried from the womb; even in your old age I am he, and to grey hairs I will carry you. I have made and I will bear; I will carry and I will save. (Is 46:3-4)

It would be worthwhile here to do the following fantasy:

> First of all quieten yourself and centre your attention on the inner room within yourself. Next, imagine God with you looking at the pictures around the walls of your inner room. These represent the story of your life. Select one picture and dwell with it to see what image of yourself it conveys to you and what good feelings you associate with it. Next, choose a name or a phrase which captures who you were in the pic-

ture. Finally, let God call you by that name, or use that phrase about you, letting him repeat it at intervals until it pervades your whole person.

One of the most attractive things about this face of God is what it manifests about his desire that we discover, and make our own of, the unique self whose name he calls.

> But my dove is unique, mine, unique and perfect. She is the darling of her mother, the favourite of the one who bore her. (Song 6:9)

As Gerard Manley Hopkins observes, all things tend to express their deep self. It is this deepest self that God wants to relate with when he calls me by my name.

> Each mortal thing does one thing and the same:
> Deals out that being indoors each one dwells;
> Selves, goes itself; myself it speaks and spells,
> Crying What I do is me: for that I came.
> (Hopkins)

Summary

Your name calls up the whole unique relationship you have with God. This relationship is always changing so that there is a special name which God calls you by at this time. God wants us to discover this very personal way he calls us.

Questions for reflection

1) Are there people who call you by name? How does this affect you? Does it mean a lot to you when someone remembers your name? Why?

2) How do you react to the fantasy, Hearing God call Your Name?

FEATURE 4

One who constantly calls you along a unique way to life

There is one basic Christian vocation – to 'change our hearts and minds and to believe the Good News.' This call, however, will be heard by each person in a unique way. This is true even of the way different people view a landscape or receive love and express it. Because of this, God calls each of us in a unique way and no two people travel exactly the same road. What is distinctive to the way we are each called will slowly emerge in a whole pattern of enlightenment and attraction that is going on in each person's life as a result of God's constant guidance. In other words, each of us receives a personal vocation from God.

> ... you shall be called by a new name which the mouth of the Lord will give. You shall be a crown of beauty in the hand of the Lord, and a royal diadem in the hand of your God. You shall no more be termed Forsaken, and your land no more be termed Desolate, but you shall be called My delight is in her, and your land Married; for the Lord delights in you and your land shall be married ... and as the bridegroom rejoices over the bride, so shall your God rejoice over you. (Is 62:2-5)

We each have a personal vocation. It is like a name God is using to call us, and it captures all that we are, as well as the very distinctive person we are destined to be.

> And now this is what the Lord says, he who created you, O Jacob, he who formed you, O Israel: Fear not, for I have redeemed you; I have called you by name, you are mine. When you pass through the waters I will be with you; and through the rivers, they shall not overwhelm you; when you walk through fire you shall not be burned, and the flame shall not consume you. For I am the Lord your God, the Holy One of Israel, your Saviour ... Because you are precious in my eyes and honoured, I love you, I give men in return for you, peoples in exchange for your life. Fear not, for I am with you. (Is 43:1-5)

The House With A Million Doors

It is as if the good news is kept for us within a house with a million doors. Because of the unique person each of us is, there will be one of these doors that will be best for each of us to enter and make our own of the good news. God is always drawing us towards that way of nourishing ourselves that is particularly suitable for us at any one time in our lives.

The following passage from the Book of Wisdom expresses the way God adapts his revelation of himself, his word, to what the unique person in each of us needs, at any stage of life.

> Instead of these things you gave your people the food of angels, and without their toil you supplied them from heaven with bread ready to eat, providing every pleasure and suited to every taste. What you gave them manifested your sweetness towards your children, with the bread conforming to the taste of the one who took it. It was changed to suit everyone's liking ... By changing into these forms it served your all-nourishing bounty, according to the desire of those who had need. So your people whom you loved, O Lord, might learn, that it is not the production of crops that feeds us, but that it is your word that preserves those who trust in you. (Wis 16:20-21,25)

Since we remain basically the same kind of person, God will work in a consistent way, modifying his approach according to circumstances and to the stage of growth at which he finds us. All through our lives he will be leading us into the extent and depth of his love. He will do this with a unique and consistent stream of enlightenment and attraction.

The personal quality of our vocation is determined by the fact that we each start out with a special gift from God. This is essential to the unique person each of us is. As we move on through life we are led by God to realise all the potential of that gift, in a very distinctive way:

> Each has his own special gift from God, one of one kind and one of another. (1 Cor 7:7)

> Now there are varieties of gifts, but the same Spirit: and there are varieties of service, but the same Lord: and God

works through different people in a variety of ways, but it is the same God who inspires them all in every one.
(1 Cor 12:4)

God is like the Master in the Indian wisdom stories. He will always make the shoe from an infinite supply of leather. The way he cuts and fashions his material however will always be in accordance with the contours of the individual foot. God is always adapting the way he enlightens and attracts us to the kind of person each of us is, at a particular time of life.

Summary

The way God calls each person is constantly changing just as his or her relationship with God is. The call will always be adapted to the unique person that is constantly emerging in us. Each of us receives a personal vocation.

Questions for reflection

1) What does the fact that you have a personal vocation tell you about this face of God? Do you find it hard to accept that God calls you in this unique way?

2) What words of scripture best express your sense of personal vocation?

FEATURE 5

One who speaks to you face to face

The personal vocation we each receive is a call to our depths, to what is most intimate in us. Its intimacy and depth is best seen in the context of the New Covenant that was announced to Jeremiah. In this, each person is called to be known and loved by God and to know and love him in return. The deeply personal relationship which Moses shared with God, when he spoke to him 'face to face as a person speaks to his friend', is now offered in a unique way to each person.

> And this is the covenant which I will make with the house of Israel after those days, says the Lord: I will put my law within them, and I will write it upon their hearts; and I will be their God and they shall be my people. And no longer shall each man teach his neighbor and each his brother saying, 'Know the Lord' for they shall all know me, from the least of them to the greatest, says the Lord. (Jer 31:33-34)

Each of us passes through the stages that the people of the Old Testament passed through in coming to know God. We reluctantly move ahead from one stage to another and are always likely to revert to an earlier stage.

Firstly, we are asked to let go of our reliance on an outer authority and to accept God revealing himself to each person, to 'the least no less than the greatest.' We like to transfer the arduous responsibility of listening to God's voice onto others.

Another step we are asked to take is to let go of our desire that God would reveal himself in extraordinary signs. This involves getting used to God making himself known in a much more intimate way, as he speaks to us with 'a still small voice'.

> And behold the Lord passed by, and a great and strong wind rent the mountains, and broke in pieces the rocks before the Lord, but the Lord was not in the wind; and after the wind an earthquake, but the Lord was not in the earthquake; and after the earthquake a fire, but the Lord was not in the fire; and after the fire a still small voice. And when Elijah

heard it, he wrapped his face in his mantle and went out and stood at the entrance of the cave. (1 Kgs 19:11-13)

Our desire for very tangible evidence may prevent us hearing the still small voice of God's efforts to reveal himself in the intimate way he wishes.

> Unless I see in his hands the print of the nails, and place my finger in the mark of the nails, and place my hand in his side, I will not believe. (Jn 20:25)

'… just as the Father knows me'

When God wishes to express how intimate is the relationship he wants with us, he most frequently uses the image of marriage. For the people with whom he used it in the Bible this was the closest of all human relationships. So when it is applied to the relationship we now have with God, it supplies a rich context within which to understand our vocation to know him face to face.

The Growth of Friendship

You might imagine two people falling in love, getting married and their relationship deepening over the years. At the silver jubilee of their marriage, they would probably notice, as they look back over their time together, that there are not the same highs and lows there were when they first fell in love.

It is not that they love each other less but it is a quieter kind of loving; it is not as physical or emotional now but they are capable of sharing at a deeper level. From the outside, their lives might appear quite uneventful, but they would not exchange the happiness they find together for anything.

Their passionate being in love has grown into – not been replaced by – a friendship in which there is a deep sharing of mind and heart, and a growing experience of understanding and concern for what matters most to each other.

Jesus adds an overwhelming depth to the personal nature of our vocation, to 'know' God, when he tells us that we are called into his own deep, personal intimacy with his Father.

> I know those that are mine and my sheep know me, just as the Father knows me and I know the Father. (Jn 10:14-15)

THE FOURTH FACE OF GOD   145

Jesus brings about this friendship with God by sharing with us, not only all he has but even all he is, in his gift of self-revelation. His friendship is precisely this gift of himself in self-disclosure.

> I have called you friends because I have told you everything I have heard from the Father. (Jn 15:15)

To get some appreciation of the intimate quality of this friend-ship, we may need to spend time with people in our own experi-ence who share themselves with us in different ways. Some may reveal only their successes, while with others we may only come to know their opinions. Some may be willing to tell us about their failures or even venture into revealing how they feel, and not just what they think. From these examples, we may get some idea of how intimately personal is God's desire to reveal to us everything about himself through Jesus.

The intimacy we are called to with God is compared by Jesus to that which he enjoys with the Father:

> The glory which you have given me I have given to them, that they may be one even as we are one, I in them and you in me, that they may be perfectly one, so that the world may know that you have sent me and have loved them even as you have loved me. (Jn 17:22-23)

The Ultimate Country
Intimacy, that's the ultimate country
My soul seeks to explore and own.
It is my birthplace and Promised Land
Whose memory haunts all this exile's days.

In it lies the burning fire
That inflames the inmost places of the heart;
The ecstasy of being your beloved
Harnessing all to a single purpose.

But there is a quieter flame within us
That burns more enduringly;
Fired by the deeper regions of the heart;
Whence springs the intimacy of friends.

I would be inspired by both these,
Be wholly and deeply touched.
Then all my concerns would centre on you
And I would be at home, at rest.

But that one place is not yet where
My scattered heart resides;
Drawn as it is to possess ephemeral things
And alas, be possessed by them.

Yet to be close, or even one with You
Is all my heart's desire,
For without you I am but half my truest self,
Ever destined to search for the other.

Summary

Our calling is to know God intimately, as he reveals himself to each person in 'a still small voice'. The Old Testament uses the image of marriage to portray the intimacy of 'knowing' God. Jesus takes as his model, the friendship he enjoys with his Father and uses it to describe the intimacy God wants with us. This involves his complete self-revelation.

Questions for reflection

1) Is there someone with whom you are truly intimate? What do they reveal to you about this Face of God? What impression do you form of God when you hear about his 'still small voice'?

2) What do the two models of marriage and friendship tell you about the face-to-face relationship God wants with you? Are there aspects of this which you find yourself resisting?

One for whom nothing about you is common

There is much in today's world that makes us feel insignificant, just one of the crowd. We may find it very difficult, therefore, to accept what is being revealed here of a very intimate and personal God. In effect, we are being told that God seeks to communicate with each of us 'face-to-face, as a person speaks with a friend.' The intimacy of this communication is the same as that between Jesus and his Father.

I have clothed you with my own splendour. (Ezek 16:14)

Each of us, though seemingly ordinary, is made in God's image and shares his glory. We have a vast potential built into us that we are called to realise.

The Immortal Diamond
The uncut diamond looks very like any other stone, being very ordinary or common. Its lustre or sparkle is unimaginable before it is cut. It is only to the discerning eye that it has got such immense potential, that its splendour can be seen beneath the drab exterior.

Then the master craftsman, with an eye for what it might be, works, with a knowing and sure hand, to uncover the riches of the diamond. It is a great labour, for the diamond is the hardest of stones and does not readily admit its glory. When, however, it is cut, this glory is a many splendoured thing for the diamond has many facets, each reflecting the light in a different way, each rivaling the others for splendour.

As we turn the diamond around in our hand there is a sense of awe at what God has fashioned so intricately and with such care.

For you formed my inmost parts;
you knit me together in my mother's womb.
For all these wonders I thank you,
for the wonder of myself and all your works.
You know me through and through;

my frame was not hidden from you,
when I was being made in secret,
intricately put together in the depths of the earth.
(Ps 139:2,9-10,13-15)

The 'wonder of our being' is confirmed by the fact that we are
invited to share in his divinity, his splendour, in a way that is beyond our wildest dreams.

> By the mystery of this water and wine, may we come to
> share in the divinity of Christ, who humbled himself to
> share in our humanity. (Offertory Prayer)

> Eye has not seen nor ear heard, nor has it entered into the
> heart of man to conceive what God has prepared for those
> who love him, but God has revealed it to us by his Spirit.
> (1 Cor 2:9-10)

The Spirit seeks to help us to realise this dream, the potential of
the image of God in us, symbolised by the diamond.

> And we, with our unveiled faces reflecting like mirrors the
> brightness of the Lord, all grow brighter and brighter as we
> are turned into the image that we reflect; this is the work of
> the Lord who is Spirit. (2 Cor 3:18)

Peter had a very powerful experience of how God reveals himself
to 'the least no less than the greatest.' It happened when he was
faced with the reality that the Holy Spirit was given to Cornelius,
a non-Jew, in exactly the same way as he was given to Peter himself.

> Could anyone refuse water or object to these men being bap-
> tised – men who have received the Holy Spirit just as we did
> ourselves? (Acts 10:47)

Call nothing common!

As a Jew, Peter would have found it hard to conceive of the idea of
the Spirit being given to anyone other than a Jew. God, however,
prepared him to let go of this belief by giving him a vision. In this
he was invited to eat what he would have considered 'unclean' or
unfit for a Jew to eat. Through this vision he came to realise that
nobody is 'common' in God's eyes. Everybody is special for God.

God has shown plainly that no man must be called common or unclean. (Acts 10:28)

There is a completely unique quality about each person's relationship with God that is captured in this quotation:

> That I am a man, this I share with other men. That I see and hear and that I eat and drink is what all animals likewise do. But that I am I is only mine and belongs to me and to nobody else; not to an angel nor to God except insomuch as I am one with him. (Eckhart)

This experience of being special comes from being loved in a very personal way; we see it in another's eyes. We, being so frail, may be able to convince just a few people that they are loved for who they are. God, however, can do this for anyone who looks into his eyes and thus learns to believe in the deeply personal and intimate love of this face of God. We may discover also that before him 'we are what Christ is, since he was what we are.'

> In a flash, at a trumpet crash,
> I am at once what Christ is, since he was what I am, and
> This Jack, joke, poor potsherd, patch, matchwood, immortal diamond, Is immortal diamond.
> (G M Hopkins)

Not getting trapped in our insignificance

Even though we are inclined to get trapped into our own insignificance as creatures and into our unworthiness as sinful, it does not affect God's vision of our worthwhileness.

> O Lord, what is man that you should care for him,
> the son of man that you should think of him.
> Man is like a breath,
> his days like a passing shadow. (Ps 144:3-4)

> Do not be afraid, Jacob, poor worm, Israel, puny mite. I will help you – it is Yahweh who speaks – the Holy One of Israel is your redeemer. (Is 41:14)

We may think that our days are full of trivia. In fact all that happens is part of a drama in which two sides of us battle it out for dominance. In this struggle we easily fall under the influence of the witch, the voice of our own insignificance. This is the illusion that dominates us when a small, dark fraction of our lives becomes the whole picture we see of ourselves. This makes it very difficult for us to accept the gospel vision of God as love and ourselves as lovable in his eyes.

What blocks our acceptance of this love, and the life and happiness it can bring us, is seen in the story of Cyrano de Bergerac. Read it again on page 12. This unbelief in the fact that one is loved, and the loneliness and the loss of peace that follow from it, is a human tragedy that caused Jesus to weep.

> And when he drew near and saw the city he wept over it, saying, 'Would that even today you knew the things that make for peace! But now they are hid from your eyes ... because you did not know the time of your visitation. (Lk 19:41-44)

Summary

Our sense of insignificance makes it difficult for us to accept being loved by the Father as Jesus was. This love is for the least no less than the greatest and is revealed in the most mundane places. No one loved by God is common, but all are, by this love, made unique. We are confirmed in this belief by those who believe in us, but there is much in our world to deny it. We easily succumb to the illusion of insignificance.

Questions for reflection

1) People imagine that God reveals himself to the chosen few. What expresses for you most strongly that this is not the case?
2) What does the image of the immortal diamond say to you? Is there a piece of Scripture that confirms you in this view? What prevents us seeing ourselves as unique? What does the story of de Bergerac suggest?

One who convinces you of how special you are

The prodigal son on his return home from 'the far country' was accepted and appreciated by his father. For this reason he must have had a much greater appreciation than he had before he went away, of how special he was to his father.

Compare this with the difficulty the elder son had with appreciating his father's touching words, 'All I have is yours.' Even though the father sees him as a partner or friend, he sees himself as a servant, for he says, 'I have slaved for you all these years.' He cannot accept the way his father sees him.

We do not have to search far to find the unloving and unlovable prodigal son in each of us. We need to let God 're-teach us our loveliness.'

> *St Francis and the Sow*
> The bud stands for all things,
> even for those things that don't flower,
> for everything flowers, from within, of self-blessing;
> though sometimes it is necessary
> to re-teach a thing its loveliness,
> to put a hand on its brow
> and re-tell it in words and in touch
> it is lovely
> until it flowers again from within, of self-blessing;
> as St Francis
> put his hand on the creased forehead
> of the sow, and told her in words and in touch
> blessings of earth on the sow, and the sow
> began remembering all down her thick length,
> from the earthen snout all the way
> through the fodder and slops
> to the spiritual curl of the tail
> from the hard spininess spiked out from the spine
> down through the great broken heart
> to the blue milken dreaminess spurting and shuddering
> from the fourteen teats into the fourteen mouths sucking

and blowing beneath them:
of long, perfect loveliness of sow.
(Galway Kinnell)

Even though our eye is often fixed on the dark side of ourselves
and others, God finds what is special and precious about us.

> When I passed by you again and looked upon you, behold,
> you were at the age for love; and I spread my skirt over you
> and covered your nakedness; yes I plighted my troth to you
> and entered into a covenant with you, says the Lord God,
> and you became mine. Then I bathed you with water and
> washed off your blood from you, and anointed you with oil.
> I clothed you with embroidered cloth and shod you with
> leather ... And I decked you with ornaments and put brace-
> lets on your arms and a chain on your neck. And I put a ring
> on your nose and earrings in your ears, and a beautiful
> crown upon your head. Then you were decked with gold
> and silver and your raiment was of fine linen and silk, and
> embroidered cloth ... You grew exceedingly beautiful and
> came to regal estate, and your renown went forth among the
> nations because of your beauty, for it was perfect through
> the splendour which I had bestowed upon you [I have
> clothed you with my own splendour], says the Lord God.
> (Ezek 16:8-14)

God gives permanent expression to his way of relating with us in
an everlasting covenant. He guarantees the permanence of the
most personal and intimate periods of our relationship. In our
human experience these periods can be rare and fleeting.

> ... yet I will remember my covenant with you in the days of
> your youth, and I will establish with you an everlasting cov-
> enant. (Ezek 16:60)

'All I Have Is Yours'
Wisdom's ultimate beauty
Goes beyond giving all she has
And makes known her inmost self
In revelation's gift of self.
But the depth of this mystery
Is that the self She reveals
Is love unto death for wayward me
That I might ever lovelier be.

There is no way that love could be more personal, and each of us more special to God, than that he should share himself with us in this way. What he shares is the riches of his glory in Christ, and his plan to fill us with all his fullness.

> ... God has planned to give a vision of the full wonder and splendour of his secret plan for the nations. And the secret is simply this; Christ in you! Yes, Christ in you bringing with him the hope of all the glorious things to come. (Col 1:27)

> For this reason I bow my knees before the Father from whom every family in heaven and on earth is named that according to the riches of his glory he may grant you to be strengthened with might through his Spirit in the inner man ... that you may be filled with all the fullness of God. (Eph 3:14-19)

Through his gift of the Spirit, God enables us to explore and make our own of 'all the fullness of God' he now makes available to everyone. The great obstacle to the belief that this is available to all is the widespread illusion that the Spirit is only given, in any significant way, to a small number of people. It is Peter's conviction that he is given to each person in the same way as he was given to himself. The Spirit's work will be to lead us into 'all the truth' or into the full extent of God's love.

> Can any one forbid water for baptising these people who have received the Holy Spirit just as we have?(Acts 10:47)

> But the counsellor, the Holy Spirit, whom the Father will send in my name, will teach you all things. (Jn 14:26)

> When the Spirit of truth comes he will guide you into all the truth. (Jn 16:13)

The Spirit is given to us so that we might become sensitive and responsive to 'the truth', i.e. to the extent and the depth of God's revelation of himself to each one of us. This is the foundation of the very personal nature of the love of God that this Face of God manifests: he reveals himself, the extent and depth of his love, to each individual, 'face-to-face as with a friend.'

> God has revealed himself to us through the Spirit. For the Spirit searches the depths of everything, even the depths of God. (1 Cor 2:10)

In this Fourth Face of God we get a glimpse of God's endless ability to focus on each of us in a most personal way. There is also an immense sensitivity to what God discovers there – our strength and weakness, what we need and how we feel. This is beautifully expressed in Patrick Kavanagh's memory of his mother, which you should re-read on page 84. Perhaps we can best see this face of God in the features of people whose faces are like hers.

Summary

We have to let God 're-teach us our loveliness' in the way the prodigal son learned, on his return home, a new appreciation of himself, from his father. God can see beyond our weakness to what is precious, and give this permanent expression. This he does by teaching us the full extent of his love and our lovableness through his Spirit. He has all the sensitivity of a mother to where we are and to how we feel.

Questions for reflection

1) What ideas in Galway's poem appeal to you most, in connection with God's way of re-teaching us our loveliness? Do you see a similarity in the way the prodigal was retaught his loveliness?
2) Is it true to say that God can see beyond our weakness to what is precious? Where do you find evidence for this?
3) What features of this Face of God does Kavanagh's poem about his mother highlight for you?

The Wisdom of God

The Key Experience:
The intimacy of self-disclosure
Resistance:
God is too mysterious to know intimately.
The Main Symbol:
God's one Word

God is a love which is not content to share all he has but wishes to share even himself. God does this by giving us the gift of himself in complete self-disclosure as love. The intimate knowledge of God which becomes possible because of this self-disclosure is called wisdom. This intimate knowledge is made known in its fullness to 'the least no less than the greatest.' (Jer 31:34) God is not deterred in his self-disclosure by our in-fidelity, but seeks to overcome it by expressing his self-revelation in human terms through Jesus. He also sends his Spirit to lead us into the full extent and depth of his self-disclosure as love for each of us.

1. *One who wants to reveal himself to us*

God wants to make himself 'known', to reveal himself completely to all who are willing to listen with their hearts.

2. *One who wants to be known intimately*

God restores a lost intimacy, by revealing himself as love, 'luring us into the desert to speak to our hearts.' He begins this by opening up a dialogue with Abraham, Moses, and the Prophets, as the model of what he wants with each of us. We thirst for this revelation of God as love, but it is a long journey to accepting it as being for 'little me.' To know this love 'face to face' just as Jesus does, involves the 'combat of dialogue.'

3. *One who wants to reveal the depth of his love for us*

Wisdom is a mysterious, intimate knowing, born of God's self-revelation as love. It comes ultimately from God's plan to make known the love he is to each person. God accomplishes this by sending Jesus, and they both send the Spirit to lead us into the depths of this knowledge.

4. *One who continues to reveal himself in the face of our infidelity*

We get a deeper understanding of the love of others for us when it remains constant in spite of our disloyalty or infidelity. Our infidelity to God may take the form of resistance to listening to him as he reveals himself to us. We resist the revelation of God's wisdom because our idea of wisdom may be too abstract, or we may see it as the source of unwelcome advice. Resistance may also arise from ingrained ideas about God which make it difficult to accept the kind of love revealed in this face of God.

5. One who incarnates wisdom in his 'one Word'

In the Bible, *wisdom* has the same meaning as *knowledge*. Both mean the intimate experience of being loved by God. This is always his gift, one resisted, yet longed for by us.

Jesus is God's one word, incarnating his wisdom or making known completely the love he is. He is love's wisdom in human terms, especially in his love of us 'to the end' on the cross. To the world this is folly.

6. One who leads us gradually into the fullness of his wisdom

Wisdom is not an abstract knowledge but one written on our hearts. We need the Spirit's gifts 'to lead us into all the truth', i.e. into God's self revelation as love, in the person of Jesus. This wisdom can be learned, bit by bit, if we obey 'the promptings of the Spirit.'

7. Wisdom which seeks the joy of intimacy

Wisdom, as an intimate knowledge born of God's love, leads to a deep union that Jesus calls friendship. The result of this union is a share in the happiness of the Father.

The kind of love we will be looking at here is that of someone who, out of love, shares not only all he or she has, but even themselves through self-disclosure. John Powell, in his book, *He Touched Me*, says that this is the most loving thing we can do for another person.

This Face of God is named the wisdom of God. There are different kinds of wisdom we might consider in order to bring into sharper focus the one we are looking at here:

1) Wisdom understood as being very knowledgeable on some subject. This kind of wisdom is often very abstract and intellectual.

2) There is also a wisdom that is perceptive in all that concerns human relationships. We can all think of a wisdom figure in our lives, one who has learned to penetrate deeply into the workings of human nature.

3) Then there is the wisdom that comes out of loving someone deeply. It has an eye for what the lover alone sees, a perceptiveness that generates an intimate knowledge of another. This is well illustrated by the story, *I'm His Wife*, (see page 85) which we have already had in the Second Face.

4) Finally, there is a wisdom that comes from being deeply known and loved by someone. This experience is all the more profound when this person shares with us, out of love, not only all they have but their very selves in self-disclosure. This is the kind of wisdom we will be looking at here.

Resistance

We may have particular difficulty with this Face of God, because of an idea that God is remote and so mysterious that we cannot know him at all. I remember coming across a book on different qualities of God and being excited by the prospect of coming to know him a bit better. However, it turned out to be so abstract that I left it down with a great sense of disappointment. I was confirmed in my belief at that time that God was too mysterious to know intimately.

Another form of resistance comes from our unease when others reveal details about themselves that are too intimate. There is a voice inside us saying, `Don't give too much of yourself away, you might regret it.' It is difficult for us therefore to let God reveal himself completely to us in the way that he wants to.

Arousing dormant experience

Spend time getting in touch with your experience by means of some or all of these exercises.

1) We each have four windows, through which wc let others get a glimpse of the kind of person we are. The first window we open to many, the second to very few, the third to ourselves alone and the fourth to nobody, as it is where our deepest selves abide.

What kinds of things do you allow others to see when you open windows 2, 3 and even 4? How intimate do you allow or expect others to be? Are there limits to what you are easy about them revealing?

2) What do you think of John Powell's statement that `The real gift of love is self disclosure?'

3) Try to relive an experience of being loved by someone in your life, and then see if what you have learned from this is a profound kind of knowledge that you would call wisdom.

The Main Symbol:
God's One Word

God's One Word

God created all with his Word, 'Let it be.' Of one part of this creation, the devil was particularly jealous: human beings and their intimacy with God. He, therefore, bound up God's tongue and mocked him for no longer being able to speak with humans and to be intimate with them.

After many eons, God pleaded to say just one word to them and this the devil conceded, thinking that God could not make up his losses with a single word. So God spoke the one word 'Jesus'. It expressed all that is God, his caring, forgiving and loving self, all that had been stored up during his long enforced silence.

When I first came across this story, it puzzled and intrigued me – it seemed so improbable that the devil could silence God. As I stayed with it, an interesting truth emerged. The dark side of each of us binds up God's tongue, when we fail to listen to him. Our unwillingness to be receptive to God's Word means in effect that God is prevented from revealing himself to us. Unless someone at the far end of the line takes up the phone and continues to listen, we cannot communicate with them.

God's desire is to reveal himself as love for each person and thus to make available the most profound kind of wisdom, the wisdom of God.

One who wants to reveal himself to us

The way God reveals himself is by opening up a conversation that is symbolised by Jacob's ladder in the Book of Genesis. There we have a description of a dream that Jacob had in which he saw a ladder stretching between heaven and earth, and angels descending and ascending the ladder. The angels descending represent God's desire to reveal himself to us, while those ascending represent his desire that we would respond to this revelation by revealing ourselves to him.

> And he (Jacob) dreamed that there was a ladder set up on the earth, and the top of it reached to heaven; and behold the angels of God were ascending and descending on it. And behold, the Lord stood above it and said ... 'See, I am with you and will keep you wherever you go, and will bring you back to this land; for I will not leave you until I have done that of which I have spoken to you. Then Jacob awoke from his sleep and said, 'Surely the Lord is in this place; and I did not know it.' And he was afraid and said, 'How awesome is this place! This is none other than the house of God; this is the gate of heaven.' (Gen 28:12-13,15-17)

One of the most awesome things about God, which this story illustrates, is his desire to be intimate with us to such a degree that he seeks to reveal himself, to disclose himself completely to us. This is central to the New Covenant that is announced in Jeremiah where God declares his desire to make his love known to each person.

> And no longer shall each man teach his neighbour and each his brother, saying, 'Know the Lord', for they will all know me, from the least of them to the greatest, says the Lord. (Jer 31:34)

Jesus, too, sees this as the main thrust of his work, when he concludes his farewell message to us with the words:

> I have made known to them your name, and I will make it known so that the love with which you have loved me may be in them, and I too may be in them. (Jn 17:26)

THE FIFTH FACE OF GOD

Our capacity to prevent God revealing himself to us by our not listening, and thus 'binding up God's tongue,' is equally awesome.

> You have apostatised from Yahweh your God ... and have not listened to my voice. (Jer 3:13)

The Parable of the Sower, which is central to all three synoptic gospels, is mainly about our unwillingness to listen to the word of God. The Father wants to reveal himself, to give each person an intimate knowledge of the love he is. He makes this available to those who are open or willing to listen to it, not just with their ears but with their hearts.

Listening With Your Heart
In his book, *The Little Prince*, Antoine de Saint-Exupery has a scene where the Little Prince comes to say good bye to the little fox. It is then that the fox imparts one of its gems of wisdom. It tells the Little Prince that our eyes are blind and that we are most perceptive with our hearts.

This thought is reflected in what must be Pascal's best known saying: 'The heart has reasons of which the reason knows nothing.' I love the poster of one of those dogs whose eyes are covered by hair and the caption reads something like 'I see best with my heart.'

We need to have 'the eyes of our hearts enlightened' if we are to see this face of God. The fact that the deepest wisdom consists in an intimate knowledge of being loved, is something that people today find it difficult to appreciate. Seeing things with the heart is foreign to us, as we belong to a tradition where the head is dominant.

> I do not cease to give thanks for you, remembering you in my prayers, that the God of our Lord Jesus Christ, the Father of glory, may give you a spirit of wisdom and of revelation in the knowledge of him, having the eyes of your heart enlightened, that you may know what is the hope to which he has called you, what are the riches of his glorious inheritance in the saints. (Eph 1:16-18

Summary
God wants to make himself 'known', to reveal himself completely to all who are willing to listen to him with their hearts.

Questions for reflection

1) Do you find the following ideas sit easily with you:
   a) That knowing God is in reality God making himself known,
   b) that this revelation takes place in a dialogue, and
   c) that this can be heard fully only with the heart?
2) How would you describe wisdom?

FEATURE 2

One who wants to be known intimately

An outline of the story of our intimacy with God might read like this:

In the beginning God was intimate with his people when it says that he walked with them in the garden. They, however, sinned and thus separated themselves from God. The rest of the Bible story is an account of the ways in which God sought to restore intimacy with them and their descendants.

We, like our first parents, walk out of that intimacy when we fail to make the space to listen to God. This is the same as refusing to listen to God, and to 'binding up his tongue.'

God, however, is not happy to leave things like this but constantly seeks new ways of restoring a lost intimacy by revealing himself. It is for this that he 'lures us into the desert to speak to our hearts.'

> Yet even now, says the Lord, return to me with all your heart, with fasting, with weeping and with mourning; and rend your hearts and not your garments. Return to the Lord your God for he is gracious and merciful, slow to anger and abounding in steadfast love. (Joel 2:12-13)

When God calls us back to intimacy it is not through making himself known to us as some abstract deity but by revealing himself as love.

> *Incarnatio est maximum Dei donum*
> So God's eternal bounty ever shined
> The beams of being, moving, life, sense, mind,
> And to all things himself communicated.
> But see the violent diffusive pleasure
> Of goodness, that left not till God had spent
> Himself by giving us himself, his treasure,
> In making man a God omnipotent.
> How might this goodness draw our souls above,
> Which drew down God with such attractive love.
> (William Alabaster)

Intimacy as the fruit of dialogue

It was to realise this dream of revealing himself, as a way of restoring a lost intimacy, that God began to make himself known in a dialogue he opened up with Abraham.

One of the richest expressions in the development of this dialogue was when, as we are told in the Book of Exodus, God spoke to Moses 'face to face as a person does with a friend.' These words never fail to excite me, as they reveal God's desire for a deep intimacy and I know how much my heart longs for that.

> Thus the Lord used to speak to Moses face to face, as a man speaks to his friend. (Ex 33:11)

The way God revealed himself to the prophets becomes the way he gradually reveals himself to each of us, if we learn how to listen to him and to discern his voice. In the First Book of Samuel there is a description of how the first of the prophets was taught to do this, and it is very symbolic of the dialogue which God wants to open up with each of us. It would be well worthwhile reading the whole of 1 Sam 3.

> Now Samuel did not know the Lord, and the word of the Lord had not yet been revealed to him.
>
> And Samuel grew and the Lord was with him and let none of his words fall to the ground. And all Israel from Dan to Beersheba knew that Samuel was established as a prophet of the Lord. And the Lord appeared again at Shiloh, for the Lord revealed himself to Samuel at Shiloh by the word of the Lord. And the word of Samuel came to all Israel.
> (1 Sam 3:7,19-21)

'They will all know me'

In Jeremiah a new era of God's self-revelation begins. Till then, God had revealed himself to the people only through leading figures such as Moses and the prophets. He would in future reveal himself face to face to every individual person.

> And no longer shall each man teach his neighbour and each his brother, saying, 'Know the Lord', for they will all know me, from the least of them to the greatest, says the Lord.
> (Jer 31:34)

It may be very hard for us to accept that God would be making himself known to 'little me', or to this 'puny mite' as Jeremiah expressed it.

... With an intimate knowledge

God not only wishes to reveal himself to each person willing to listen to him, but he wishes to do this in a most intimate way. This is expressed in the words, 'They shall all know me' used in Jer 31:34. The word 'know' here, has a rich meaning, accumulated from the time God first began to speak to Abraham.

God's desire to reveal himself, as expressed by the symbol of the ladder in Genesis 28, is not sufficient for us to know God. We on our part, have to 'wrestle with God', like Jacob did, if we are to make God's revelation of himself as love our own. This wrestling is the condition of seeing him face to face, or reaching an intimate knowledge of him.

> Jacob named the place Peniel, 'Because I have seen the face of God,' he said, 'and I have survived.' (Gen 32:30)

The symbolism of the ladder of Jacob's dream is drawn out further for us in the life of Moses. There we are told that God spoke with him 'face to face as a person speaks with a friend.' 'Wrestling with God' has become what someone has called 'the combat of dialogue', and this dialogue has become the model of Christian prayer.

This dialogue is the way God wishes to reveal himself, not just to Moses, but to his whole people. This desire for self-disclosure springs from the love God has for his people. Jesus opens up the possibilities of coming to know God's revelation of himself as love when he says that we can now know the Father in the intimate way he does.

> Jesus said, 'I know my own and my own know me, as the Father knows me and I know the Father.' (Jn 10:14-15)

> That the world may realise that you sent me and have loved them as you loved me. (Jn 17:23)

NINE FACES OF GOD

Summary

God restores a lost intimacy, by revealing himself as love, 'luring us into the desert to speak to our hearts.' He begins this by opening up a dialogue with Abraham, Moses, and the Prophets, as the model of what he wants with each of us. We thirst for this revelation of God as love, but it is a long journey to accepting it as being for 'little me.' To know this love 'face to face' just as Jesus does, involves the 'combat of dialogue.'

Questions for reflection

1) Does it seem strange to you to put wisdom in the context of God's desire to restore intimacy with us? Do you find yourself reaching for some other way of understanding salvation?

2) What strikes you, about the way God started restoring his relationships with Abraham?

3) Why is it so difficult for us to accept God's revelation of himself as love for each of us? What is it in us that wants to stay with and overcome this difficulty?

4) What do you learn from people like Jacob, about coming to know God?

One who wants to reveal the depth of his love for us

Wisdom I Ask
I descend wisdom's winding stair
Down to the vast regions of the mind,
and thence to the depths of the heart.
To go further I must be led by love
Into the inmost places of the soul,
To glimpse there what only love can disclose:
The features of wisdom's face
And my truest self mirrored there.

As a way of developing a clearer picture of God's Wisdom, it
might be helpful now to distinguish four different ways of understanding wisdom.

'For my thoughts are not your thoughts'

1) The first way we could understand the wisdom of God is that it
is a very extensive knowledge God has of all his creation. He
knows everything about everything. This is a very factual and
conceptual way of understanding wisdom. It sees God's wisdom
as something that reflects the transcendent and mysterious side of
God.

> For my thoughts are not your thoughts, nor are your ways
> my ways, says the Lord. For as the heavens are higher than
> the earth, so are my ways higher than your ways and my
> thoughts than your thoughts. (Is 55:8-9)

> O the depth of the riches and wisdom and knowledge of
> God! How unsearchable are his judgments and how inscrut-
> able are his ways! (Rom 11:33)

In the way that God reveals himself here as Wisdom there is a
sense of utter mystery, an experience of the 'fullness of God' that
surpasses knowledge. While this does reflect a great truth about
God's wisdom, it is a very intellectual way of seeing this Face of
God. A more intuitive approach, like that of Moses at the burning
bush, would be more helpful.

There is a feature of Wisdom
That appeals to our mind's thirst
For the all-inclusive insight
And to delve into the mystery of all.
Here we find a knowledge of things
Past, present and to come,
A knowledge that springs from
Being made, sustained and provided for.

The heart's reasons

2) A second way of understanding wisdom is more intuitive than the previous one. It is more concerned with the way we relate with people than it is with ideas. From this point of view, this Face of God reveals the kind of person God is, who we are in his eyes and the wondrous plans he has in mind for us. Even though God's wisdom is still a knowledge beyond the reaches of our minds, God has now opened it up for us.

Call to me and I will answer you, and tell you great and hidden things you have not known. (Jer 33:3)

If you seek me, you shall find me; if you seek me with all your heart, I will let you find me. (Jer 29:13-14)

No eye has seen, no ear has heard, no mind has conceived what God has prepared for those who love him, but God has revealed it to us by his Spirit. (1 Cor 2:9-10)

Another feature of Wisdom's face
Is best glimpsed by the heart;
Like the intuitive grasp of life
That comes with the wisdom of years.
Its concern is people and providence
And is the intimate understanding
Mirrored to us in the loving gaze
Of the One who knows us through and through.

Wisdom as knowing his love

3) The third way of understanding more fully the wisdom revealed in this Face of God, is one born of the our belief in his love. Re-read the story *I'm his Wife* on page 85.

Being deeply concerned for another person can make us very sensitive and perceptive in the way we know them. The intense love God has for us gives him a most intimate knowledge of each person. Where many things are hidden to the gaze of those around us, God, like the wife in the incident above, with his loving gaze, knows us through and through.

> Yahweh, you examine me and know me, you know if I am standing or sitting, you read my thoughts from far away, whether I walk or lie down, you are watching, you know every detail of my conduct ... Such knowledge is beyond my understanding, a height to which my mind cannot attain ... You know me through and through. (Ps 139:1-3,6,15)

When it is said in Jer 31:34 that the new covenant will consist in knowing God, it is very important to understand the meaning of the word 'knowing.' Knowledge of God is primarily an interior knowledge of being loved by God. There is a note in the Jerusalem Bible which says, 'In the wisdom literature 'knowledge' and 'wisdom' are practically synonymous.'

> He who does not love does not know God; for God is love ...
> In this is love, not that we loved God but that he loved us and sent his Son to be the expiation for our sins. (1 Jn 4:8-10)

Knowledge (wisdom) here is not an abstract or merely intellectual knowledge but what one might call a felt knowledge. This, for example, is what we pray for when we say in the *Anima Christi:* 'Blood of Christ inebriate me.'

> No one ever became drunk
> on an intellectual understanding of the word 'wine'.

> Gazing more deeply into Wisdom's face
> We may discover the mystery
> of an intimate knowledge seen in eyes
> That love us wholly and deeply.
> Perceptive of all that is good in us
> And accepting of all that is weak
> A deep appreciation inspired by deep love
> That relishes all we are and may become.

Making known his inmost self

4) The fourth way of understanding wisdom is very closely con-

nected with the previous one. It is an intimate knowledge of one who wishes to make himself known to each person willing to listen. God plans to share with us, not just all he has, but all he is. It is this self-disclosure of God that makes possible the knowledge that is ultimate Wisdom. The revelation of this wisdom is the work of the Trinity, who conspire to lead us into the 'extent and depth' of their love, into 'all the fullness of God.' (Eph 3:18-19) Just as it is Jesus who is the truth (Jn 14:6), the one who puts the self-revelation of God in human terms, it is the Spirit who leads us 'into all the truth'.

> When the Spirit of truth comes, he will guide you into all the truth (i.e into the full extent and depth of God's love) ... All that the Father has is mine; therefore I said he will take what is mine and declare it to you. (Jn 16:13-15)

> Wisdom's ultimate beauty
> Goes beyond giving all she has
> And makes known her inmost self
> In revelation's gift of self.
> But the depth of this mystery
> Is that the self She reveals
> Is love unto death for wayward me
> That I might ever lovelier be.

Summary

Wisdom is a mysterious, intimate knowing, born of God's self-revelation as love. It comes ultimately from God's plan to make known the love he is to each person. God accomplishes this by sending Jesus, and they both send the Spirit to lead us into the depths of this knowledge.

Questions for reflection

1) What does the incident entitled *I'm his wife* tell you about wisdom?

2) Do you feel that people get more wisdom from being loved than from loving?

3) Describe the four different ways of understanding of God's wisdom which we have seen in this feature. Which aspect did you warm to most?

One who continues to reveal himself in the face of our infidelity

There is a sense in which we do not really appreciate the extent and depth of God's love until we acknowledge that it is a 'love to the loveless shown.'

> My song is love unknown;
> My Saviour's love to me;
> Love to the loveless shown,
> That they might lovely be.
> O, who am I,
> That for my sake
> He should become
> Frail flesh, and die?

> I will love Unloved; I will say to Not My People, 'You are my people', and he will say, 'You are my God.' (Hos 2:23)

God does not give up disclosing himself, in spite of our failure to listen to him. The strongest expression of this 'faithful or steadfast love' is in the story of Hosea. His own repeated taking back of a wife who was unfaithful to him became an experience through which God revealed to Hosea the constancy of his love. He was led to see his experience in terms of the intimacy of the marriage of God to his people, and especially when God repeatedly remained faithful to unfaithful Israel. The infidelity of the people to their marriage with God was a new revelation of the strength and depth of the love of God for his people.

If people continue to share the most intimate areas of their lives with us, in spite of our repeated disloyalty to them, it reveals a whole new dimension of their love.

> But our fathers grew proud ... they refused to obey and were not mindful of the wonders which you performed among them; ... But you are a God ready to forgive, gracious and merciful, slow to anger and abounding in steadfast love and you did not forsake them ... but so gently loving,

you did not forsake them in the wilderness; the pillar of cloud which led them in the way did not depart from them by day, nor the pillar of fire by night which lighted for them the way by which they should go. You gave your good Spirit to instruct them and did not withhold your manna from them and gave them water for their thirst. (Neh 9:16-20)

When people are unfaithful to us, especially after we have revealed to them our intimate selves, our desire to be intimate with them, to reveal anything further to them, dries up. In this context we can appreciate God's willingness to continue to reveal his intimate self.

Pierre in Tolstoy's novel, *War and Peace*, discovered in his wife's love for him what was really good about himself. He had already experienced in an earlier marriage how fickle was his own love.

After seven years of married life, Pierre had a firm and joyful consciousness that he was not a bad fellow, and he felt this because he saw himself reflected in his wife. In himself he felt all the good and bad mingled together, and obscuring one another. But in his wife he saw reflected only what was really good; everything not quite good was left out. And this result was reached not by way of logical reflection, but by way of a mysterious, direct reflection of himself.

There is a kind of infidelity that is associated with this Face of God. It consists in our failure to listen to God's revelation of himself. There are a number of ways in which we hinder or prevent God speaking to us, and in this sense 'bind up God's tongue'.

In spite of the fact that we long deep down to see the Face of God, there is a huge amount of resistance in us to seeking it. We need to grow in awareness of the nature of this resistance or it will block our vision of God. This resistance will limit the life and happiness God wants for us when he seeks to reveal his face to us.

One form of resistance occurs when our idea of wisdom is abstract and thus leaves us uninvolved. God's wisdom is seen as dispassionate or cold. Unless we do something about this, we will not be able to let God be so intimate as to reveal himself to us. As a result we will deprive ourselves of the life-giving experience of being open to God's revelation and coming to know him intimately in the way he wishes us to. (Jn 17:3)

THE FIFTH FACE OF GOD 175

Another form of resistance is that God's wisdom is associated with someone who is always telling us what to do. We may therefore resist this idea of wisdom just as we resist anyone who gives us a lot of advice.

Perhaps the biggest source of our resistance to God revealing himself to us are false ideas about God that have become ingrained in our minds and hearts. We resist what God reveals about himself if that differs from our pre-conceived ideas about him. All that we receive must fit the mould of our mind; if it does not, it has to be cut down to size or stretched until it does. God constantly challenges these illusions of ours that make his revelation of himself, of his wisdom, seem so unreal to us.

> Can a woman forget her sucking child, that she should have no compassion on the son of her womb? Even these may forget, yet I will not forget you. Behold, I have carved you on the palms of my hands. (Is 49:14-16)

Being loved in this way is our deepest human longing. Yet it seems so improbable that God would want to continue revealing his love when we are so seldom at home when he comes.

> *Visitation*
> Love calls many times each day
> but finds me preoccupied,
> not able to make the time
> to be at home for her.
>
> I let the signs of her visitation
> Come and go unnoticed:
> And am not nourished
> by a love that is not recognised or named.
>
> So I continue to live in a world
> That deadens with its indifference:
> Alas, that I cannot be here when you call
> And have time to be at home together.

Summary

We get a deeper understanding of the love of others for us when it remains constant in spite of our disloyalty or infidelity. Our infidelity to God may take the form of resistance to listening to him as he reveals himself to us. We resist the revelation of God's wisdom because our idea of wisdom may be too abstract, or we may see it as the source of unwelcome advice. Resistance may also arise from ingrained ideas about God which make it difficult to accept the kind of love revealed in this face of God.

Questions for reflection

1) How can acknowledging our sinfulness give us a better appreciation of God's wisdom?

2) Which of the kinds of resistance mentioned above do you identify with most? How would you express your experience of this resistance in your prayer?

3) What is your reaction to the fact that God continues to reveal himself to you in spite of the ways you resist this and 'bind up God's tongue'?

FEATURE 5

One who incarnates wisdom in his 'one Word'

Jesus not only speaks this Word of God but he *is* this word. In him the self-revelation of God is 'made flesh' or put in human terms. In this way the Father makes his wisdom known to us in Jesus.

He who has seen me has seen the Father. (Jn 14:9)

... but we preach ... Christ the power of God and the wisdom of God. (1 Cor 1:24)

Jesus returns to the image of Jacob's ladder to express the role he plays as the one through whom God has chosen to reveal himself completely; as his all-embracing Word.

Truly, Truly, I say to you, you shall see heaven opened and the angels of God ascending and descending upon the Son of man. (Jn 1:51)

And the Word became flesh and dwelt among us, full of grace and truth. (Jn 1:14)

These words, 'grace and truth' mean that Jesus puts in the flesh and blood terms of a human body, all the 'loving kind and faithful love' of the Father. Jesus does not just preach the wisdom of God, he is this wisdom, in that he reveals the Father to us and makes his love known in his very person.

(Who) will separate us from the love of God made known to us in Christ Jesus our Lord? (Rom 8:39)

Philip said to him, 'Lord, show us the Father, and we will be satisfied.' Jesus said to him, 'Have I been with you so long and yet you do not know me, Philip? He who has seen me has seen the Father; how can you say, "Show us the Father?" Do you not believe that I am in the Father and the Father in me?' (Jn 14:8-10)

Jesus as the Word

Jesus, the one who expresses the love which the Father is in human terms, is the wisdom of God. C. H. Dodd, in his interpretation of the fourth gospel, says that what expresses most closely the meaning of 'wisdom' in the Old Testament is 'the Word' as used in a piece of scripture like the following:

And the Word became flesh and dwelt among us, full of grace and truth (i.e. full of loving-kind and faithful love). (Jn 1:14)

It is this wisdom of the Father that Jesus wishes to share with us when he invites us to come and meet him. There is a lot more behind Jesus' inviting the two disciples to 'Come and see' (Jn 1:39) than we might at first notice. It includes a wide-ranging invitation to come and get to know him and the love of his Father which he makes visible in the most ordinary of ways.

They saw his glory, the glory of the only begotten Son of God, full of grace and truth (full of loving-kind and faithful love). (Jn 1:14)

The greatest manifestation of the Father's wisdom, however, is in the death and resurrection of Jesus. It is in this that God's love is given supreme expression. To appreciate this love and its wisdom, we have to overcome the world's 'common sense' reaction to it as the height of folly.

Where is the wise man? ... Has not God made foolish the wisdom of this world? For since in the wisdom of God the world did not know God through wisdom, it pleased God through the folly of what we preach to save those who believe. For Jews demand signs and Greeks seek wisdom, but we preach Christ crucified, a stumbling block to Jews and folly to Gentiles, but to those who are called, both Jews and Greeks, Christ the power of God and the wisdom of God. For the foolishness of God is wiser than men, and the weakness of God is stronger than men. (1 Cor 1:20-25)

It is your being lifted up on a tree
That enthralls us, making all creation yours
Seducing us, to become our universal king.

It is on the cross that we see the supreme manifestation of the glory of God, in the revelation of his loving kind and faithful love. It is as if Jesus on the cross is a musical instrument giving the fullest expression to God's love and wisdom. This is the image that R.S.Thomas uses in his poem, *The Musician*. He compares Christ on the cross to Kreisler playing the violin. Just as Kreisler strained every muscle in his body to interpret the music he was playing, so Christ on the cross expressed a music to which no one listened more intently than God.

Summary

In the Bible, *wisdom* has the same meaning as *knowledge*. Both mean the intimate experience of being loved by God. This is always his gift, one resisted, yet longed for by us.

Jesus is 'God's one word', incarnating his wisdom or making known completely the love God is. He is love's wisdom in human terms, especially in his love of us 'to the end' on the cross. To the world this is folly.

Questions for reflection

1) Why is Jesus called 'the wisdom of God'? Does this name for Jesus reveal to you anything significant about this Face of God?
2) Why is the Cross seen by some people as the wisdom of God and by others as folly? Is there a part of you that sympathises with each of these views?

One who leads us gradually into the fullness of his wisdom

It is very difficult for us to make our own of, 'the folly of the Cross.' Though it is seen in Scripture as the supreme expression of the wisdom of God, it can easily remain 'written on stone.' To really have it 'written on our hearts' we need to receive an interior knowledge of it by making our own of the Spirit's essential gift.

> Already we have some experience of the love of God flooding through our hearts by the Holy Spirit given to us.[P] (Rom 5:5)

There are things we can see only with the heart

We have seen how the death and resurrection of Jesus is the ultimate expression of the Father's wisdom. The Spirit's gift of love and wisdom gives us the capacity to experience this wisdom in a most personal and profound way.

> The wisdom we speak of is that mysterious secret wisdom of God which he planned before the creation for our glory today. None of the powers of this world have known this wisdom – if they had, they would never have crucified the Lord of glory ... But God has, through the Spirit, let us share his secret. For nothing is hidden from the Spirit, not even the deep wisdom of God ... The spiritual man, on the other hand, has an insight into the meaning of everything, though this insight may baffle the man of the world. This is because the former is sharing in God's wisdom. (1 Cor 2:7-15)

What the Spirit opens up for us is not visible to the eye of common sense. It is 'a secret wisdom', a gift he can give us only gradually, as we are ready to receive it. Tony de Mello, when making this point, used to quote an Indian proverb:

> To teach a person who is not ripe is waste of words;
> not to teach someone who is ripe is waste of a person.

The Dragonfly

There lived at the bottom of a pond some grubs which were puzzled by the sudden way their friends disappeared and were never seen again. So they made an agreement that the next one to depart would make sure to come back and tell the others what had happened.

Soon after that, one of them felt drawn to climb the stem of a plant to the surface of the pond. Then, an extraordinary change began to take place and the grub slowly became a dragonfly. It tried to keep its promise, flying low time and again over the surface of the water. It failed however to attract the attention of the grubs at the bottom of the pond for they could not recognise their companion in the dragonfly nor could they hear its message.

It eventually realised that they would never recognise such a radiant creature as one of themselves or what they were becoming.

God will be gradually leading us into this 'wisdom from above' so that what we are ripe for will be well within our reach.

> For the commandments which I command you this day is not too hard for you, neither is it far off ... But the word is very near you; it is in your mouth and in your heart, so that you can do it. (Deut 30:11,14)

The Spirit guides us on our journey of faith into the Father's wisdom. Through his gifts he guides us 'into all the truth', i.e. into the complete revelation of himself that the Father makes in Jesus.

> When the Spirit of truth comes, he will guide you into all the truth ... All that the Father has is mine; therefore I said he will take what is mine and declare it to you. (Jn 16:13-15)

We can appreciate and make our own of this 'truth' only if we are mature or ripe enough to take it in. We will be led into it, if we are willing to be obedient 'to the promptings of the Spirit' guiding us.

> (God sent Christ) ... in order that the just requirements of the law might be fulfilled in us who walk not according to the flesh but according to the promptings of the Spirit. (Rom 8:4)

We always want things now and without much effort. But the reality is that we must wait for God who, like any teacher, can only teach us bit by bit. He will, therefore, be able to reveal himself to us and let us see his face only if we, with 'a noble and generous heart ... hear the word and take it to ourselves and yield a harvest through our perseverance.' (Lk 8:15)

> *To Let Be*
> O to be satisfied
> with that fleeting glimpse
> of your face,
> and the gentle pace
> of your grace growing.

Summary

Wisdom is not an abstract knowledge but one written on our hearts. We need the Spirit's gifts 'to lead us into all the truth', i.e. into God's self revelation as love, in the person of Jesus. This wisdom can be learned, bit by bit, if we obey 'the promptings of the Spirit.'

Questions for reflection

1) Why do we need the Spirit to help us appreciate fully this Face of God?

2) What has the story, *The Dragonfly*, to tell us about the wisdom revealed to us in this Face of God?

Wisdom which seeks the joy of intimacy

Gift better than himself God doth not know;
Gift better than his God no man can see.
This gift doth here the giver given bestow;
Gift to this gift let each receiver be.
God is my gift, himself he freely gave me;
God's gift am I, and none but God shall have me.
(Robert Southwell)

In his self-revelation, the Father shares with us all that he has and is. He says to us what was said to the elder brother in the Parable of the Prodigal Son:

You are always with me and all I have is yours. (Lk 15:31)

This sharing is a fulfillment of what God often promised would be part of the new covenant: there would be a total sharing and belonging; he 'would be our God and we would be his people'; he would be ours and we would be his.

My beloved is mine and I am his. (Song 2:16)

I am my beloved's and his desire is for me. (Song 7:10)

The way this sharing is fulfilled is through our coming to know the love God is and our response to this in the way we share ourselves with him. The development of these two sides of the relationship is what Jesus is referring to, when he uses the word 'known' in his final message to us in John's gospel.

I made known to them your name, and I will make it known, that the love with which you have loved me may be in them, and I in them. (Jn 17:26)

Jesus sees a deep relationship between his revelation of God – what we have called the wisdom of God – and an intimacy or union that results from it. He calls this union friendship.

I have called you friends because I have told you everything I have heard from the Father. (Jn 15:15)

In our experience we will have noticed how quickly two people become intimate when they share themselves, even to a limited degree. This is a conviction that we come across repeatedly in the books and tapes of John Powell. He believes that people who communicate honestly with each other cannot fail to become intimate.

The intimacy which God seeks with us is beautifully expressed in the spiritual exercises of St Ignatius.

> Love consists in mutual interchange on either side. That is to say, in the lover giving to and sharing with the loved one that which he has or can attain. And so in the same way, the loved one doing the same for the lover; so that if one has knowledge, he gives it to the other who does not have it. One does the same with honours and riches, always sharing with the other. (No 231)

Then follows this prayer:

> I will ponder with much affection how much God our Lord has done for me, and how much he has given me of what he has, and finally, how much, as far as he can, the same Lord desires to give himself to me according to his divine plan. (No 234)

This intimacy is had through assimilating or 'eating' God's word.

> And he said to me, 'Son of man, eat this scroll that I give you and be satisfied with it.' Then I ate it; and it was in my mouth as sweet as honey. (Ezek 3:13)

A striking connection between the wisdom revealed in this Face of God and the happiness that will result from our contemplation of it, is drawn by Jesus when he says:

> I have told you these things (i.e. his revelation of the Father as love) that you might share my joy and that your happiness may be complete. (Jn 15:11)

The purpose of God's opening up of himself to us is that, by assimilating what he reveals of himself, we would share his happiness, 'and that will be heaven at last, the first unclouded seeing.'

And that will be heaven
and that will be heaven
and that will be heaven
at last – the first unclouded seeing

to stand like the sunflower
turned full face to the sun, drenched
in light, in the still centre
held, while the circling planets
hum with an utter joy

seeing and knowing
at last, in every particle
seen and known, and not turning away
never turning away again
(Evangeline Patterson)

Summary

Wisdom, as an intimate knowledge born of God's love, leads to a deep union that Jesus calls friendship. The result of this union is a share in the happiness of the Father.

Questions for reflection

1) What is the connection between wisdom and happiness? How is this connection expressed by Jesus, and in the poem *And that will be heaven*?

The faithfulness of God

The Key Experience:
The vowing of fidelity in marriage
Resistance:
The instinct to retaliate when others let us down
The Main Symbol:
Love proved by infidelity

This Face reveals the fidelity of God's love, a fidelity which becomes all the more obvious when we become aware of our own infidelity. God's loyalty is enduring and all-pervasive and it is guaranteed by an everlasting covenant. We can be confident that, no matter how unfaithful we may have been, we need have no fear, for God is steadfast in his devotion to our best interests. Like the Good Shepherd, God cares for all our needs. The supreme manifestation of this devotion is that he gives up his own Son to death to prove how faithful his love is.

1. One whose fidelity is highlighted by our infidelity

The story of Hosea illustrates how faithful God is, in the light of our infidelity and ingratitude. Though we do not expect it, we long for a love that endures.

2. One whose love is enduring, all-pervasive yet unobtrusive

God's fidelity pervades the past, the present and the future, for he always stands by us, no matter what. Love wants to save us from the destructive effects of life's pain, but not to obstruct the way they can help us to grow.

3. One whose love is everlasting

God guarantees his fidelity with an everlasting covenant. This, in spite of our waywardness, retains all the warmth of a marriage-like intimacy. We resist being face to face with a love like Ruth's, even though our heart longs for it.

4. One whose love is proved in adversity

Life's hardships question our belief in God's fidelity and can thus broaden and deepen our conviction of faith. Through our darkness God can open our eyes to a new understanding of his fidelity. He will be with us through life's darkness, even when this is caused by our own sinfulness. Through acknowledging our sinfulness, if we allow him, he will lead us into a deeper intimacy than before. He promises to be with us in this way for ever. Fear is a sign of unbelief in God's abiding love and all-pervading providence.

5.One whose devotion and loyalty are beyond all doubt

The image of God as Shepherd expresses his faithful devotion to all our needs. The ultimate proof of this is that he sent Jesus to live with us and 'gave him up' to death that we might share his life.

In a marriage ceremony we hear the pair saying that they will love and honour each other in marriage all the days of their lives. They promise to be true to each other in good times and bad, in sickness and in health, till death parts them. They give each other a ring as a sign of their fidelity.

We all know something of the difficulty of being faithful to another but we also recognise that 'love is not love, that alters when it alteration finds.'

Resistance

The mystery of a love that endures is that it can withstand disloyalty and even prolonged coldness. This is at odds with the spontaneous reaction in us to retaliate, to give as good as we get. When trust and loyalty are betrayed, our natural expectation is that others will not take it lying down. We feel justified in backing out when another breaks a contract. Since this is so much part of our reaction when others let us down, we find it hard to conceive that God is different and does not retaliate, punish, or give us the cold treatment when we let him down.

Arousing dormant experience

1) Spend time trying to get in touch with, and articulate, the kinds of fidelity you find in your own life towards others and God. See how many of the qualities, such as trust, loyalty or constancy, you would identify in your own fidelity to God and others. Which qualities do you find it most difficult to identify with?

2) Notice how many of these qualities you have experienced from others and finally from God. Do you find yourself resisting them being shown to you by others, or by God?

3) How do you react if people are grossly or repeatedly disloyal? Do you find yourself angry, unwilling to forgive, rejecting people, cutting them out of your affection or being cold with them?

4) Do you find God reacting to you in the same way as you notice yourself reacting to others? Does he get angry with you or give you the cold treatment?

The Main Symbol:
Love Proved by Infidelity

One of the most moving moments in Leo Tolstoy's *War and Peace*, is where Prince Andrew returns after giving Natasha a year to make up her mind whether she wants to marry him. He is devastated when he finds out that she has been unfaithful to him by eloping with a good-for-nothing fellow who later abandons her. Yet later in the story when he meets her, Andrew can say that he loves her even more than before, in spite of her infidelity. Under the influence of this love, she is able to leave the twilight world of self doubt and remorse she has lived in. She gradually learns to believe what his love is saying to her and she becomes supremely happy.

Our lives are so full of infidelity that we live with a lot of guilt and a poor image of ourselves. This can take away much of the joy of living. The experience of God loving us in spite of this infidelity is very important for our happiness.

The supreme happiness in life
is the conviction of being loved for oneself
or, more correctly, being loved in spite of oneself.
(Victor Hugo)

One whose fidelity is highlighted by our infidelity

One of the most powerful ways the fidelity of God to unfaithful Israel is expressed is in the story of Hosea and his unfaithful wife. After their first child was born, she left him and had two other children by someone else. She then became a temple prostitute and was eventually sold into slavery.

It was only when Hosea saw God's faithfulness to the people of Israel, in spite of their constant breaking of the bonds he established with them, that he felt inspired to take his wife back.

> ... and she went after her lovers and forgot me, says the Lord. Therefore, behold, I will allure her, and bring her into the wilderness, and speak tenderly to her. And there I will give her vineyards, and make the Valley of Achor a door of hope. And there she shall answer as in the days of her youth, as at the time when she came out of the land of Egypt. And in that day, says the Lord, you will call me 'My husband', and no longer will you call me 'My Ba'al.' For I will remove the names of the Ba'als from her mouth, and they shall be mentioned by name no more. And I will make for you a covenant on that day with the beasts of the field, the birds of the air, and the creeping things of the ground; and I will abolish the bow and the sword and war from the land; and I will make you lie down in safety. And I will betroth you to me for ever; I will betroth you to me in righteousness and in justice, in steadfast love, and in mercy. I will betroth you to me in faithfulness; and you shall know the Lord. (Hos 2:13-20)

Hosea was led to see the people of Israel's sin as infidelity to the One to whom they were married. In reality they had become the prostitutes of 'false gods.' After Hosea, there was no prophet who could express this tragedy more powerfully than Jeremiah.

> I thought how I would set you among my sons and give you a pleasant land, a heritage most beauteous of all nations. And I thought you would call me 'My Father' and would not turn from following me. Surely, as a faithless wife leaves

her husband, so have you been faithless to me, O house of Israel, says the Lord ... From our youth even to this day, we have not listened to the voice of our God. (Jer 3:19-20,25)

God's reaction to this infidelity is extraordinary, for our infidelity seems only to emphasise his fidelity. His 'abounding, steadfast love' is intent, not on showing his reactions to this kind of disloyalty, but on our returning to him.

> Yet even now, says the Lord, return to me with all your heart, with fasting, with weeping and with mourning; and rend your hearts and not your garments. Return to the Lord your God for he is gracious and merciful, slow to anger and abounding in steadfast love. (Joel 2:12-13)

To be able to accept this overwhelming love from God, we must become aware of what is resisting it in us, and say this as honestly as we can. Like John Donne, we need to ask God about the reality of his fidelity, especially in the light of our own infidelity.

> *A Hymn to God the Father*
> Wilt thou forgive that sin where I began,
> Which is my sin, though it were done before?
> Wilt thou forgive those sins through which I run,
> And do them still, though still I do deplore?
> When thou hast done, thou hast not done,
> For I have more.
>
> Wilt thou forgive that sin by which I won
> Others to sin, and made my sin their door?
> Wilt thou forgive that sin which I did shun
> A year or two, but wallowed in a score?
> When thou hast done, thou hast not done,
> For I have more.
>
> I have a sin of fear, that when I've spun
> My last thread, I shall perish on the shore;
> Swear by thyself that at my death thy Sun
> Shall shine as it shines now, and heretofore;
> And having done that, thou hast done,
> I have no more.
> (John Donne)

Another image Hosea uses is the frightful insensitivity of the adolescent in each of us. This part of us so easily tends to forget all that has been done for us, and the gratitude this calls for. This attitude ignores how indebted we are to parents and others whose kindness we so easily forget.

> I am the Lord your God from the land of Egypt; you know no God but me, and besides me there is no saviour. It was I who knew you in the wilderness in the land of drought; but when they had fed to the full, they were filled, and their heart was lifted up; therefore they forgot me. (Hos 13:4-6)

> When Israel was a child I loved him, and out of Egypt I called my son. The more I called them, the more they went from me; they kept sacrificing to the Ba'als and burning incense to idols. Yet it was I who taught Ephraim to walk, I took them in my arms; but they did not know that I healed them. I led them with cords of compassion, with the bands of love, and I became to them as one who eases the yoke on their jaws [I was like someone who lifts an infant close against his cheek JB] and I bent down to them and fed them. (Hos 11:1-4)

It is a very painful experience when others never advert to all that we have done for them. Yet, in spite of this kind of insensitivity on our part, God remains utterly faithful to his promises.

> And now I am about to go the way of all the earth, and you know in your hearts and souls, all of you, that not one thing has failed of all the good things which the Lord your God promised concerning you; all have come to pass for you, not one of them has failed.(Josh 23:14)

The scope and intensity of this faithful love blows open the limits set by our human expectations. In the light of our human experience, we find it hard to conceive why God would not abandon us in the way we abandon him, or forget us in the way we forget him.

> But Zion said, 'The Lord has abandoned me, my Lord has forgotten me.' Can a woman forget her sucking child, that she should have no compassion on the son of her womb? Even these may forget, yet I will not forget you. Behold I have graven you on the palms of my hands. (Is 49:14-16)

Though we have no claim to it, we long for a love that does not 'alter when it alteration finds.' It is no surprise that young people who are getting married choose this sonnet of Shakespeare as part of the readings for the ceremony. It must echo the permanence of a love we all long for.

> Let me not to the marriage of true minds
> Admit impediments, love is not love
> Which alters when it alteration finds,
> Or bends with the remover to remove;
> O no! it is an ever fixed mark
> That loads on tempests and is never shaken
> It is the star to every wand'ring bark,
> Whose worth's unknown, although his height be taken.
> Love's no Time's fool, though rosy lips and cheeks
> Within his bending sickle's come;
> Love alters not with his brief hours and weeks,
> But bears it out even to the edge of doom –
> If this be error and upon me proved;
> I never writ nor no man ever loved.
> (Shakespeare)

He is not a lover who does not love forever. (Euripides)

The gift and the call of God are irrevocable. (Rom 11:29)

Summary

The story of Hosea illustrates how faithful God is, in the light of our infidelity and ingratitude. Though we do not expect it, we long for a love that endures.

Questions for reflection

1) How was Hosea led to discover this Face of God? What aspect of it struck him most? Why has Hosea's story so fascinated people?

2) Are you ever struck by the thoughtlessness of many adolescents or of the adolescent in yourself? Why is Shakespeare's poem on faithful love so popular with people who are getting married?

One whose love is enduring, all-pervasive yet unobtrusive

God sticks by us, no matter what. He has always been with us along the way we have travelled, he is with us now, and will be to the end.

> ... the Lord your God bore you as a man bears his son, in all the way that you went until you came to this place. Yet in spite of this word you did not believe the Lord your God, who went before you in the way to seek you out a place to pitch your tents, in fire by night, to show you by what way you should go, and in the cloud by day. (Deut 1:31-33)

> Listen to me, House of Jacob, all the remnant of the House of Israel, who have been borne by me from your birth, carried from the womb; even in your old age I am he, and to grey hairs I will carry you. I have made, and I will bear; I will carry and will save. (Is 46:3-4)

This steadfast love is constantly with us to teach and guide, to support and carry, to provide all our needs along the way.

> O God, from my youth you have taught me,
> and yet your wonders stretch out beyond me still. (Ps 71:17)

> God has revealed only one reality:
> that to him alone belongs the power
> of a love that endures forever. (Ps 62:11-12)

In Jacob's dream about the ladder stretching between heaven and earth, he came to realise how profoundly God is with each person as an abiding, all-pervasive presence.

> 'Behold I am with you and will keep you wherever you go, and will bring you back to this land, for I will not leave you until I have done that of which I have spoken to you.' Then Jacob awoke from his dream and said, 'Surely the Lord is in this place and I did not know it.' And he was afraid and said, 'How awesome is this place! This is none other than the house of God, and this is the gate of heaven.' (Gen 28:15-17)

In that day, a pleasant vineyard, sing of it! I, the Lord, am its keeper; every moment I water it. Lest any one harm it, I guard it night and day ... Or let them lay hold of my protection, let them make peace with me. (Is 27:2,3,5)

Our human experience would lead us to believe that God comes and goes in our lives, as the best of friends do.

Footprints

A man was once on a journey and he began to notice that when things were going well there were two sets of footprints, his and God's. When, however, things got difficult, there appeared to be only one set.

When he brought this to God's attention, God said that when there was only one set of footprints, it did not mean that he had deserted him, but that in fact he was carrying him.

There is an art in staying by the side of people who are finding life very difficult. We have to strike a balance between, on the one hand, trying to save them from life's pain and, on the other, ensuring that the pain does not become a frustration rather than an invitation to grow.

In all their affliction he was afflicted, and the angel of his presence saved them; in his love and in his pity, he redeemed them; he lifted them up and carried them all the days of old. (Is 63:9)

Summary

God's fidelity pervades the past, the present and the future, for he always stands by us, no matter what. Love wants to save us from the destructive effects of life's pain, but not to obstruct the way they can help us to grow.

Questions for reflection

1) How do you feel about fair weather friends? Have you a special place in your heart for those whom you can rely on, no matter what happens?
2) Do you feel that there are healthy and unhealthy ways of 'carrying' people in their troubles?

One whose love is everlasting

God's presence with us on life's journey is guaranteed by an everlasting covenant which he makes with each of us. This presence is a love that never leaves us and is as durable as the everlasting hills.

> For the mountains may depart and the hills be removed, but my steadfast love shall not depart from you, and my covenant of peace shall not be removed, says the Lord who has compassion on you. (Is 54:10)

When we think of how easily we cool towards people who let us down and how our trust in them can be weakened, it is wondrous how whole-hearted God can remain in staying with us.

> I have loved you with an everlasting love, and I am constant in my affection for you. (Jer 31:3)

> And I will betroth you to me for ever ... in steadfast love ... I will betroth you to me in faithfulness. (Hos 2:19-20)

When Cain murdered his brother, God put a mark on him as a symbol of his concern for him. It was a symbol of God's fidelity in protecting him even from the effects of his own weakness and waywardness.

> And the Lord put a mark on Cain, lest any who came upon him should kill him. (Gen 4:15)

The Mark of Cain

A swallow found a strange egg along with her own, but she did not pay much attention to it. When it was hatched out as a robin, even though it was now not strictly one of her own, she gave it the same care as the others. Under her attentive eye it learned to fly, though it was more inclined to stay at home than her own young were.

When Winter was approaching, the swallow began to tell them of the joys of the land she would shortly bring them to. She noted that the robin was not very interested and so when the day for departure came she was not surprised that

198   NINE FACES OF GOD

it decided to stay at home. She was sad that it would not see the land she had promised them but, then, that was the inevitable consequence of its not being able to leave where it was.

In her concern for the robin she got some red paint from the peacock and smeared it on the robin's breast so that people would notice and care for it during the long winter months while she herself was away.

A very touching reflection of the warmth and intensity of God's constant affection and devotion is the friendship of Ruth with Naomi. After the death of her husband, Ruth refused to leave her mother-in-law and return to her own people, as her sister had done.

> And she (Naomi) said, 'See, your sister-in-law has gone back to her people and to her gods; return after your sister-in-law.' But Ruth said, 'Entreat me not to leave you or to return from following you; for where you go I will go, and where you lodge I will lodge; your people shall be my people, and your God my God; where you die I shall die, and there will I be buried. May the Lord do so to me and more also if even death parts me from you.' (Ruth 1:15-18)

Ruth symbolises an essential feature of this face of God, the reality of the very personal quality of his fidelity to each of us. When someone treats us in this way, as part of a group, it is difficult enough to handle. When, however, we experience it face to face from *The Divine Lover*, (see page 77) we are likely to resist.

Nehemiah, recording the story of God's dealings with us, discerns this same capacity of God to stay with us in a 'gently loving' way. This is in spite of our giving him every reason for leaving us, because of our perversity.

> But our fathers grew proud ... they refused to obey and were not mindful of the wonders which you performed among them ... But you are a God ready to forgive, gracious and merciful, slow to anger and abounding in steadfast love and you did not forsake them ... but so gently loving, you did not forsake them in the wilderness; the pillar of cloud which led them in the way did not depart from them by day,

nor the pillar of fire by night which lighted for them the way by which they should go. You gave your good Spirit to instruct them and did not withhold your manna from them and gave them water for their thirst. (Neh 9:16-20)

'Wherever you go, I will go'

On our journey God has been, is and always will be with us in the most profound way, no matter where this journey takes us.

Be strong and of good courage; be not frightened, neither be dismayed; for the Lord your God is with you wherever you go. (Jos 1:9)

If I ascend to heaven, you are there! If I make my bed in Sheol you are there! If I take the wings of the morning and dwell in the uttermost parts of the sea, even there your hand shall lead me, and your right hand shall hold me. If I say, 'Let only darkness cover me, and the light about me be night,' even the darkness is not dark to you, the night is bright as the day; for darkness is as light to you. (Ps 139:8-12)

God as an abiding loving presence, as a friend, is something we hardly dare to hope for, even though it is what the heart needs all the time.

Summary

God guarantees his fidelity with an everlasting covenant. This, in spite of our waywardness, retains all the warmth of a marriage-like intimacy. We resist being face to face with a love like Ruth's, even though our heart longs for it.

Questions for reflection

1) When you hear about God's everlasting covenant, does it give rise to a feeling of intimacy? Do you think it is a hard-headed agreement? Does your experience of broken agreements make it difficult for you to accept God's fidelity as being everlasting?
2) What does Ruth symbolise for you about God? Do you resist God saying to you, 'Wherever you go I will go?' Is there a way to overcome this resistance?

One whose love is proved in adversity

> Prosperity asks fidelity;
> adversity exacts it.

When we walk on a dark night, we often become uneasy. Questions arise about our security and we imagine the worst. When we walk in the valley of darkness, we are questioned in a similar way. Are we alone in a dark, hostile world? Are there lacunae in our belief in the constancy of God's providence? Our faith is challenged by the darkness of life. It is not so easy then to believe that God is present.

> For a brief moment I forsook you, but with great compassion I will gather you ... I hid my face from you, but with everlasting love I will have compassion on you, says the Lord, your Redeemer. (Is 54: 4-8)

God's seeming absence during times of hardship, questions us as to what we really believe about his faithful love and his providence. Our belief, by being questioned, is challenged to grow. At times like these God is like a teacher broadening and deepening our faith in his steadfast love.

> Therefore the Lord waits to be gracious to you ... and though the Lord give you the bread of adversity and the water of affliction, yet your Teacher will not hide himself any more, but your eyes shall see your Teacher, and your ears will hear a word behind you, saying, 'This is the way, walk in it,' when you turn to the right or when you turn to the left. (Is 30:18-21)

Often it is only by means of this darkness that God can dislodge our illusion that when life is dark God has deserted us.

> Whatever happens to you, accept it, and in the uncertainties of your humble state, be patient, since gold is tested in the fire and God's chosen in the furnace of humiliation. (Sir 2:4-5)

God is guiding us to find a new sense of his presence in times of hardship, and thus to 'make the foul December flowery May.'

> See I am black as night,
> See, I am darkness: dark as hell.
> Lord, thou more fair than light;
> Heaven's sun thy shadow; can suns dwell
> With shades? `Twixt light and darkness what commerce?
> True thou are darkness, I thy Light; my ray
> Thy mists and hellish fogs shall pierce
> With me, black soul, with me converse;
> I make the foul December flowery May.
> Turn thou thy night to me; I'll turn thy night to day.
> (Phineas Fletcher)

This poem takes the form of a dialogue in which we 'reason together' in the way God calls us to. It is in this kind of honest sharing that we will best overcome the resistance of our prejudices to this face of God.

> Come now, let us reason together, says the Lord: Though your sins are like scarlet, they shall be as white as snow.
> (Is 1:18)

We live at two levels, at an emotional level, and at a level of conviction of what is worthwhile. We tend to think that because something is felt emotionally it is real, and that what is not thus experienced is not real. This was Thomas' problem when he would not believe in Jesus unless he could see and touch him. Jesus, however, invited him to move to the conviction of faith, when he said, 'Thomas, you believe because you have seen. Happy are those who have not seen but have believed.' (Jn 20:29)

Much of life's education comes through knowing how to stay with what we have experienced at times of emotional involvement with God and others. By doing this we can learn to find God with us in times of hardship, when we are left with only the conviction of faith.

> Never doubt in the dark
> what God told you in the light.

What God hopes to teach us through life's hardship and darkness is a new way of deepening our conviction of his enduring presence and providence. This is what he taught Job through the great hardships of his life, so that Job was able to say:

> I have heard of you by the hearing of the ear (hearsay) but now my eye sees you; therefore I despise myself and repent in dust and ashes.' (Job 42:5-6)

Through his experience Job found someone who would stay with him through thick and thin, one who, in spite of his ugly moods, would come down into the pit of his despair with him. He learned of one who would also be with him to sustain and strengthen him until he made his way back out of the pit again. Such a one is portrayed in the father of the prodigal son:

> There was a man who had two sons; and the younger said to his father, 'Father, give me the share of property that falls to me.' And he divided his living between them. Not many days later, the younger son gathered all he had and took his journey into a far country and there he squandered his property in loose living ... But while he was yet at a distance, his father saw him and had compassion, and ran and embraced him and kissed him. And the son said to him, 'Father, I have sinned against heaven and before you; I am no longer worthy to be called your son.' But the father said to his servants, 'Bring quickly the best robe and put it on him ... Bring the calf we have fattened and kill it; we are going to have a feast, a celebration because this son of mine was dead and has come back to life, he was lost and is found; and they began to celebrate. (Lk 15:15-22)

In the father of the prodigal son, we have a portrayal of how Jesus saw the fidelity of God. An outline of this portrait is sketched for us in Ezek 16:

> When I passed by you again and looked on you, behold, you were at the age for love ... I bound myself to you by oath and made a covenant with you, says the Lord God, and you became mine ... I clothed you with embroidered cloth and shod you with leather ... I decked you with ornaments, put bracelets on your arms and a chain on your neck ... You

grew exceedingly beautiful and became a queen. And your name spread among the nations because of your beauty, for it was perfect through the splendour with which I had clothed you, says the Lord God. (Ezek 16:8-14)

There follows a description of how, like the Prodigal Son, Israel abandoned her God and squandered the riches God had shared with her. In spite of this God receives her back into the intimacy of a covenant that 'will last for ever.'

For the Lord Yahweh says this ... I will remember the covenant I made with you when you were a girl, and I will conclude a covenant with you that will last for ever.
(Ezek 16:59-60)

I will love Unloved; I will say to No People of Mine, 'You are my people,' and he will answer, 'You are my God.' [JB]
(Hos 2:25)

Like Israel, we too are meant to experience 'love to the loveless shown that we might lovely be.' This is powerfully portrayed for us in a love that becomes 'frail flesh' and dies for each one of us.

My song is love unknown;
My Saviour's love to me;
Love to the loveless shown,
That they might lovely be.
O, who am I,
That for my sake
He should become
Frail flesh, and die? (*Samuel Crossman*)

The experience of the love we see in this Face of God, especially as it is shown us in the passion and death of Jesus, can change our whole view of life.

You sent him (Christ) as one like ourselves ... that you might see and love in us what you see and love in him.
(Preface of the Mass)

'Do not be afraid; I am with you'

A sure sign that we are not accepting God's abiding love and all-pervasive providence is fear or anxiety. God is constantly reminding us of how groundless these are, since he is always present to care for us.

Therefore, I tell you, do not be anxious about your life, what you shall eat, nor about your body, what you shall put on. For life is more than food, and the body more than clothing. Consider the ravens: they neither sow nor reap, they have neither storehouse nor barn, and yet God feeds them. Of how much more value are you than the birds! And which of you by being anxious can add a cubit to his span of life. If then you are not able to do as small a thing as that, why are you anxious about the rest?

Consider the lilies, how they grow; they neither toil nor spin; yet I tell you, even Solomon in all his glory was not arrayed like one of these. But if God so clothes the grass which is alive in the field today and tomorrow is thrown into the oven, how much more will he clothe you, O men of little faith. And do not seek what you are to eat and what you are to drink, nor be of anxious mind. (Lk 12:22-29)

Cast your care upon the Lord
and he will sustain you. (Ps 55:22)

Destructive feelings such as anxiety or undue fear can easily become ingrained in us. It is only the conviction that we are loved with an everlasting love that can set us free from the paralysing effects of this fear.

Fear knocked on the door.
Faith answered.
There was nobody there.

Be strong and courageous; do not be frightened or dismayed; for the Lord your God is with you wherever you go. (Josh 1:6,9)

I, I am he that comforts you; who are you that you are afraid of man who dies, of the son of man who is made like grass, and have forgotten the Lord, your Maker, who stretched out the heavens and laid the foundations of the earth?
(Is 51:12-13)

I said to you, 'Have no dread or fear of them. The Lord your

God, who goes before you, is the one who will fight for you,
just as he did for you in Egypt before your very eyes, and in
the wilderness, where you saw how the Lord your God carried you, just as one carries a child, all the way that you travelled until you reached this place. But in spite of this, you
have no trust in the Lord your God, who goes before you on
the way to seek out a place for you to camp, in fire by night
and in cloud by day, to show you the route you should take.'
(Deut 1:29-33)

I seek you in darkness
Or, better, wait for you.
I, a creature of the sun,
Fear the clouds and darkness.
Yet in the desert of myself
I can find you in the cloud by day
And in the fire of suffering by night.

Summary

Life's hardships question our belief in God's fidelity and can thus
broaden and deepen our conviction of faith. Through our darkness
God can open our eyes to a new understanding of his fidelity. He
will be with us through life's darkness, even when this is caused
by our own sinfulness. Through acknowledging our sinfulness, if
we allow him, he will lead us into a deeper intimacy than before.
He promises to be with us in this way for ever. Fear is a sign of
unbelief in God's abiding love and all-pervading providence.

Questions for reflection

1) How can life's hardships give you a deeper understanding of
God's fidelity?
2) What do the parable of the Prodigal Son and Ezekiel 16 tell you
about love's fidelity?
3) Why does God speak so often about fear in connection with his
providence? What do your fears say to you about your reaction to
God's faithful love?

FEATURE 5

One whose devotion and loyalty are beyond all doubt

We should not be fearful because God cares for each of us. He is an abiding presence and providence. One of the most often repeated statements that God makes in the Bible is, 'Fear not, for I am with you.'

> Because you are precious in my eyes and honoured, and I love you, I give men in return for you, peoples in exchange for your life. Fear not, for I am with you. (Is 43:4-5)

To this constancy of God's caring we must add his devotion to our needs. This is richly portrayed for us in the image of the shepherd used in Ezekiel. Here we see that God lives with us as a shepherd does with his sheep and loyally devotes himself to every detail concerning our welfare.

> I myself will search for my sheep, and I will seek them out. As a shepherd seeks out his flock when some of his sheep have been scattered abroad ... and I will rescue them from all the places where they have been scattered on a day of clouds and thick darkness ... and I will feed them on the mountains of Israel ... I myself will be the shepherd of my sheep, and I will make them lie down, says the Lord God. I will seek the lost and I will bring back the strayed, and I will bind up the crippled and I will strengthen the weak, and the fat and the strong I will watch over, I will feed them in justice.
>
> ... I will save my flock, they shall no longer be a prey; and I will judge between sheep and sheep ... And I will make with them a covenant of peace ... and I will send down showers in due season, and they shall be showers of blessing ... and they shall be secure in their land ... when I break the bars of their yoke and deliver them from the hand of those who enslave them ... And you are my sheep, the sheep of my pasture, and I am your God, says the Lord God.
> (Ezek 34:11-16,22-31)

This theme of one who refuses to leave us and seeks to heal us from woundedness is echoed for us in many a story.

The film *Frankie and Johnnie* centres on a relationship between two people who work in a cafe. Both have been married but are now separated and living alone. The focus of the film is Frankie's reluctance to enter into another relationship and Johnnie's efforts to overcome this. Her reluctance is based on a loss of belief in herself. This manifests itself in a sense of depression or deadness that is written all over her, and makes her proof against all his efforts to enter her life.

Johnnie, on the other hand, is determined to enter her life. He loves her and thinks she is beautiful. Apart from a brief relationship with one of the other women who work in the cafe, his life centres on Frankie and on how he might win her. So he works away at this throughout the film, gently trying to gain her attention and get her involved.

It is as if he has to take down a huge wall of resistance to him brick by brick. At times he seems to be making progress, only to find that she builds up the wall almost as quickly as he takes it down. The wall is largely her image of herself as worthless and this blocks his best efforts to tell her otherwise. Anytime he tries to enter her life she presents him with this picture of herself that contradicts all that he is trying to say about all she means to him, how worthwhile she is in his eyes. He refuses to give up in spite of what seems at times a fruitless struggle, and by the end of the film she has allowed him into her life. We are left hoping that neither of them will give up the struggle.

The ultimate proof of love's fidelity

The strongest possible sign of God's faithful love is the fact that he sent Jesus and in him loved us 'to the end.'

> While we were still weak, at the right time Christ died for the ungodly … God shows his love for us in that while we were yet sinners Christ died for us. (Rom 5:6-8)

In the gospel of John, the death and resurrection of Jesus is seen as the ultimate proof not only of Jesus' faithful love but also of that of the Father. When John introduces the second part of his gospel, which is about the death and resurrection of Jesus, he takes as his theme the first verse of chapter 13:

Now before the feast of the Passover, when Jesus knew that his hour had come to depart out of this world to the Father, having loved his own who were in the world, he loved them to the end.(Jn 13:1)

Other ways of expressing 'He loved them to the end' are: 'He showed them how perfect his love was', 'He loved them utterly', or 'He loved them to death'.

This giving up to death of one he loves so deeply and intensely is the most powerful sign and proof of the Father's fidelity to us. We see a reflection of this love in the way that parents sacrifice themselves so that their children may have a better life.

For God so loved the world that he gave his only Son, that whoever believes in him should not perish but have eternal life. For God sent the Son into the world, not to condemn the world, but that the world might be saved through him. (Jn 3:16-17)

When Jesus uses the words, 'he gave his only Son' to describe the Father's love, it is a reference to one of the most awesome moments in the Old Testament. This was when Abraham was willing to sacrifice his only son Isaac out of love for God. St John sees God's willingness to sacrifice his only Son as that which demonstrates to us the fidelity that is at the heart of God's love.

In this the love of God was made manifest among us, that God sent his only Son into the world, so that we might live through him. (1 Jn 4:9)

A Hymn to God the Father
Who more can crave
Than thou hast done,
That gav'st a son
To free a slave,
First made of nought,
With all since bought?
(Ben Jonson)

Summary

The image of God as Shepherd expresses his faithful devotion to all our needs. The ultimate proof of this is that he sent Jesus to live with us and 'gave him up' to death that we might share his life.

Questions for reflection

1) What does the image of God as shepherd say about his steadfast love?
2) Why is the death of Jesus such a profound revelation of this Face of God?

The happiness of God

The Key Experience:
Our joy at the happiness of those we love
Resistance:
Our happiness is not a priority for God
The Main Symbol:
Bread and cheese or a Banquet?

God desires to share his happiness with us. He delights in everything he has made. His delight is mainly in his people and this joy is not diminished by the fact that, like the prodigal son, we see much in ourselves that is not delightful. God plans that we would enjoy life to the full. (Jer 29:11) He even commits himself to fulfilling this plan in a covenant of peace which he enters into with each person. He undertakes the long and arduous journey with us to find happiness, not in spite of life's hardships, but through them. In all circumstances, no matter how trivial or adverse, ours is the 'God of all consolation'.

1. One for whom our happiness is a priority

We are urged by God to enter into his happiness which is symbolised by a banquet. There is an inexhaustible quality to this invitation.

2. One who delights in all things and especially in us

Our appreciation of God's delight in what we already are in his eyes, should not be dominated by the desire for what we might become.

God's desire for us is that by revealing himself to us we might become his and he ours. Along with this would come the happiness of our possessing him in this way. Our lack of faith in our happiness being God's main concern, resists this.

3. One who seeks to satisfy our thirst for happiness

God reveals himself as satisfying the thirst we are for him, and for the happiness that this brings us. Gratifying this thirst is the purpose of Jesus' revelation of the Father and of their both sending the Spirit of truth to us. The condition of enjoying the happiness God wants for us is that we make our own of his Word and thus come to know and 'have' him who is the source of our basic happiness.

4. Always seeking to broaden and deepen our happiness

Our essential happiness is had through the conviction of faith. This need not be tangible or felt, even though we tend to think that only what is felt is real.

5. One who wants us to be happy even in times of hardship

Hardship invites us to go on an inner journey into faith, and to deepen and make more permanent our conviction of being loved. Our joy always follows, and is proportionate to this conviction.

6. 'I am the one who comforts you'

The danger of suffering is that it captures our attention and prevents us seeing life in the context of faith. God would have life's hardships deepen our faith and thus our joy. He is our consoler in that he frees us from the deadening effect of suffering, by helping us see it in a wider perspective. God commits himself to our happiness in a covenant of peace.

7. One who seeks our happiness in the here and now

Nothing is too small or too great for God, where our happiness is concerned. Like the Good Shepherd he seeks the best interests of all in the most practical ways. Nothing falls outside his plan for our peace: he is 'the God of peace'.

It has always puzzled me that even though happiness or joy is central to the Bible's way of seeing things, it is not so in the minds of most Christians. I grew up with the belief that happiness was something I should expect to find in the next life, but that suffering and the cross were much more the stuff of this present life. I have since learned to see happiness in other ways, which excite me and which are closer to the Bible's viewpoint. One of these is that we are made for happiness; it is not just that we need a certain amount of happiness, but that we are a thirst for it, especially for the fullness of happiness which we find in God.

> All the animals except man know that the principle business of life is to enjoy it.

I have also come to realise how important for me is the happiness of those I love, and how central my happiness is for them. I find this very helpful in contemplating God. For surely he is at least as concerned for my happiness as my best friends are.

Resistance

The main block to our acceptance of this seventh Face of God is the common image of him as one whose main concern for us in this life is not our happiness. Many people have a very dark view of life and feel more at home with 'weeping and wailing in this valley of tears' than with the joy which Jesus tells us is the object of his revelation.

> These things I have spoken to you, that my joy may be in you, and that your joy may be complete. (Jn 15:11)

Again, we may have an image of God as humourless and very serious. This image is part of a strong puritanical or jansenistic strain in our view of life.

Arousing dormant experience

The following exercises may help you get in touch with areas of your experience which will lead to a greater appreciation of the features of this Face of God:

1) Since we are prone to focusing a lot of attention on the dark side of life, we need to become aware that there are a lot of good things going on as well. To do this, begin by listing on paper some of the things that give you most joy in life.

2) Select one of the experiences you have listed, and re-live it. This involves recreating the scene where it took place, watching what happened and listening to what was said. This is very different from simply thinking about the experience.

3) After you have spent some time quietening yourself and focusing your attention, allow a sense of God's presence to grow. Let him ask you about some joyful experience and, after you have told him about it, ask him if he shares your sense of joy. After listening to what he replies, notice how he appears – whether he is happy, and if he wants to share your happiness.

The Main Symbol:
Bread and cheese or a Banquet?

There was once a family which decided to emigrate from Eastern Europe to the United States. They sold their home and land and had just enough money to pay their fare. Their neighbours were poor people, but they gave them lots of bread and cheese for the journey.

On the second week, when they were well on their journey across the Atlantic, one of the children could no longer take any more bread and cheese, so his father gave him a little money to buy himself an apple. When he did not come back, the father went searching for him, and at last found him in the dining hall, surrounded by all kinds of food.

When he complained that they could never afford this meal, he was told that the whole family could have had it three times every day, as it was all included in the price of their ticket.

FEATURE 1

One for whom our happiness is a priority

The banquet is an image God frequently uses to convey an idea of the abundance of good things – the fullness of life and happiness which is available to us all the days of our lives.

> The Lord is my shepherd
> I will not know need
> Fresh and green are the pastures
> where he gives me repose ...
> You have prepared a banquet for me ...
> Surely goodness and kindness shall follow me
> all the days of my life. (Ps 23:1-2,5-6)

> O Lord, you are my God; I will exalt you, I will praise your name; for you have done wonderful things, plans formed of old, faithful and sure ... On this mountain the Lord of hosts will make for all peoples a rich banquet. (Is 25:1,6)

> ... that you may be filled with all the fullness of God ... who, by the power at work within us, is able to do far more abundantly than all we ask or think. (Eph 3:19-20)

In the parable of the prodigal son Jesus paints a picture of the Father as one who entreats us to come to the banquet. He wants us to enter the fullness of life which the banquet symbolises and to enjoy the resulting happiness. He is prepared to go to great lengths to bring this about.

> But he (the elder son) was angry and refused to go in. His father came out and entreated him ... And he said to him, 'Son, you are always with me, and all that is mine is yours. It is fitting to make merry and be glad, for this your brother was dead and is alive, he was lost and is found. (Lk 15:28-32)

This 'fullness of all good things' which the banquet symbolises is called, in the Bible, happiness, joy and, sometimes, peace. All these words refer to what the Jerusalem Bible calls, 'the perfect happiness which God promised the Messiah would bring.'

> Learn where there is wisdom, where there is strength, where there is understanding, that you may at the same time discern where there is length of days and life, where there is light for the eyes and peace. (Bar 3:14-15)

> For surely I know the plans I have for you, says the Lord, plans for your welfare [peace JB] and not for harm, to give you a future with hope. (Jer 29:11)

How essentially Christian it is to enter this peace, to 'array ourselves in all joy', can be seen from one of the earliest of our Christian writings:

Revel Thou Therein

'Put sadness away from thee, for truly sadness is the sister of half-heartedness and bitterness, Array thee in the joy that always finds favour in God's sight and is acceptable with him; yes, revel thou therein. For everyone that is joyous worketh those things that are good, and despiseth sadness. But he that is sad doth always wickedly; first, because he maketh sad the Holy Spirit that had been given to man for joy; and secondly, he worketh lawlessness, in that he neither prays to God nor gives thanks. Therefore, cleanse thyself from this wicked sadness, and thou shalt live with God. Yea, unto God all they shall live who have cast out sadness from themselves and arrayed themselves in all joy.'
(The Shepherd of Hermes)

An inexhaustible invitation

God issues an inexhaustable invitation to the banquet. He really wants for us the happiness that the banquet symbolises.

> Enter into the joy of your master.(Mt 25:21)

> The father came out and pleaded with him to enter (the banquet he had prepared for his younger brother). (Lk 15:28)

It is an invitation that is urgent and inexhaustible.

> A man once gave a great banquet and invited many ... Come, for all is now ready ... compel people to come in that my house may be filled. (Lk 14:16-23)

Another interesting feature of the banquet is that it is often associated with a wedding.

> The kingdom of heaven, he said, is like a king who arranged a wedding for his son. He sent his servants to summon those who had been invited to the festivities, but they refused to come. (Mt 22:23)

This association with a wedding is important, because each of us personally is the one in whose honour the banquet is held. God invites us to remember that each of us is involved in a marriage-like relationship with him.

Origen, one of the most influential early Christian writers, saw the marriage of Christ and ourselves as central to Christian belief. This intimacy or union with God is the source of our deepest happiness.

> I will betroth you to myself for ever ... betroth you with tenderness and love. (Hos 2:19)

God wants us to keep alive the reality that he has betrothed himself to us for ever, and his delight in that.

> ... as the bridegroom rejoices over the bride, so shall your God rejoice over you. (Is 62:5)

This is a very important symbol, for it is often at weddings that we experience the essential joy of life that is symbolised in the love of two young people.

Summary

We are urged by God to enter into his happiness which is symbolised by a banquet. There is an inexhaustible quality to this invitation.

Questions for reflection

1) What are the main things that God is saying to you by his use of the banquet symbol in the Bible?
2) John Shea, a theologian with a special interest in biblical imagery, says that one of the main qualities we notice about God is his 'inexhaustible invitation' to enter his banquet. What evidence do you see for that?

One who delights in all things and especially in us

Scripture sees God taking great joy in his creation, in us and in all that we already are, exulting 'with shouts of joy' over us. To exult means to rejoice greatly or to be jubilant.

> ... he will rejoice over you with gladness, he will renew you in his love; he will exult over you with loud singing as on a day of festival. (Zeph 3:17)

> Great is the Lord who delights in the peace of his servant. (Ps 35:27)

God finds great joy in us and to describe this he uses the very colourful image of the joy a bridegroom finds in his bride.

> You shall no more be termed Forsaken, and your land shall no more be termed Desolate; but you shall be called My Delight Is In Her, and your land Married; for the Lord delights in you, and your land shall be married ... as the bridegroom rejoices over the bride, so shall your God rejoice over you. (Is 62:4-5)

> It is God's will that we should rejoice with him in our salvation, and that we should be cheered and strengthened by it. He wants our soul to delight in its salvation, through his grace. For we are the apple of his eye. He delights in us for ever as we shall in him, by his grace. (Julian of Norwich.)

One of the things that can prevent us appreciating God's delight in us is our tendency to see God's will as centred on what we *should* be or do.

If we have only got eyes for the way things might be, we can fail to appreciate and be content with what is.

Magical City
There was once a man who was convinced that the humdrum nature of his life was due to where, not what he was. So he set off for Magical City, where he felt all would be new and exciting. At sunset on the first day of his journey, he found himself in a forest, so before he went to sleep he point-

ed his shoes towards where he thought Magical City lay. During the night someone reversed the direction of the shoes so that at the end of the second day of his journey he found himself back in familiar surroundings.

Even though he never arrived in the city of his dreams, he learned to see his own street, house and family in a new way, and to realise that happiness is not always on the far side of the hill.

... And Desires What We May Be

Not only is God happy with what we are, but he plans to share, to an ever greater extent, his own happiness with us, by inviting us to become more intimate with him, the source of true happiness.

> Behold the days are coming, says the Lord, when I will make a new covenant with the house of Israel ... I will put my law within them and I will write it upon their hearts; and I will be their God and they shall be my people. (Jer 31:31-33)

> My Beloved is mine and I am his. (Song 2:16)

> You are always with me and all I have is yours. (Lk 15:31)

> When anyone loves me, he follows my teaching. Then my Father will love that person and we will come and make our home there. (Jn 14:23)

God will lead us into 'the promised land' of this relationship and its joy.

> For the Lord your God is bringing you into a good land ... in which you will lack nothing. And you shall eat and be full, and you shall bless the Lord your God for the good land he has given you. (Deut 8:7-10)

> The best is yet to be,
> The last of life, for which the first was made;
> Our times are in His hand
> Who saith, 'A whole I planned,
> Youth shows but half; trust God: see all,
> Nor be afraid!'
> (Robert Browning)

It is the reality of 'God being ours and we being his' that consti-tutes the new promised land. It is in making our own of the richness which God makes available to us, in revealing himself, that we enter the fullness of all good things he wants for us. This is the peace or perfect happiness for which we are made and we will be restless until our hearts rest in that peace.

> God cannot give us happiness and peace apart from himself, because it is not there. There is no such thing. (C S Lewis)

> (You) may have power to comprehend with all the saints what is the breadth and length and height and depth, and to know the love of Christ which surpasses knowledge, that you may be filled with all the fullness of God. (Eph 3:18-20)

We have a strong tendency to make God in our own image, to limit the vision we have of his love to our human experience. We come to the conclusion, early on in life, that we will only get what we have earned. Therefore, we do not expect God to be the utterly bountiful and generous person he is, urging us to come to his banquet.

The biggest obstacle to our accepting this invitation is our lack of faith in his plan for our happiness. We have learned to live with a God not noticeably happy, nor intent on our happiness.

One of the saddest moments in the gospels is when Jesus weeps over Jerusalem because it has failed to enter the peace God has intended for it.

> Would that even today you knew the things that make for peace! But now they are hid from your eyes. (Lk 19:42)

The consequences of not entering God's joy are of our making, not his.

> Because you did not serve the Lord your God with joyfulness and gladness of heart, that comes from an abundance of all things, therefore you will serve your enemies whom the Lord will send against you. (Deut 28:47-48)

The 'enemies' we serve are subtle ones, like success or prosperity. As Paul says, 'We become the slaves of the powers we obey', and so if prosperity is this power, we become its slave.

Summary

Our appreciation of God's delight in what we already are in his eyes, should not be dominated by the desire for what we might become.

God's desire for us is that by revealing himself to us we might become his and he ours. Along with this would come the happiness of our possessing him in this way. Our lack of faith in our happiness being God's main concern, resists this.

Questions for reflection

1) How do you feel about God delighting in you? Is it something you imagine him doing for others, who are better placed on the spiritual ladder than yourself? What does the story, Magical City, say to you?

2) What does God's plan for your happiness consist in? There are two reasons given above for why you resist this plan. Do you identify with either of them?

One who seeks to satisfy our thirst for happiness

God does not just desire our peace, but plans to share the fullness of his own joy with us and `a future full of hope.' This is hard to believe if we have grown up with a God whose joy is not obvious and who does not seem intent on ours, at least not in this life.

The plan God has for our happiness is built into our make-up. We are made for joy. This is often compared to a hunger or thirst for the food and drink without which we would not survive. It is also a thirst that God alone can satisfy and in this sense he, and he alone, is our happiness.

> O Lord, we wait for you; your name, your memory is the desire of our soul. My soul yearns for you in the night, my spirit within me earnestly seeks you. (Is 26:8-9)

> Like the deer that yearns for running streams,
> so my soul is thirsting for you my God.
> My soul thirsts for God, for the living God.
> When shall I come and behold the face of God.
> (Ps 42:1-2)

> *'My spirit longeth for thee'*
> My spirit longeth for thee
> Within my troubled breast;
> Although I be unworthy
> Of so divine a Guest.

> Of so divine a Guest,
> Unworthy though I be;
> Yet has my heart no rest,
> Unless it comes from thee.

> Unless it come from thee,
> In vain I look around;
> In all that I can see,
> No rest is to be found.

> No rest is to be found,
> But in thy blessed love;

O let my wish be crowned,
And send it from above.
(John Byrom)

This in-built thirst is compared to the parched land which must
have water to bring it back to life again.

O God, you are my God, for you I long;
my soul thirsts for you;
My body pines for you,
like a dry, weary land without water. (Ps 63:1)

God plans to satisfy this thirst through making himself known to
'the least no less than the greatest'.

For he satisfies him who is thirsty,
and the hungry he fills with good things. (Ps 107:9)

They shall all know me, the least no less than the greatest.
(Jer 31:34)

Jesus tells us that the revelation of the Father which he expresses
in human terms, especially in his own person, is given as part of
their plan that we would be abundantly happy.

I have told you these things that you might share my joy and
that your happiness may be complete. (Jn 15:11)

This story helped me to understand this parting wish of Jesus to
share his joy with us:

'I want you to be happy'
Karl Rahner, the famous German theologian, tells the very
moving story of his final visit to his mother before she died.
When she knew she was soon to die, she asked him to do
something special for what she knew would be his last visit
to her.

He was to bring a bottle of wine and two glasses, and when
he did, and they were sitting enjoying the wine together, she
said that her parting wish for him, on this his last visit to her,
was that he would be a joyful priest all his remaining days.

It is to satisfy this thirst that God sends the Spirit, to give us an intimate knowledge of himself.

If any one thirsts let him come to me, as the scripture has

said, 'Out of his heart shall flow rivers of living water.' Now this he said about the Spirit, which those who believed in him were to receive. (Jn 7:37-39)

> They feast on the abundance of your house,
> and you give them drink from the river of your delights.
> Yours is the fountain of life;
> in your light do we see light. (Ps 36:8-9)

This face of God expresses his essential happiness and his desire to share this, by revealing himself as love for each person. The condition of our entering into his plan is what is called in scripture 'keeping his commandments.' We easily associate this with keeping rules and regulations, whereas in the Bible it has a much richer meaning. It includes the effort of making our own of the vision and values that are expressed in God's word. 'Keeping his commandments', in this sense then, means that we have to make our own of his revelation of himself if we wish to share his happiness.

> As the Father has loved me, so have I loved you, abide in my love. If you keep my commandments, you will abide in my love, just as I have kept my Father's commandments and abide in his love. These things I have spoken to you, that my joy may be in you, and that your joy may be full. (Jn 15:9-11)

Seeing the face of God as love for us, and making our own of this vision through faith, helps us to experience to the full the joy God intends when he reveals himself as joyful and celebrating:

> 'Let us eat and make merry.'
> 'It is right to make merry and be glad.' (Lk 15:24,32)

Our main symbol, the banquet, is one that makes us feel that 'it is right to make merry and be glad' in God's presence. He is not as serious or solemn as many imagine him to be, and above all not one to be feared.

> Love bade me welcome; yet my soul drew back,
> Guiltie of dust and sinne.
> But quickey'd Love, observing me grow slack
> From my first entrance in,
> Drew nearer to me, sweetly questioning,
> If I lack'd any thing.

A guest I answer'd, worthy to be here:
Love said, you shall be he.
I the unkinde, ungrateful? Ah my deare,
I cannot look on thee.
Love took my hand, and smiling did reply,
Who made the eyes but I?

Truth Lord, but I have marr'd them: let my shame
Go where it doth deserve.
And know you not, sayes Love, who bore the blame?
My deare, then I will serve.
You must sit down, says Love, and taste my meat;
So I did sit and eat.
(George Herbert)

Summary

God reveals himself as satisfying the thirst we are for him, and for the happiness that this brings us. Gratifying this thirst is the purpose of Jesus' revelation of the Father and of their both sending the Spirit of truth to us. The condition of enjoying the happiness God wants for us is that we make our own of his Word and thus come to know and 'have' him who is the source of our basic happiness.

Questions for reflection

1) What is meant by saying, we are a thirst for God? How does he plan to satisfy this thirst?
2) How is the work of Jesus, and of the Spirit, connected with this plan of God for our peace?
3) What have you to do, for your part, in order to enter into this plan?
4) What do the poems of Byrom and Herbert, or the story about Karl Rahner's mother, have to say to you?

Always seeking to broaden and deepen our happiness

The vision of God which we will have when we see him face to face in heaven, is described as 'beatific' – one that will make us supremely happy. With Thomas the apostle, we long for that face-to-face vision of God in the form of a tangible experience – one that we get by means of our senses and emotions. Jesus, however, explains, that we can get a more profound glimpse of God, which will make us really happy, through faith.

> You believe because you can see me. Happy are those who have not seen and yet believe. (Jn 20:29)

We tend to assume, like Thomas did, that the deepest experience comes through 'seeing' or through what is very tangible. The Letter to the Hebrews, however, assures us that it comes through the conviction of faith, and that this need not be tangible:

> Now faith is the assurance of things hoped for, the conviction of things not seen. (Heb 11:1)

Without the vision of faith, we can miss the jewel at the heart of all as illustrated in the story on page 57.

Is it real only if I feel it?

Think of the way two people experience each other as a marriage develops. Initially, romantic love seems to be the essence of their life together. Like Thomas, they are inclined to say, 'If I feel it, it is real, but if I do not, there is nothing there.' Yet romantic love is the most impermanent of loves. The pair are in ecstasy while it lasts, but when it is gone, there will be the agony of doubt. In the light of this, we may be able to understand Jesus' warning about the impermanence of the tangible experience of him that we, like Thomas, are inclined to rely on too much.

> A little while and you will see me no more; again a little while and you will see me ... Truly, truly, I say to you, you will weep and lament but the world will rejoice; you will be sorrowful but your sorrow will turn into joy. (Jn 16:16,20)

Jesus is anxious to help us, as he helped Thomas, to reach a happiness that is deeper and more permanent. This is like what the married pair find when they begin to experience committed love. Then the satisfaction they get from each other is not the criterion of the relationship. They begin to live more with a conviction of the love there is between them, and find a deeper and more lasting contentment in this.

Summary

Our essential happiness is had through the conviction of faith. This need not be tangible or felt, even though we tend to think that only what is felt is real.

Questions for reflection

1) Do you see a difference between the way Thomas wanted to experience Jesus after the Resurrection and the way Jesus wanted him to, through faith? Do you notice your own preference between these two ways of relating with God and other people? Do you find as time goes on that you rely more on your convictions than on your emotions?

One who wants us to be happy even in times of hardship

The happiness Jesus promises Thomas, and each of us, rests on the growing conviction of God's love – on faith. It is often life's hardship that helps us find this deeper, more permanent joy in life, the jewel at the heart of all things.

> When a woman is in travail she has sorrow, because her hour has come; but when she is delivered of the child, she no longer remembers the anguish, for joy that a child is born into the world. So you have sorrow now but I will see you again and your hearts will rejoice, and no one will take your joy from you. (Jn 16:21-22)

Hardships can have a very salutary effect on us, for through them we are encouraged to explore resources we never previously thought we possessed.

> A bird used to live in an old tree, that was the best it could find in a very desolate place. One day, the tree was destroyed by lightning and the bird had to find a new home. This involved a long search, but it meant that the bird eventually found a forest where the trees were rich with fruit for it to live on.

It is often through the hardship and darkness of life that we are invited, like the bird in the story, to go on a journey. Times of great difficulty challenge us to be resourceful and patient in our search for the promised land.

> I have seen the affliction of my people who are in Egypt and have heard their cry ... I have come down to deliver them out of the hand of the Egyptians and to bring them up out of that land to a good and broad land, a land flowing with milk and honey. (Ex 3:7-8)

Reaching this land 'flowing with milk and honey' — a symbol for the fullness of the life and happiness which God wants for us – involves passing through life's desert periods. It is only these that breed a real conviction of faith, the sureness of being loved, which is the rock on which our deepest happiness rests.

So we know and believe the love God has for us. God is love, and he who abides in love abides in God, and God abides in him. (1 Jn 4:16)

Our Autumn Glory Is Forever
Autumn's wonderful world of leaves
Alas, in such a short, though glorious show
Of yellow and brown, of green and gold,
Soon to be stripped in winter starkness.
So, ravaged by cruel wind, frost and dreary rain,
Amid this all-encompassing greyness
It will be hard to imagine there was a Summer
And the brilliance of this Autumn glory.

But it was not this sorry tale
Or to feed nostalgia for the Summer past
That inspired this picture of a passing show,
But the hope of my own Autumn years.
That these may capture the beauty of this scene
And hold its glory, for my remaining years,
Less through my own all too feeble effort
Than by the growing appreciation of Your Grace.

Summary
Hardship invites us to go on an inner journey into faith, and to deepen and make more permanent our conviction of being loved. Our joy always follows, and is proportionate to this conviction.

Questions for reflection
1) Do you feel that hardship can bring about growth? Does the story about the bird help you see the possibilities for this kind of growth?
2) Do you feel that your happiness can be fashioned by the hardships of your life? How would you explain this?

FEATURE 6

'I am the one who comforts you'

The experience of life's hardships can be a major obstacle to our seeing this face of God. They can, like the clouds that cross the moon, impede our vision of it. All can appear dark, as if the object of our delight were no longer there. Thus the darkness brought on by hardships can dominate our attention and leave us desolate.

> The fascination of evil obscures what is good. (Wis 4:12)

We have a strange tendency to let the dark areas of life dominate our attention, even if they are only a small fraction of our experience. For example, if I get angry during the day, by nightfall I tend to see little else. A small fraction of my experience, maybe five per cent of it, tends to be all that I see. I get cut off from the things that are for my peace.

The role adversity or affliction should play in life is not to obscure our vision of God and the happiness this brings, but to deepen it. God portrays himself as a Teacher nourishing us with 'the bread of adversity', opening up our minds, so that we might see him in a deeper way.

> Therefore, the Lord waits to be gracious to you ... He will surely be gracious to you at the sound of your cry; when he hears it, he will answer you. And though the Lord give you the bread of adversity and the water of affliction, yet your Teacher will not hide himself any more, but your eyes shall see your Teacher. (Is 30:18-20)

In this way God wants to 'turn our mourning into dancing', to deepen our vision of faith and the joy that is always its sequel.

> You have turned my mourning into dancing;
> ... and clothed me with gladness,
> that my soul may praise you and not be silent.
> O Lord my God, I will give thanks to you for ever.
> (Ps 30:11-12)

The desert periods of life can easily obscure our vision of the God, whose primary interest is that we would live joyfully. We tend to live with a god who works on the principle of postponed gratification, one who says that we must be willing to forego joy in this life in order that we may have it in the next. Paul says something very different when he tells us, 'Rejoice in the Lord always.'

> Rejoice in the Lord always; again I will say, Rejoice. Let your gentleness be known to everyone. The Lord is near. Do not worry about anything, but in everything, by prayer and supplication with thanksgiving, let your requests be made known to God. And the peace of God, which surpasses all understanding, will guard your hearts and minds in Christ Jesus. (Phil 4:4-7)

> If you want to be happy, begin where you are.
> Don't wait for some rapture that's future and far.

Hardship is not something God sends but it is a part of life. God, however, can use it to deepen our vision of faith, by questioning our belief in the extent of his love and providence. God is portrayed in the Bible as a refiner intent on using the fire of life's sufferings to purify, or bring out the best in us. The 'best' here means the 'life and peace' or 'happiness' that come from the vision of faith.

> For he is like the refiner's fire ... He will take his seat as refiner and purifier; he will purify the sons of Levi and refine them like gold and silver. (Mal 3:2-3)

> My covenant with him was a covenant of life and peace, and I gave them to him. (Mal 2:5)

It is in this context especially that God presents himself as our consoler, wishing to deliver us from a tendency to let life's hardships deaden us and make us sad.

> I, I am he that comforts you; who are you that you are afraid of man who dies ... and have forgotten the Lord, your Maker, who stretched out the heavens and laid the foundations of the earth. (Is 51:12-13)

> Blessed be the God and Father of Our Lord Jesus Christ, the Father of mercies and the God of all consolation.
> (2 Cor 1:3-4)

God wants to set us free from fear, especially from that of walking 'in the valley of darkness.'

Near restful waters he leads me,
to revive my drooping spirit.
He guides me along the right path;
he is true to his name.

If I should walk in the valley of darkness
no evil would I fear.
You are there with your crook and your staff;
with these you give me comfort. (Ps 23:2-4)

When we walk in the valley of darkness, it is easy to drift into dull resignation to our lot, to grin and bear it. The way along which God wants to lead us, the 'Holy Way', is one where people will walk with 'everlasting joy on their faces'.

And a highway shall be there, and it shall be called the Holy Way; the unclean shall not pass over it, and fools shall not err therein ... the redeemed shall walk there. And the ransomed of the Lord shall return and come to Zion with singing; everlasting joy on their faces; they shall obtain joy and gladness and sorrow shall flee. (Is 35:8-10)

We have to keep alive the memory of God's commitment to our happiness. We need, especially in dark times, to return to our roots in 'the God of peace'.

The Flower
Who would have thought my shrivelled heart
Could have recovered greenness? It was gone
Quite underground; as flowers depart
To feed their mother-root, when they have blown;
Where they together
All the hard weather,
Dead to the world, keep house unknown.
(George Herbert)

* * *

The covenant of peace

At times of dryness or darkness, it is hard to believe that God is more committed to our peace (happiness) than we are to our own. He reminds us of the reality of this when he speaks of his 'covenant of peace.' This is a profound commitment and, no matter how dark things may appear, God is intent on sharing his happiness with us.

NINE FACES OF GOD

I will make a covenant of peace with them. (Ezek 34:25)

Behind this covenant is his 'everlasting love', guaranteeing us that, come what may, the source of our peace will not be removed.

> For a brief moment I forsook you, but with great compassion I will gather you. In overflowing wrath for a moment I hid my face from you, but with everlasting love I will have compassion on you, says the Lord your Redeemer ... For the mountains may depart and the hills be removed, but my steadfast love shall not depart from you, and my covenant of peace shall not be removed, says the Lord, who has compassion on you. (Is 54:7-8,10)

Summary

The danger of suffering is that it captures our attention and prevents us seeing life in the context of faith. God would have life's hardships deepen our faith and thus our joy. He is our consoler in that he frees us from the deadening effect of suffering, by helping us see it in a wider perspective. God commits himself to our happiness in a covenant of peace.

Questions for reflection

1) In what way does the 'fascination of evil obscure what is good'? What would God have the evil of suffering do in your life?
2) Most people connect sadness with suffering. In what way can we let hardship deepen our faith?
3) Is there some way that suffering or hardship can deepen your sense of joy?

One who seeks our happiness in the here and now

Even if we believe that God is concerned for our happiness in general, it is almost incredible that he is concerned with everything that contributes to this happiness.

> He who did not spare his own Son but gave him up for us all, will he not also give us all things with him ... can we not trust such a God to give us, with him, everything else we can need?[P] (Rom 8:32)

Jesus tells us of the Father's desire to give us the fullness of joy in every area of life, if we but seek it.

> Truly, Truly I say to you, if you ask anything of the Father, he will give it to you in my name. Hitherto you have asked nothing in my name; ask, and you will receive that your joy may be full. (Jn 16:23-24)

It is in the ordinary everyday things that God will be working out his plan for our peace. The real joy of life lies at our feet.

The Great Land Is Here

The count lived in a great castle filled with books. He was one of the wisest men in the world. One day he came across a little child playing on the sea shore, trying to fill a hole in the sand with sea water. The count did not think this made sense but, after talking to the child, he began to realise that the child lived in a place he called The Great Land.

This stirred the count's curiosity, so he asked how he might get to this Great Land. The little boy pointed to the blank page of a book that lay beside him on the strand. The count felt very foolish, but asked the book about how he might get to The Great Land. To his surprise he was told to learn to laugh, and when he had mastered this, to learn how to play, to dance, to cry. Having mastered all these, he still had not reached the great land.

One day when he had almost given up hope of getting what he wanted, he saw some children playing and decided to join them. It was then, through their childlike games, in learning to laugh and to play and to appreciate the very simple things of life, that he realised the Great Land is here.

He is a wise man who does not grieve for the things he has not, but rejoices for those he has. (Epictetus)

Nothing will be too insignificant for God to concern himself with.

Therefore I tell you, do not be anxious about your life, what you shall eat, nor about your body, what you shall put on, for life is more than food and the body more than clothing. Consider the ravens, they neither sow nor reap, they have neither storehouse nor barn, and yet God feeds them. Of how much more value are you than the birds? (Lk 12:22-24)

The manna (food) for the banquet which God wants us to enter and to celebrate with him, is available each day at our very doors.

Happiness is like manna; it is to be gathered in grains, and enjoyed every day. It will not keep, it cannot be accumulated; nor have we to go out of ourselves or into remote places to gather it, since it is rained down from heaven, at our very doors.

* * *

The God of peace

God seeks our happiness in the most mundane of things. He gives us a symbol of this in portraying himself as our shepherd. As such, he is concerned about the welfare of each one of us in the most practical ways and in the most ordinary circumstances. He intends to work every detail of our lives into the covenant of peace he makes with us.

I myself will be the shepherd of my sheep ... I will seek the lost and bring back the strayed, and I will bind up the crippled, and I will strengthen the weak. I will make with them a covenant of peace ... I will send down the showers in their season; they shall be showers of blessing ... I will break the bars of their yoke and deliver them from the hand of those who enslave them ... And you are the sheep, the sheep of my pasture, and I am your God, says the Lord God. (Ezek 34:15-31)

In this face of God we see one who is essentially happy, and who in all kinds of ways seeks to share this happiness with us. He does this, as St Francis did with the sow, by 're-teaching us our loveliness' in his eyes. Re-read that poem on page 152.

In his letter to the Christians in Rome, Paul tells us how central the gifts of peace and joy are for us.

> The kingdom of God is not food and drink but righteousness, peace and joy in the Holy Spirit ... Let us then pursue what leads to peace. (Rom 14:17,19)

God is 'the Lord of peace' who seeks our joy and happiness always and everywhere.

> In his days may righteousness flourish
> and peace abound till the moon be no more!
> May he have dominion from sea to sea,
> and from the River to the ends of the earth! (Ps 72:7-8)

> May the Lord of peace himself give you peace at all times in all ways. (2 Thes 3:16)

Perhaps what seems an over-optimistic view of life is, in fact, most realistic. 'All the way to heaven is heaven.' (St Catherine)

Summary

Nothing is too small or too great for God, where our happiness is concerned. Like the Good Shepherd he seeks the best interests of all in the most practical ways. Nothing falls outside his plan for our peace: he is 'the God of peace'.

Questions for reflection

1) What point does the story, *The Great Land Is Here*, make for you concerning God's plan for your peace or happiness? What does the image of the Good Shepherd say to you about this?

2) Is there some experience in your own life that you find hard to place inside God's covenant of peace?

God: lover and Lord

The Key Experience:
Intense, all-absorbing falling in love
Resistance:
It is too soft, erotic and impermanent for God
The Main Symbol:
Stages of falling in love

God's love is passionate and he loves wholeheartedly and intensely. We are lured out into the desert by him so that he might win our hearts and become our lover. By winning our hearts with his overwhelming attractiveness, God becomes our Lord. His intense and passionate love never lessens; he wants to 'take you for his wife forever', (Hos 2:19) He will do this by loving so intensely that he will win our hearts and become our Lord.

1. One who is lover and we his beloved
God is portrayed in the Bible as one seeking to win our hearts, loving us wholly and deeply, with all the intensity of a lover. Our image of a more dispassionate and non sexual God, resists this.

2. One who loves us wholly and passionately
Seeing God portrayed as a lover, as in the Song of Songs, seems too romantic in a hardheaded world. Yet, he must love as wholly and intensely as do those who are made in his image. The ultimate proof that God is a burning fire and loves with his whole heart, is in his sacrificing Jesus for those so undeserving of this love.

3. One who invites us into an overwhelming intimacy
As his beloved, God invites us into the love he has for Jesus, his only beloved Son. This is an overwhelming reality, challenging the great illusion of our insignificance. God gives us a new heart, capable of accepting the intimacy of he being ours and we his.

4. One who delights in us as he does in Jesus
God's delight in us centres on the reality that he shares with us the relationship he enjoys with Jesus. Therefore, God delights in us as he does in his Beloved Son. This reality makes the least of us greater than John the Baptist.

5. One whose love is truly generative
There is great energy in this Face of God, as it seeks to realise all that we may be, with a passion. It is generative in the intensity of its love, seeking to open up new areas of our dream and gradually to bring us to full flower.

6. One whose love is transforming

Love has a radically transforming effect on us. This is especially true of the healing and life-giving power of God's love, which is given supreme expression in the death of Jesus out of love for us.

7. One who wins our heart to become its Lord

To the degree that someone wins our heart they become our lord. In this same way God seduces us, winning our hearts to become our Lord. This is very different from God being demanding.

8. One whose intense love is respectful of our freedom

Even though God's love has all the passion of falling in love and the permanence of a marriage relationship, it is not pushy in spite of its intensity. God remains 'gently loving' in his deference to our freedom.

9. One who wins our heart and soul, mind and strength

Loving with our whole mind, heart and strength means that we:
1) 'Walk humbly with our God.' This involves acknowledging him as Lord, and it invites the response of our whole heart
2) 'Love tenderly,' in response to his love.
3) 'Act justly' by letting God, not success etc, become the Lord of every area of life.

The Key Experience

Falling in love can be the least permanent of loves, but while it lasts it is most intense and all-absorbing.

We might be quite scattered in our interests before we fall in love but once we do, all our energies become focused on the person with whom we are in love. It is an experience that stirs our depths, touching us wholly and deeply. Because it can touch us in this way romantic love has a power to arouse the sexual side of us. Since being moved sexually is often so suspect, it is not easily seen as a way God loves us or wishes us to love him. I have come across a writer recently who holds that falling in love is the biggest source of energy in people today. We miss a very important side of God if we fail to find him passionately loving.

Resistance

The very male image of God that is prevalent today may make it inappropriate to attribute romantic love to him. It may appear too soft, or not manly enough to attribute to God.

The kind of love we are dealing with here has also got erotic overtones. This may make it seem inappropriate to talk about God loving in this way. It is the same kind of experience that makes us uneasy about seeing God portrayed as the Lover in the Song of Songs.

Resistance to attributing passionate love to God may also come from our experience that it can be the least permanent of loves. If we have much experience of it, we will know that it waxes and wanes and cannot be lived with its initial intensity for very long.

Arousing dormant experience
1) Notice some of the ways that falling in love does people good.

Single out one of the good effects you have noticed it having on them and dwell with the circumstances in which you noticed it. It is always better to relive experiences like this than to think about them.

2) Can you let God react to you in any of the ways you have noticed people doing when they are in love? For example, you may have noticed how much they enjoy each other's company. You might, like Teresa of Avila recommends, let God look on you lovingly. You might, however, find it easier to let him say, in some way that seems right to you, that you are his beloved.

3) Spend time trying to become aware how you feel when God looks on you in this way. Some of the feelings you will notice will be positive, in the sense that you may feel a sense of wonder. But you will also feel a certain amount of resistance to what he is saying as it may, for example, sound unreal. It would help your relationship with God a lot if you could share with him how you feel.

The Main Symbol:
Stages of falling in love

When two people fall in love they pass through a number of stages. These range from an initial strong attraction, to the commitment of marriage and leaving home to be permanently with the other.

1) The boy and the girl meet, get interested in, and find their lives centering on each other.

2) They ask themselves how much they know about each other: love begins blind but becomes wide-eyed.

3) They try to change what makes them unsuitable to be together. A clean-up begins.

4) They find out all they can about each other, to know whether their love can overcome their differences.

5) They each ask if they really love sufficiently to leave everything to be together.

6) They are ready to leave home and commit themselves to each other.

FEATURE 1

One who is lover and we his beloved

There is something intriguing about the experience of two people falling in love and the way it affects them, how it seems to touch them wholly and deeply.

> So Jacob served seven years for Rachel,
> but they seemed to him but a few days
> because of the love he had for her. (Gen 29:20)

> … he fell so deeply in love with her
> that he could no longer call his heart his own. (Tob 6:18)

> Many waters cannot quench love, neither can floods drown it. If a man offered for love all the wealth of his house, it would be utterly scorned. (Song 8:7)

It always fascinates people when God portrays himself in these terms. The following are some of the ways in which God expresses how he finds himself wholly and deeply moved by his love for us:

> I am going to lure her, and bring her into the wilderness, and speak tenderly to her. (Hos 2:16)

> You have seduced me, Yahweh, and I have let myself be seduced; you have overpowered me, you were the stronger. (Jer 20:7)

> I have loved you with an everlasting love, so I am constant in my affection for you. (Jer 31:3)

> How do I love thee? Let me count the ways,
> I love thee in the depth and breadth and height
> My soul can reach, when feeling out of sight
> For the end of Being, and ideal grace.
> I love thee to the level of everday's
> Most quiet need, by sun and candlelight.
> I love thee freely, as men strive for Right;
> I love thee purely as they turn from Praise.
> I love thee with the passion put to use
> In my old griefs, and with my childhood's faith.

I love thee with a love I seemed to lose
With my lost saints – I love thee with the breath,
Smiles, tears of all my life – and if God choose,
I shall but love thee better after death.
(Elizabeth B Browning)

We may find this face of God difficult to appreciate if we have grown up with an image of him that is colder and more remote than the one portrayed here.

There is also a strong element of the sexual associated with romantic love. So, if we feel that the sexual is of doubtful spiritual value, we may find it inappropriate to hear God spoken of as loving us passionately.

Summary
God is portrayed in the Bible as one seeking to win our hearts, loving us wholly and deeply, with all the intensity of a lover. Our image of a more dispassionate and non sexual God, resists this.

Questions for reflection
1) How do you feel about God being in love with you? What ways would you allow him to express the fact that he loves you wholly and deeply?

One who loves us wholly and passionately

This face of God is so striking that when we see it portrayed in a book like the Song of Songs we may find it exaggerated and un-real. Yet, it is common in the Bible to find God relating to us as his beloved. Because of the difficulty we have in looking at and ac-cepting God as portrayed in this way, we tend to shy away from it; it seems so soft or romantic in a hardheaded world.

> The mystic and the lover seem foolish.

> Once I was deaf to the music, so the gyrations of the dancer seemed ludicrous. Then one day I heard the music and the dance was beautiful.

This romantic or passionate love is essential to the way that God reveals himself. It may help us realise how much it is part of him, if we consider how profoundly it is part of those whom he has made in his own image.

> Then God said, 'Let us make man in our image, after our likeness ... So God created man in his own image, in the im-age of God he created him. (Gen 1:26-27)

> And we all with unveiled face beholding the glory of the Lord, are being changed into his likeness from one degree of glory to another; for this comes from the Lord who is the Spirit. (2 Cor 3:18)

One of the implications of being made in God's image is that any kind of loving we find in people must also be, to a supreme de-gree, in God. He could not give to us something that is not part of his own way of loving. God must be as passionately loving as those who are made in his image or likeness.

> Romantic love is the single greatest energy system in the Western psyche. In our culture it has supplanted religion as the arena in which men and women seek meaning, transcen-dance, wholeness and ecstasy. (Robert A Johnson)

There are people from whom life and energy seem to emanate, so that they engage others and enliven them with their own vitality. This was how Jeremiah felt about God, whom he describes as 'a burning fire' deep within himself which he found hard to contain.

> If I say, 'I will not mention him, or speak any more in his name,' there is in my heart as it were a burning fire shut up in my bones, and I am weary with holding it in, and I cannot. (Jer 20:9)

Jesus reflects this when he says that he has come to cast fire on the earth.

> I have come to cast fire on the earth, and would that it were already kindled. (Lk 12:49)

Hosea experienced the intensity of God's love in its wholeheartedness.

> I will heal their faithlessness, I will love them with all my heart.(Hos 14:5)

Distinctive of our human experience of falling in love, is the fact that it does not last or endure. C.S. Lewis, in *The Four Loves*, speaks of it as the most impermanent of loves. With God, however, the power or passion of his love endures forever.

> God has revealed only one reality
> that to him alone belongs the power
> of a love that endures forever. (Ps 62:11-12)

It is above all in the death of Jesus that the Father reveals the intensity of his love for each of us. We need to love someone or some cause with a passion to be willing to give up all we possess for them.

> For God so loved the world that he gave his only Son, that whoever believes in him should not perish but have eternal life. (Jn 3:16)

What highlights the intensity of this love is that it is willing to sacrifice the life of one who is profoundly loved. This is all the more striking, if the one for whom the sacrifice is made is completely undeserving.

> But God shows his love for us in that while we were yet sinners Christ died for us. (Rom 5:8)

Summary

Seeing God portrayed as a lover, as in the Song of Songs, seems too romantic in a hardheaded world. Yet, he must love as wholly and intensely as do those who are made in his image. The ultimate proof that God is a burning fire and loves with his whole heart, is in his sacrificing Jesus for those so undeserving of this love.

Questions for reflection

1) What words would you use to name your positive and then your negative feelings, when you hear God spoken of as a lover, or in such romantic terms?
2) Do you find it convincing to have God loving us as wholly and intensely as we love, who are made in his image?
3) Do you easily associate the death of Jesus with the passionate love of God for you?

One who invites us into an overwhelming intimacy

One of the things we noticed above about two people falling in love, was their desire to know each other better, their growing intimacy. So, besides the intensity of God's love that is like 'a burning fire,' there is an intimacy about it that is difficult for us to handle. God does not just place us down beside the fire of his love but within the very heart of it.

> But now in Christ Jesus you who once were far off have been brought into intimacy with God through the blood of Christ. (Eph 2:13)

God wants to be always intimately present to his 'beloved,' 'encompassing her all the day long.'

> Of Benjamin he said, 'The beloved of the Lord, he dwells in safety by him; he encompasses him all the day long, and makes his dwelling between his shoulders.' (Deut 33:12)

God is one who wishes to make his home within us.

> If anyone loves me, he will follow my teaching. Then my Father will love him, and we will come and make our home within that person. (Jn 14:23)

It is important to keep in mind, that what is said to Israel as a people, is now said to each of us personally, to 'the least no less than the greatest.' (Jer 31:34)

> It was not because you were more numerous than any other people that the Lord set his heart on you and chose you, you were the fewest of all peoples; but it is because the Lord loves you, and is keeping the oath which he swore to your fathers, that the Lord has brought you out with a mighty hand and redeemed you from the house of bondage. (Deut 7:7-9)

Most people keep us at a distance, with the result that the experiences of those who take us to their hearts, and let us take them to ours, are as memorable as they are rare. The intimacy and intensity of God's love is so personal and strong that it is very hard to believe. This is especially so when we consider that, as Jesus tells us, it is exactly the same as the love that the Father has for him.

> The glory you have given to me, I have given them, that they may be one even as we are one, I in them and you in me, that they may become perfectly one, so that the world may know that you have sent me and have loved them even as you have loved me. (Jn 17:22-23)

When we are faced with the reality that God says he loves us, even as he loves Jesus, our mind is overwhelmed, and may even relegate this experience to the realm of unreality. There is a certain level of affirmation we can handle and anything beyond that sounds unreal and is likely to be rejected.

John Powell uses the image of a little black box we have in our heads. Anything that does not easily fit into this is rejected. So if God says he loves us passionately, we cut that down to a size we can easily handle. This means that we exclude most of God's love and are essentially impoverished by this tendency to squeeze him into our mould.

> In the beginning God made us in his image
> but ever since we have been making him in ours.

> Do not be conformed to this world but let your minds be remoulded. (Rom 12:2)

The reason for our difficulty in accepting what the intensity of God's love reflects back to us is that we accept uncritically the illusion of our insignificance or worthlessness. It is sufficient that we do not hear ourselves affirmed much, for our sense of a lack of worth to grow.

> Linus tells Charlie Brown that he believes that life has passed him by and asks him whether he ever feels this way. Charlie replies that it has not only passed him by but knocked him down and walked all over him as well.

Our feeling of insignificance fosters in us the great illusion that runs directly counter to what God has destined us to be.

> He destined us in love to be his sons through Jesus Christ, according to the purpose of his will, to the praise of his glorious grace which he freely bestowed on us in the Beloved. (Eph 1:5-6)

You sent him as one like ourselves, though free from sin, that you might see and love in us, what you see and love in him. (Preface of the Mass)

The main work of God in our lives is to open our hearts to receive the revelation of this 'one reality,' to open our hearts to the depth of the intimacy where we become his and he ours. (Song 2:16)

I will give them a new heart, and put a new spirit within them; I will take the stony heart out of their bodies and give them a heart of flesh, that they may walk in my statutes and keep my ordinances and obey them; and they will be my people and I will be their God. (Ezek 11:19-20)

The Ultimate Country
Intimacy, that's the ultimate country
My soul seeks to explore and own.
It is my birthplace and Promised Land
Whose memory haunts all this exile's days.

In it lies the burning fire
That inflames the inmost places of the heart;
The ecstasy of being Your beloved
Harnessing all to a single purpose.

But there is a quieter flame within us
That burns more enduringly;
Fired by the deeper regions of the heart;
Whence springs the intimacy of friends.

I would be inspired by both these,
Be wholly and deeply touched.
Then all my concerns would centre on you
And I would be at home, at rest.

But that one place is not yet where
My scattered heart resides;
Drawn as it is to possess ephemeral things
And alas, be possessed by them.

Yet to be close, or even one with You
Is all my heart's desire,
For without You I am but half my truest self,
Ever destined to search for the other.

Summary

As his beloved, God invites us into the love he has for Jesus, his only beloved Son. This is an overwhelming reality, challenging the great illusion of our insignificance. God gives us a new heart, capable of accepting the intimacy of he being ours and we his.

Questions for reflection

1) What does being intimate with another mean for you?
2) Have you difficulty applying what you notice in your intimacy with others to that which Jesus wants with you?
3) What ways do you notice yourself resisting this intimacy which God wants with you?

One who delights in us as he does in Jesus

God delights in us in the way that those who fall in love delight in each other. We can see this delight, not just at the initial stages of falling in love, but also in people who remain in love with each other. When this kind of love matures, it learns to move beyond the quest for satisfaction to appreciate the goodness of the other person.

This face of God reveals deep appreciation of who we are, and how he delights in us. We may expect to find a lot of resistance to this, especially when we find him telling us that we are delightful, wholly beautiful and ravishing (i.e. that we enrapture, charm, entrance and fill him with delight).

> You are beautiful, my love, and without blemish ... You have ravished my heart, my sister, my bride, you have ravished my heart with a glance of your eyes. (Song 4:7,9)

> Behold, you are beautiful, my beloved, truly lovely (and how delightful). (Song 1:16)

> ... as the bridegroom rejoices over the bride, so shall your God rejoice over you. (Is 62:5)

Jesus does not use the image of the marriage relationship very much, for he speaks rather of the reality that it symbolises. To describe his intimacy with us he uses the same word as that which expresses his own relationship with the Father. So, he speaks about 'knowing' the Father and being known by him and then adds to this the startling reality that the Father knows us, just as he does Jesus.

> I know my own and my own know me, as the Father knows me and I know the Father. (Jn 10:14-15)

The wondrous nature of this may not strike us unless we appreciate the profound meaning of the word 'knowing.' This biblical word gathers together all the richness of the image of the marriage relationship, used by prophets like Hosea. It means that we can be known and loved by the Father and know and love him in return, with all the intensity and intimacy of the way he knows and loves Jesus.

> I made known to them your name, and I will make it known, that the love with which you have loved me may be in them and I in them. (Jn 17:26)

When Jesus says he will make the Father's name known to us, he means that he will reveal all the love that God is. In this way, we are brought into the very life of the Trinity and 'are made welcome in the everlasting love God bears towards his Beloved.' (Eph 1:6) When the Father looks at us he says the words he spoke of Jesus at his baptism in the Jordan.

> This is my Beloved in whom I delight. (Mt 3:17)

If God delighted in his people in the old Covenant, how much more full of meaning for us now are the words he used of Israel.

> ... he will rejoice over you with gladness, he will renew you in his love; he will exult over you with loud singing as on a day of festival. (Zeph 3:17)

Jesus puts the comparison between the new covenant and the old in a very striking way when he says that the least in the new is greater than the greatest in the old. The change of mind and heart involved in adjusting to this reality will mean that we will have to do violence to ourselves in order to accept it. It is hard enough to bring our mind around to seeing ourselves as greater than John the Baptist, but even more so to bring ourselves to feel it. We have only to notice how difficult it is for us to change our ways of behaving, to know how we have to struggle to change deeply ingrained ways of seeing things and feeling about them.

> Believe me, among those born of woman there has risen no one greater than John the Baptist; yet he who is least in the kingdom of heaven is greater than he. From the days of John the Baptist until now, the kingdom of heaven has suffered violence, and men of violence take it by force.' (Mt 11:11-12)

This experience of the love of God overwhelms us; it is difficult to grasp or express fully as 'it is beyond all knowing.'

> ... may have power to comprehend with all the saints what is the breadth and the length and height and depth, and to know the love of Christ which surpasses knowledge. (Eph 3:18-19)

Hopkins, in his poem on St Alphonsus Rodriguez, (see page 121) expresses how God can 'crowd career with conquest' in the midst of what appears insignificant. God appreciates and delights in the great dignity he finds in us.

Summary

God's delight in us centres on the reality that he shares with us the relationship he enjoys with Jesus. Therefore, God delights in us as he does in his Beloved Son. This reality makes the least of us greater than John the Baptist.

Questions for reflection

1) When Jesus uses the word 'know' to describe his own relationship with the Father, the one he wants us to enter, what does this mean for you?

2) How do you feel about being greater than John the Baptist? Do you feel Jesus was exaggerating when he used this comparison?

One whose love is truly generative

The young man and woman in the process of falling in love delight in what they find in each other. With time, it is to be hoped that everything that contributes to the other's growth will become increasingly important. God also not only delights in us but has a dream, 'a plan for our peace'. (Jn 29:11) This is that we would work with him to realise all the potential he has built into us, in making us capable of `knowing' the extent and depth of his love for us. His ultimate goal is that we might be filled with all his fullness.

> may have power to comprehend with all the saints what is the breadth and the length and height and depth, and to know the love of Christ which surpasses knowledge, that you may be filled with all the fullness of God. (Eph 3:18-19)

If we look at our human experience, we will realise the energy that being deeply loved gives to us. It is like the realisation of our wildest dreams when we grasp something of the extent and depth of God's love.

> Eye has not seen, nor ear heard, neither has it entered into our hearts to conceive what God has prepared for those who love him. (1 Cor 2:9)

There is a very limited amount of this 'fullness' that we are ripe for at any point in our lives, but it is towards this that God will be drawing us in a very gentle, yet powerful way. He will, as he did with Jeremiah, 'seduce' us or win our hearts by his attractiveness.

> You have seduced me, Yahweh, and I have let myself be seduced; you have overpowered me, you were the stronger. JB (Jer 20:7)

He will be 'luring' or enticing us out into the desert, so that we would make space to meet and come to know his lifegiving love.

> That is why I am going to lure her and lead her out into the wilderness and speak to her heart. (Hos 2:16)

God will be constantly seeking to open up new ground, drawing us into areas where we are ready for growth or to realise some part of his dream for us. This will not be without a lot of resistance on our part. We all want to be left with old, superficial dreams, with which we are comfortable.

Gerard Manley Hopkins, in *The Wreck of the Deutschland*, sees God as a skilled craftsman fashioning our lives. He sees God bringing about our conversion in a way peculiar to each one of us. Read again *With anvil ding* on page 60.

An image Jesus uses is of the Father as a gardener pruning his vine. He has an expert eye for what he must cut away, to foster new growth and make us more fruitful.

> I am the true vine and my Father is the vinedresser. Every branch of mine that bears no fruit, he takes away, and every branch that does bear fruit he prunes that it may bear more fruit. (Jn 15:1-2)

Summary

There is great energy in this Face of God, as it seeks to realise all that we may be, with a passion. It is generative in the intensity of its love, seeking to open up new areas of our dream and gradually to bring us to full flower.

Questions for reflection

1) What, in very practical terms, is God's dream for you?
2) What piece of God's word best expresses for you the intensity with which God wants to bring you to full flower?
3) Are there people in your life who are generative and who know the right amount of pressure to put on you to help you grow?
4) What do people, who give you an impression of this Face of God, tell you about it?

One whose love is transforming

There seems to be something particularly life-giving about the experience of falling in love. According as the two people involved realise they are the object of the other's intense love, they can be transformed by this. I am the second last of a family of ten, so this has given me a vantage point from which to observe the way being love-stricken affected my brothers and sisters. I can vouch for its transforming effects. It is like the third of the stages of falling in love that we saw in the main symbol at the beginning, where the pair change their ways in order to fit in better with each other.

The most transforming expression of this love is when God sacrificed his only Son for our sakes. In this we experience the full extent and depth of God's intense love of us and its life-giving power. Jesus compares the helping and life-giving power of his being 'lifted up' on the cross to the Bronze Serpent which Moses raised up before the people of Israel in the desert.

> And as Moses lifted up the serpent in the wilderness, so must the son of man be lifted up, that whoever believes in him may have eternal life. For God so loved the world that he gave his only Son, that whoever believes in him should not perish but have eternal life. (Jn 3:15-16)

> ... and I, when I am lifted up from the earth, will draw all men to myself. (Jn 12:32)

This face of God radiates such life and energy that it has the power to undo the effects of sin that cause us, like the prodigal son, to wander into the far country.

> So it is the magnetic power of this
> That draws us together and onto you
> Undoing the disintegrating power of sin.

This passionate love of God is so strong that not even gross infidelity can deter him from winning back our hearts. It is a very striking feature of falling in love that the two people who do so will most likely find its intensity hard to maintain. They can fall out of love just as quickly as they have fallen in love, especially at the early stages. Against this background of our human experience, the enduring quality of the passionate love we experience in this face of God satisfies a deep human longing.

Summary

Love has a radically transforming effect on us. This is especially true of the healing and life-giving power of God's love, which is given supreme expression in the death of Jesus out of love for us.

Questions for reflection

1) What ways have you noticed falling in love changing people?
2) Why can God's love bring about even more dramatic changes?

One who wins our heart to become its Lord

God becomes Lord or King by winning our hearts with his love. The truth of this is echoed by the words of the song which say, 'love is Lord of all.' Anyone or anything that exercises a strong attraction for us gains a certain hold on our heart.

> Answer me, O Lord, answer me, that this people may know that you, O Lord, are God and are winning their hearts. (1 Kgs 18:37)

> You belong to the power you choose to obey. (Rom 6:16)

It was Hosea who made the connection between God being lover and, as a direct result of that, Lord. He is the one 'beside whom there is no other.'

> Thus says the Lord, the King of Israel and his Redeemer, the Lord of hosts: I am the first and I am the last; besides me there is no god. (Is 44:6)

> For the sake of my servant Jacob, and Israel my chosen, I call you by your name, I surname you though you do not know me. I am the Lord, and there is no other, besides me there is no God; I gird you, though you do not know me, that men might know from the rising of the sun to its setting in the west that there is none besides me; I am the Lord and there is no other. (Is 45:4-6)

What often blocks our appreciation of this face of God is the illusion that ours is a demanding God. With this preconception we cannot see one who wishes 'to lure us into the desert,' to win back our hearts. This he wishes to do 'with cords of compassion, with bands of love.'

> It was I who taught Ephraim to walk, I took them up in my arms; yet they did not know that it was I who healed them. I led them with cords of compassion, with the bands of love. (Hos 11:3-4)

Even though there is a passion and an intensity about this Face of God, its effect on us must not be the strain of meeting ever new

---

demands. He always remains one who seduces us, i.e. 'wins us by attractiveness'.

> You have seduced me, God, and I have allowed myself to be seduced; you are stronger than I, and you have prevailed. (Jer 20:7)

A Strange Kind Of King
It is a strange kind of king
That comes riding on a donkey
Winning our hearts to become their Lord.

'Tis the power of God in manger born,
Becoming for me weak flesh and blood,
Amid the animals in a winter cold cave.

You first showed your glory as our king
At wedding feast, to save that poor pair's name
With a miracle of unobtrusive kindness.

Since you came on a donkey to claim us as your own
The whole world has been running after you,
Our hearts won by your quiet attractiveness.

It is no pushing of your authority then
That makes you King of our inconstant hearts,
But a love we will always be struggling to tell.

So it is the magnetic power of this
That draws us together and onto you
Undoing the disintegrating power of sin.

It is your being lifted up on a tree
That enthrals us, making all creation yours
Seducing us, to become our Universal King.

Summary

To the degree that someone wins our heart they become our lord. In this same way God seduces us, winning our hearts to become our Lord. This is very different from God being demanding.

Questions for reflection

1) What is the meaning for you of the words, 'love is lord of all?'
2) Do you feel there is a connection between them and Jeremiah's experience of being seduced by God?

FEATURE 8

One whose intense love is respectful of our freedom

God most frequently expresses his passionate love in terms of the intensity and intimacy of a man and woman who fall in love and marry. When we see two people getting married we wonder will the intensity of their love quieten and deepen into a love that is permanent. Will their love break up in the storms that lie ahead, or outlast them?

> For your Maker is your husband, the Lord of hosts is his name; and the Holy One of Israel is your Redeemer, the God of the whole earth he is called. For the Lord has called you like a wife forsaken and grieved in spirit, like a wife of youth when she is cast off, says your God. For a brief moment I forsook you, but with great compassion I will gather you. In overflowing anger for a moment I hid my face from you, but with everlasting love I will have compassion on you, says the Lord, your Redeemer. (Is 54:5-8)

This image of God may not fit very well with the very masculine one we have grown up with. Even women who reflect this face of God, in the great energy of their passion for the truth, can come across as bossy or pushy. So, it is as well to recognise the difficulty we are going to have, believing that God is one who seeks to transform us in a very intimate and deferential way.

This deference is imaged in the story of God patiently waiting for more room in our house (see page 52), and God's consistent and gentle love is reflected in the *Frankie and Johnnie* story on page 208. Re-read one of these and, in the light of it, ponder prayerfully chapter 9 of the Book of Nehemiah or the following extract from it. Throughout this chapter, we hear the refrain of God being 'gently loving' running through the history of God's passionate love of Israel and of each of us.

> But our fathers grew proud ... they refused to obey and were not mindful of the wonders which you performed among them ... But you are a God ready to forgive, gracious and merciful, slow to anger and abounding in steadfast love and you did not forsake them ... but so gently loving, you

did not forsake them in the wilderness; the pillar of cloud which led them in the way did not depart from them by day, nor the pillar of fire by night which lighted for them the way by which they should go. You gave your good Spirit to instruct them and did not withhold your manna from them and gave them water for their thirst. (Neh 9:16-20)

Your first showed your glory as our king
At a wedding feast, to save that poor pair's name
With a miracle of unobtrusive kindness.

Since you came on a donkey to claim us as your own
The whole world has been running after you,
Our hearts won by your quiet attractiveness.

It is no pushing of your authority, then
That makes you King of our inconstant hearts,
But a love we will always be struggling to tell.

Summary

Even though God's love has all the passion of falling in love and the permanence of a marriage relationship, it is not pushy in spite of its intensity. God remains 'gently loving' in his deference to our freedom.

Questions for reflection

1) Do you know of anyone who can combine a great depth and intensity of love with deep feeling and respect for where you are?
2) What do you notice about falling in love, marrying and remaining faithful, that says something about God's love for you?

One who wins our heart and soul, mind and strength

The more God wins our hearts and thus becomes Lord, the more we will experience the need to acknowledge him as God in a number of ways. In the following verse, we might notice that God draws us to himself by winning back our minds, our hearts and the deep instinctive side of us, out of which we act.

> He has showed you, O man, what is good; and what does the Lord require of you but to act justly, to love tenderly and to walk humbly with your God. (Mic 6:8)

We are constantly being challenged by God to accept the reality that he is not just lover, but also the Lord. The awesome fact we all have to face when we approach God is that he is holy. Moses was dramatically confronted with this when he experienced God in the burning bush.

> God called to him out of the bush, 'Moses, Moses!' And he said, 'Here I am.' Then he said, 'Do not come near; put off your shoes from your feet, for the place on which you are standing is holy ground.' And he said, 'I am the God of your fathers, the God of Abraham, the God of Isaac and the God of Jacob' and Moses hid his face, for he was afraid to look at God. (Ex 3:4-6)

This attitude of reverence, of acknowledging God as God, leads to a willingness to listen to him, and to the surrender of true obedience. This involves 'walking humbly with our God' and learning the wisdom of the child.

Learning The Wisdom Of The Child
Mali was a very clever child and when he was ready to start his formal education his parents sent him to the best school in their area. It was a long way away, and involved travelling through a forest where there were a lot of wild animals. So every day the little boy would travel through the forest but he was not afraid for he put his hand in the hand of Krishna.

His teacher at school was amazed at the faith and courage of the child and asked him, 'Would I meet Krishna, if I went to the forest?' So in order to get an answer he accompanied the little boy on his journey home. When they had passed through the forest together several times, the teacher was disappointed that he did not meet Krishna. Then one day he heard a voice saying, 'When you have learned the wisdom of the child you will meet Krishna.'

The attitude, like that of the child Mali, which we need to adopt to meet God, is expressed in the story of the boy Samuel. There Elijah helps Samuel to discern the attitude he must adopt to hear God's revelation of himself. Read chapter 3 of 1 Sam, and stay with this verse:

Now the Lord came and stood there, calling as before, 'Samuel! Samuel!' And Samuel said, 'Speak, Lord, your servant is listening.' (1 Sam 3:10)

It was for their lack of this 'perception' of God as God, for not walking humbly with their God, that the people of Israel went into exile. This was not a punishment imposed by God but a consequence of their failure to live with the reality of this Face of God.

... but they do not regard the deeds of the Lord, or see the work of his hands. Therefore, my people go into exile for their lack of perception; their honoured men are dying of hunger, and their multitude is parched with thirst. (Is 5:12-13)

Loving tenderly

Another result of God winning our hearts and becoming Lord is that we feel the need to return love for love, especially for the tender love he lavishes on us.

Nevertheless in your great love you did not make an end of them or forsake them; for you are a gracious and merciful God.(Neh 9:31)

The call to respond to God's love with our whole heart and soul, mind and strength is central to the message of the Bible and is the great commandment.'

This call to love God with our whole heart is a response that our being loved wholly and passionately by him calls out of us.

Teacher, what shall I do to inherit eternal life? He said to him, 'What is written in the law? How do you read?' And he answered, 'You shall love the Lord your God with all your heart and with all your soul, and with all your strength and with all your mind; and your neighbour as yourself.' And he said to him, 'You have answered right; do this and you will live.' (Lk 10:27-28)

Acting justly

A large part of acknowledging God as God, as the Lord of the whole of creation, is our effort to make this effective in every area of our lives. It is one thing to make the initial choice but another to hold ourselves to it, so that our hearts are not seduced, as was Solomon's, by other gods.

For when Solomon was old his wives turned his heart after other gods; and his heart was not wholly true to the Lord his God as was the heart of David his father. (1 Kgs 11:4)

We easily get side-tracked, seduced by false gods. Our quest for success or prosperity leaves our search for God very little time or energy. Jesus constantly insists on not just listening to the word of God, but doing it or living consistently with it. This is what is implied in loving God with our whole heart and soul, mind and strength. The Good News must penetrate to every area of our lives, 'to the whole of creation.'

God invites us to enter the fullness of life symbolised by the promised land. What prevents us accepting this invitation is our attachment to something that leads to the neglect of so much else in life. If, for example, a career becomes a priority, all else may become secondary. We can be very impoverished by this decision because we may fail to develop many more important areas of our lives, such as our relationship with God or with friends. In this way our career is a source of great injustice, and we fail, as a result, to 'act justly.' We can easily fail to see the real consequence of the loss of life involved in this decision.

See, I have set before you this day life and good, death and evil. If you obey the commandments of the Lord your God … by loving the Lord your God, by walking in his ways … then you will live and multiply.

But if your heart turns away, and you will not hear, but are drawn away to worship other gods and serve them, I declare to you this day, that you shall perish, you will not live long in the land which you are entering. ... I have set before you life and death, blessing and curse; therefore choose life that you and your descendants may live, loving the Lord your God, obeying his voice and clinging to him; for that means life to you and length of days. (Deut 30:15-20)

The Whirlpool
The four furrowed plough
Turned the sod with feverish efficiency
Within a day of harvest's end
Where well-earned rest used follow
Our time of reaping.
Now the unrelenting cycle of activity
Means little root room for rest,
And alas, this but reflects
The harrowing of the heart
When leisure falls victim to activity
Dove-tailing task ended with task begun.

Reflected too is the whirlpool of my heart
That knows not any other world
Than the intensity of ceaseless striving.
I am sucked in by the seductive swirl
Of the unrelenting demands of service
That fill even the crevices of each day
With endless desires and what must be done.
My prayer is now for liberty
From the tyranny of misguided zeal
I long to come apart and rest awhile
Lured into the desert by One
Who is the heart's essential quest.

God confronts us with the seriousness of his invitation to enter his banquet. Ours is the responsibility for the consequences of not entering. God does not punish us for not doing so; we punish ourselves.

You have stayed long enough at this mountain; you must move on and continue your journey ... Behold I have set the land before you; go and take possession of the land which the Lord swore to your fathers. (Deut 1:6,8)

See, I set before you the way of life and the way of death. (Jer 21:8)

So the Lord calls us to the banquet of his peace but challenges us to enter into it wholeheartedly, and to take pains with all that is involved in living fully and happily.

For I know the plans I have for you, says the Lord, plans for welfare and not for evil, to give you a future and a hope. Then you will call upon me and come and pray to me, and I will hear you. If you seek me, you will find me; when you seek me with all your heart, I will be found by you, says the Lord. (Jer 29:11-14)

The poem, *Batter My Heart*, by John Donne, expresses well the struggle involved in seeking to know the face of the passionate God which we are contemplating here. There is a lot of resistance in us to this, to letting God be Lover and Lord. The only way to become free of this is to let him gradually 'enthral' us.

Batter my heart, three person'd God; for, you
As yet but knock, breathe, shine, and seeke to mend;
That I may rise, and stand, o'erthrow mee, and bend
Your force, to breake, blowe, burn and make me new.
I, like an usurpt towne, to another due,
Labour to admit you, but Oh, to no end,
Reason your viceroy in mee, mee should defend,
But is captiv'd, and proves weake or untrue.
Yet dearly I love you, and would be loved faine,
But am betroth'd unto your enemie:
Divorce mee, untie, or breake that knot again,
Take mee to you, imprison mee, for I
Except you enthral mee, never shall be free,
Nor ever chaste, except you ravish mee.
(John Donne)

Summary
Loving with our whole mind, heart and strength means that we:
1) 'Walk humbly with our God.' This involves acknowledging him as Lord, and it invites the response of our whole heart
2) 'Love tenderly,' in response to his love.
3) 'Act justly' by letting God, not success etc, become the Lord of every area of life.

Questions for reflection
1) What do the words, 'Act justly, love tenderly, and walk humbly before your God,' mean for you? What do they reveal to you about this eighth Face of God?
2) What does the poem *Batter My Heart* say to you about the features of this Face of God?
3) Do you challenge others or confront them? Do you allow them to do this to you? What feelings arise in you when you come up against the way God challenges and confronts you?

The friendship of God

The Key Experience:
Friendship
Resistance:
We resist being at this depth with one so superior
The Main Symbol:
The growth-path of friendship.

The friendship which God seeks with us is a very profound kind of intimacy based on the mutual gift of self-disclosure. Achieving this will involve restoring an intimacy which we have lost and befriending what has been estranged. God appreciates us as a good friend does and he discovers in us the deep worth which often lies buried beneath our human poverty. We see also his desire for our happiness. His love is not just one-way or salvific for he seeks a return of the love he has expressed for us. We are invited to become God's friends by sharing our deepest selves with him. This involves an on-going commitment to speak to God 'face to face as a person does with a friend'. (Ex 33:11)

The Main Features of the Ninth Face of God

1. One who seeks to restore a lost intimacy

The intimacy, which we lost in the Fall and which God now seeks to restore, is described in the Bible as friendship. It is like the friendship which God established with Abraham, Moses and the prophets. It is above all in Jesus that God lays the foundations of the reality that we are friends of God. It is a profoundly intimate and permanent relationship which God establishes in our hearts.

2. One who seeks to befriend all who are estranged

God's plan is to reconcile all things to himself. The result is that we are being drawn into an intimacy which has the deep and permanent nature proper to a profound 'fellowship' or friendship.

3. One who gives himself in self-disclosure

Our friendship with God is based on a mutual sharing that is initiated by his self-revelation. Coming to know this revelation is possible only through coming to know Jesus in the intimate way which the Spirit makes available to us.

4. One who delights in us as a friend does

God appreciates all the good in us and welcomes us to the love which he has for his Beloved Son in whom he delights. He 'sees and loves in us what he sees and loves in Christ.

5. One who accepts our weakness as a friend does

We are invited by God as our friend to accept his acceptance of our weakness and waywardness, the prodigal in each of us.

---

6. One who, as a friend, wants the very best for us

God plans our peace, that we should share in the fullness of life which he enjoys. He never gives up in his efforts to realise all the potential there is in us.

7. One who wants our friendship

Friendship is a mutual gift. Being known and loved by God calls out of us the desire to know and love him in return. God's gift of himself in self-disclosure calls for our revelation of ourselves to him, by responding honestly to what he has revealed.

8. One who knows the value of genuine communication

Friendship with God involves an on-going dialogue in which we listen and respond honestly to what he reveals of himself. The quality of this communication will be a measure of our friendship. We have to wrestle, like Jacob did, with our weakness and infidelity, if we are to accept God's invitation to the banquet of intimacy with him.

The kind of love we are looking at here is that which we experience between ourselves and our friends. It is a much quieter love than that experienced when we fall in love, but much more permanent.

Essential to friendship is the practice of sharing, and according to what is shared, we meet people at different levels. So we have all kinds of friends, with some of whom we may share superficially, while with others, our minds and hearts, our deepest selves. This involves a dialogue in which we gradually reveal more and more of ourselves and share the essential gift of friendship, i.e. the mutual gift of ourselves in self-disclosure. It may be with very few that we reach the deeper levels of friendship, but it is there that God wants to meet each of us.

Resistance

We resist the call to friendship with God because it is hard to conceive having such an intimate relationship between persons so unequal as ourselves and God. Cicero believed that you could not have a friendship between a master and a slave or between ourselves and the gods. This belief has a profound influence on our thinking about friendship with God. He is so superior to us in every way that it is hard to conceive of a friendship with him.

We may also have difficulty sharing our mind and heart with God because we may not be in touch with this level of ourselves. We resist being drawn into a relationship where we feel out of our depth. For example, we may be more at ease sharing our thoughts rather than how we feel, but in saying only what we think, we do not share much of ourselves.

Arousing dormant experience

1) Recall a time when you had a heart-to-heart talk with someone and relive the situation as far as you can. What did this experience do for your relationship with that person at the time?

2) Meet God in a place where you like to be, and when you are at ease in his presence, let him ask you to share something about which you feel strongly. When you have expressed yourself on this, ask him how he feels about what you have said and then respond to this as honestly as you can.

At the end, become aware of how you feel towards God as a result of listening and talking to him in this way. Notice the way he relates to you in your dialogue, e.g. whether he gives a lot of advice, is remote or close, or if he really likes listening to you.

3) Recall a time when you opened your mind and heart to a very close friend and how he or she reacted. Then ask God if he is at least as good as the best of your friends, in the way he listens and talks to you. Dwell with his reply and see how you feel like responding.

The Main Symbol:
The Growth-path of Friendship

Imagine two people falling in love, getting married and their relationship deepening over the years. At the silver jubilee of their marriage, they would probably notice, as they look back over their time together, that there are not the same highs and lows that they experienced when they first fell in love.

It is not that they love each other less, but it is a quieter kind of loving; it is not as physical or emotional, but a sharing at a deeper level. From the outside, their lives might appear quite uneventful, but they would not exchange the happiness they find together for anything.

Their passionate being in love has grown into – not been replaced by – a friendship in which there is a deep sharing of mind and heart, and an understanding and concern for what matters most to each other.

One who seeks to restore a lost intimacy

God draws each of us along a path which leads us through the passionate being-in-love, of the Eighth Face, into a friendship that should be as intimate as we have with the best of our friends.

How God leads us into this has to be seen in the context of the whole story of the Bible, for there we find the pattern of the way he deals with each one of us. This story begins with a description of creation and the intimacy into which God drew his people, as they walked with him in the garden. Then follows the story of the Fall, as a result of which people experienced the terrible effects of separating themselves from God, of walking out of the intimacy for which they were made. But God was not prepared to leave things like that. Through people like Abraham and Moses, he began to restore that lost intimacy.

> Thus the Lord used to speak to Moses face to face, as a man speaks to his friend. (Ex 33:11)

When God announces his new covenant through Jeremiah, it is clear that he wishes to have this intimate 'face to face' relationship with each person. No matter how insignificant we may appear to be in our own estimation, God wants this relationship with 'the least no less than the greatest.'

> Behold the days are coming, says the Lord, when I will make a new covenant with the house of Israel and the house of Judah, and like the covenant which I made with their fathers when I took them by the hand to bring them out of Egypt, my covenant which they broke, though I was their husband, says the Lord. But this is the covenant which I will make with the house of Israel after those days, says the Lord: I will write it upon their hearts; and I will be their God and they shall be my people. And no longer shall each man teach his neighbour and each his brother, saying, 'Know the Lord,' for they will all know me, from the least of them to the greatest. (Jer 31:31-34)

The way God made himself known 'face to face' to Moses, became the model for his dealing with each person in the New Covenant. He realises the promise he made through Jeremiah by revealing himself completely through Jesus. Thus, he makes us his friends, by giving us the gift of himself in self-disclosure.

> No longer do I call you servants for the servant does not know what his master is doing; but I have called you friends, for all that I have heard from my father I have made known to you. (Jn 15:15)

This gift of self-disclosure, in which friendship consists, is received mainly by the heart. This is because what God wants to reveal is less a message than a relationship which he wants to establish with us. We tend to analyse what God says with our head, whereas God wants to write on our hearts.

> But this is the covenant which I will make with the house of Israel after those days, says the Lord: I will write it upon their hearts... (Jer 31:33)

God is trying to help us discover our heart, and there to initiate this deep relationship where we may speak to him face to face as with a friend.

'A Flower, Mister!'
A wealthy business man on his way to work heard an old lady, selling flowers, say to him, 'A flower, Mister!' He brushed her aside, but was afterwards troubled about this, as it appeared to him on reflection that he had lost something of the composure he liked to portray.

On subsequent days he began to notice the old lady, even though she still disturbed his usual calm control. She with her gentle smile, in spite of her age and occupation, confronted him with something that made him uneasy. She was such a contradiction of all he stood for, his cold brusque manner, his youth and his successful career.

As the days went by, he noticed that he was less irked by her and that he made it his business to pass her way each day. It was as if she had something important to say to him.

Then one day he found himself planning a surprise for her. At their next meeting, he returned her smile with a rose he had gone to great trouble to buy, as it was the first of the season, and of the new season in his heart. He was, through her, invited into a wider world, where he could speak to others face to face as with friends.

Like the woman, God wants us to discover our hearts and to take possession of the intimacy which he wants to establish with us. The richness and permanence of this relationship is intimated in Ezekiel 16. The whole chapter is worth reading for in it this feature of God is powerfully portrayed.

> When I passed by you again and looked on you, behold, you were at the age for love ... I bound myself to you by oath and made a covenant with you, says the Lord God, and you became mine ... I clothed you with embroidered cloth and shod you with leather ... I decked you with ornaments, put bracelets on your arms and a chain on your neck ... You grew exceedingly beautiful and became a queen. And your name spread among the nations because of your beauty, for it was perfect through the splendour with which I had clothed you, says the Lord God. (Ezek 16:8-14)

The splendour with which God clothes us is grace – the wedding garment we must wear to the banquet. (Mt 22:1-14) A way of understanding this gift of God is to see it as friendship. Friendship is the model which Thomas Aquinas chooses when he seeks to explain what is central to being a Christian – that each person is a friend of God.

Summary

The intimacy, which we lost in the Fall and which God now seeks to restore, is described in the Bible as friendship. It is like the friendship which God established with Abraham, Moses and the prophets. It is above all in Jesus that God lays the foundations of the reality that we are friends of God. It is a profoundly intimate and permanent relationship which God establishes in our hearts.

Questions for reflection

1) What is the basis of our claim to be the friends of God?
2) What is your reaction to the idea that God is your closest friend?

FEATURE 2

One who seeks to befriend all who are estranged

God desires to restore the intimacy for which we are made. He seeks to be reconciled with us.

Through Jesus, God reconciles us to himself and gathers together again, into an intimate union, what had been torn apart and scattered by sin.

> He did not say this of his own accord, but being high priest that year he prophesied that Jesus should die for the nation, and not for the nation only, but to gather into one the children of God who are scattered abroad. (Jn 11:51-52)

This reconciliation, or 'befriending of what was estranged', is God's dream or plan for us. To fulfil it he sends Jesus, who goes around making friends, drawing us into his own relationship with the Father. The friendship that Jesus draws us into is a union or an intimacy that he prays will be as close as that which he has with the Father.

> Holy Father, keep them in your name which you have given me, that they may be one, even as we are one ... I do not pray for these only, but also for those who believe in me through their word, that they may be one even as you, Father, are in me, and I in you, that they also may be in us, so that the world may believe that you have sent me. The glory which you have given me I have given to them, that they may be one even as we are one, I in them and you in me, that they may become perfectly one, so that the world may know that you have sent me and have loved them even as you have loved me. (Jn 17:11,20-23)

The words 'that they may be one' may be better understood today as an expression of God's desire for intimacy. All Nine Faces involve some aspect of intimacy, but the one that friendship focuses on is *being deeply touched by another*. This differs from the aspect emphasised in the Eighth Face which is *being wholly touched by another*. The intimacy of friendship may not involve our whole person, as being in love does, but it is more permanent and deeper.

Both have a key role in helping us on our way to *The Ultimate Country*. (see page 146)

In the first letter of John, Jesus is seen as one who makes the Father tangible. The purpose of this is that we would be drawn into the 'fellowship' or friendship that he enjoys with his Father.

> That which was from the beginning, which we have heard, which we have seen with our own eyes, which we have looked upon and touched with our hands, concerning the word of life – the life was made manifest, and we saw it, and testify to it, and proclaim to you the eternal life which was with the Father and was made manifest to us – that which we have seen and heard we proclaim also to you, so that you may have fellowship with us; and our fellowship is with the Father and with his Son Jesus Christ. And we are writing this that our joy may be complete. (1 Jn 1:1-4)

Summary

God's plan is to reconcile all things to himself. The result is that we are being drawn into an intimacy which has the deep and permanent nature proper to a profound 'fellowship' or friendship.

Questions for reflection

1) Is there a relationship which you enjoy in which you can identify *the intimacy proper to friendship*? Does God want to relate this way to you?
2) How do you feel about being called into the 'fellowship' or friendship which the Father enjoys with Jesus? Do you feel they would be good company?

One who gives himself in self-disclosure

God seeks an intimacy or 'fellowship' with us, that has been compared very helpfully to friendship. We all know what friends are like, though we might be hard put to it to say what makes a person a friend, or what it means to say that God is a friend. We can have different kinds of friends with whom we share in a variety of ways. With some we may share superficially, while with a few, we may share at a deep level. What is common to each however, is that we open up to them in different ways, with a certain degree of self-revelation, the basic gift of ourselves in friendship.

This is God's gift in the relationship of friendship he seeks with each of us, the gift of himself in selfdisclosure : 'God is my gift, himself he freely gave me.'

> *The Nativity of Christ*
> O dying souls, behold your living spring;
> O dazzled eyes, behold your sun of grace;
> Dull ears, attend what word this Word doth bring;
> Up, heavy hearts, with joy your joy embrace.
> From death, from dark, from deafness, from despairs,
> This life, this light, this Word, this joy repairs.
>
> Gift better than himself God doth not know;
> Gift better than his God no man can see.
> This gift doth here the giver given bestow;
> Gift to this gift let each receiver be.
> God is my gift, himself he freely gave me;
> God's gift am I, and none but God shall have me.
> (Robert Southwell)

By taking the initiative and revealing himself, God invites us to do the same with him, to return his gift in kind. This mutual sharing of ourselves, forms the foundation of our friendship. The following words of Jesus are often seen as referring to our side of the relationship exclusively. In fact, they refer first of all to the need we have to be loved. It is only when we have fulfilled this half of the commandment that we will have the energy to return this love in kind.

> You shall love the Lord your God with all your heart and
> with all your soul and with all your strength and with all
> your mind and your neighbour as yourself. (Lk 10:27)

The initiative that God takes, when he loves us with all his being,
is symbolised by what the father says to the elder brother in the
parable of the prodigal son.

> You are always with me and all that is mine is yours.
> (Lk 15:31)

> Wisdom's ultimate beauty
> Goes beyond giving all she has
> And makes known her inmost self
> In revelation's gift of self.
> But the depth of this mystery
> Is that the self She reveals
> Is love unto death for wayward me
> That I might ever lovelier be.

When the New Covenant is announced in Jeremiah the words
used to express it are: 'They shall all know me, the least no less
than the greatest.' The word *know* can mislead us into thinking
that the effort to know God is mainly ours. In fact, it is God who
takes the initiative in knowing and loving us, so that we may be
able to know and love him in return.

> In this the love of God was made manifest among us, that
> God sent his only Son into the world, so that we might live
> through him. In this is love, not that we loved God but that
> he loved us and sent his Son to be the expiation for our sins.
> (1 Jn 4:9-10)

> We love, because he first loved us. (1 Jn 4:19)

Jesus says that the friendship he is inviting us into consists in our
coming to know the Father as he does. This is what was foretold
by Jeremiah when he said that the new covenant would be based
on God making himself known to the least no less than the greatest. (Jer 31:34)

> I have called you friends, for all that I have heard from my
> Father I have made known to you. (Jn 15:15)

It is only through Jesus that God's self-revelation, on which our
friendship with God depends, becomes possible.

THE NINTH FACE OF GOD   283

I am the way, the truth and the life; no one comes to the Father except through me. (Jn 14:6)

Coming to See the King

There were three people who wanted to see the king but were told that the only way this was possible was through the influence of the king's son. However, he was also quite difficult to see. If they were really determined however, they would be prepared to take the time to meet and come to know the son, for that was the surest way to get to see the king.

The first of the three people was too busy to take the time it needed to come to know the son. The second took the time to see the son once or twice but never really got to know him. It was only the third that was determined enough to make the time available to come to know the son and so he was the only one who saw the king.

Revealing himself in Jesus

Jesus invites each of us to come to know him, he says, 'Come and see' Jn 1:39, and assures us that in 'seeing' him we see the Father. It is important to remember that the words 'know' and 'see' used here have all the rich meaning they had in the Old Testament. There they were used to describe a whole new relationship into which God was leading his people.

> Philip said to him, 'Lord, show us the Father, and we will be satisfied.' Jesus said to him, 'Have I been with you so long, and yet you do not know me, Philip?' He who has seen me has seen the Father .(Jn 14:8-9)

It is the Spirit who leads us into an interior knowledge of the love of the Father or the 'truth' which Jesus makes visible.

The meaning of the word 'truth' here is very different from what it normally calls up for us. Jesus uses it to mean the revelation of the Father, the love he is, that is disclosed in human terms by himself. It is into this revelation of God's love that the Spirit gradually guides us.

> When the Spirit of truth comes, he will guide you into all the truth; for he will not speak on his own authority, but what-

ever he hears he will speak, and he will declare to you the things that are to come. He will glorify me, for he will take what is mine and declare it to you. All that the Father has is mine; therefore, I said that he will take what is mine and declare it to you. (Jn 16:13-15)

This interior knowledge of the Father's love which the Spirit leads us into makes it possible for our friendship with God to be at least as good as that which we enjoy with the best of our friends.

It would be interesting and instructive for each of us to list some of the things that friends mean to us, in the way that Elizabeth Browning does, in the poem on page 245. We could then test whether God is at least as good as the best friend we have. If he is not, then this may clarify for us what a poor impression we have of God as our friend.

Summary

Our friendship with God is based on a mutual sharing that is initiated by his self-revelation. Coming to know this revelation is possible only through coming to know Jesus in the intimate way which the Spirit makes available to us.

Questions for reflection

1) What is the basis of the friendship God invites us into? What is distinctive about friendship, compared to other ways of relating with God?
2) What role do Jesus and the Spirit have in revealing this Face of God to us? Have our friends a role?

FEATURE 4

One who delights in us as a friend does

The reality of Jesus calling us to be friends in Jn 15:15, combined with the fact that he makes the Father visible, has given Christians the courage to accept that God wants to be our friend. St Thomas Aquinas gave this aspect of God a central place in his theology, and to help us understand it he presents us with three elements of friendship. These he took from a larger number that the Greek philosopher, Aristotle, had worked out.

The first element is that God takes the initiative in revealing himself as love and ourselves as lovable in his eyes.

> ...and (you) have loved them even as you have loved me. (Jn 17:23)

The second is that God wants us to respond to this gift of himself with a corresponding gift of ourselves to him.

> We love, because he first loved us. (1 Jn 4:19)

The third consists in maintaining the mutual sharing of friendship by meeting regularly to speak 'face to face.'

> The Lord used to speak to Moses face to face, as a man speaks to his friend. (Ex 33:11)

Being loved and lovable

We see the first of these elements in the face of God that gazes on us lovingly. Where there was a passion in the gaze of God as Lover and Lord, here there is a peace and a depth in his gaze. This is beautifully portrayed in the Rublev Icon. There, the gaze of the Trinity is one of contentment with what they see in each other, and in us. They speak to us from the Icon with the 'still small voice of calm.'

> Breathe through the beats of our desire
> The coolness of thy balm;
> Let sense be dumb, let flesh retire;
> Speak through the earthquake, wind and fire,
> O still, small voice of calm.
> (Whittier)

In this picture of the Trinity, sitting at table, there is a place left for each of us to join the 'circle of God's love in Christ Jesus.' (Eph 2:13) We are encircled by the utter conviction of our lovableness.

> You shall be called by a new name which the mouth of the Lord will give. You shall be a crown of beauty in the hand of the Lord, and a royal diadem in the hand of your God. You shall no longer be termed Forsaken, and your land shall be no more termed Desolate; but you shall be called My Delight Is In Her, for the Lord delights in you. (Is 62: 2-5)

God will be always trying to educate us to the reality that he 'is the one who has made us so lovely' (Ezek 16:14) and that our own efforts to distinguish ourselves come to nothing compared to this. We are all like the apple tree in the following story, in that we find it hard to penetrate the apparent ordinariness and drabness of ourselves, to accept the way that God delights in us, just as we are.

Being True To Our Roots

Two trees grew alongside each other. The younger of these, an apple tree, was always complaining to its neighbour, a venerable old pear tree. Its main complaint was that it always wanted to be other than it was. The pear tree's answer to this centred around the belief that we are happiest in getting in touch with our deepest dream, with our roots. Living that out to the full was the secret of life.

The apple tree, living in another world from all of this, was not very taken by the answer. With time, however, it began to feel more and more that there was a certain wisdom in what the pear tree said. A lot of our unhappiness could very well be in trying to be other than we are, and in not appreciating the inner eventfulness of our lives.

Unless we get in touch with the inner eventfulness of our lives, the wonder of our being, we can easily be overcome by a sense of our insignificance. We can thus miss the delight God finds in every area of our lives, filling them with the wonder of his love, and our lovableness in his eyes. Because we now live in Christ, the words spoken to Jesus at his baptism are now said to us:

You are my Son, the Beloved: with you I am well pleased. (Mt 3:17)

Here is my servant whom I uphold, my chosen in whom my soul delights; I have put my spirit upon him; he will bring forth justice to the nations. (Is 42:1)

But by the grace of God I am what I am, and his grace toward me was not in vain. (1 Cor 15:10)

So great was your love that you sent your Son as our redeemer. You sent him as one like ourselves, though free from sin, that you might see and love in us what you see and love in Christ. (Preface of the Mass)

Summary

God appreciates all the good in us and welcomes us to the love which he has for his Beloved Son in whom he delights. He 'sees and loves in us what he sees and loves in Christ.'

Questions for reflection

1) Think of a number of things that God would really appreciate in your life. As you let God say these to you, what way do you welcome what is said and how do you find yourself resisting it?
2) What does the illustration about the apple tree say to you in the light of 1 Cor 15:10?

FEATURE 5

One who accepts our weakness as a friend does

There is also in this face of God a very gentle acceptance of what is wayward in us. This challenges us, more than anything can, to have the courage to 'change our minds and hearts and to believe the Good News.'

> Faith is the courage to accept acceptance (Van Breeman)

This courage is fed by the reassurance that God does not change his attitude towards us. He remains gracious, compassionate and steadfast like the father of the prodigal son.

> The Lord is gracious and merciful,
> slow to anger and abounding in steadfast love.
> The Lord is good to all,
> and his compassion is over all that he has made.
> (Ps 145:8-9)

God is at least as accepting of us as the friends we have met during our lives.

> A friend is one to whom one may pour out all the contents of one's heart, chaff and grain together, knowing that the gentlest of hands will take and sift it, keep what is worth keeping and with a breath of kindness blow the rest away.
> (Arabian Proverb)

> Who is a God like you, pardoning iniquity and passing over the transgression of the remnant of your possession? He does not retain his anger forever, because he delights in showing clemency. (Mic 7:18)

There is always the assumption, based on hard human experience, that our waywardness means that God distances himself from us. He assures us that this is not so, and tries to allay the fear that this illusion causes.

> I have chosen you, not rejected you, do not be afraid for I am with you; stop being anxious and watchful for I am your God. For I Yahweh your God, I am holding you by the right hand ... (Is 41:8-14)

290

NINE FACES OF GOD

God not only wants to allay our fear as sinners in his presence. He also wants us to believe that he finds joy in being with the prodigal son in each of us.

> I tell you there will be more joy in heaven over one sinner who repents than over ninety nine good people who have no need of repentance. (Lk 15:7)

> ... And when she has found it, she calls together her friends and neighbours, saying, 'Rejoice with me, for I have found the coin which I had lost.' Just so, I tell you, there is joy before the angels of God over one sinner who repents. (Lk 15:9-10)

> But while he was yet at a distance, his father saw him and had compassion, and ran and embraced him and kissed him ... let us eat and make merry, for this my son was dead; and is alive again. (Lk 15:20-24)

Jesus is the love of the Father in human terms, yet, with all the 'weakness' of being human. As such he can 'sympathise with our weaknesses as one who has been tempted in every respect as we are.' He also 'can deal gently with the ignorant and wayward, since he himself is beset by weakness.'

> For because he himself has suffered and been tempted, he is able to help those who are tempted. (Heb 2:18)

> For we have not a high priest who is unable to sympathise with our weaknesses, but one who in every respect has been tempted as we are, yet without sin. Let us then with confidence draw near to the throne of grace, that we may receive mercy and find grace to help in time of need. For every high priest chosen from among us is appointed to act on behalf of us in relation to God, to offer gifts and sacrifices for sins. He can deal gently with the ignorant and wayward, since he himself is beset with weakness. (Heb 4:15-5,3)

As we saw in the Main Symbol for the First Face, God is like the master craftsman who can make a feature of our mistakes in the tapestry he is weaving in our lives.

> We know that all things work together for good for those who love God, who are called according to his purpose. For those whom he foreknew he also predestined to be con-

formed to the image of his Son, in order that he might be the firstborn within a large family. (Rom 8:28-29)

The 'good' that God is working is that he wants us to discover, in our weakness and infidelity, the extent of his power and of his faithful love. Though we may appear loveless in our own eyes, in the light of his faithful love we become lovely.

Fidelity
Fresh fall of snow, soon blotched
And turning to a world of slush.
Creeping tepidity makes inroads
On first fervour.

Through it is worked
Spring and fresh call,
Of the Other's fidelity
In our lack of it.

Depth of disloyalty
May discover another
Loving us to the end
And making the loveless lovely.

Three times I appealed to the Lord about this, that it would leave me, but he said to me, 'My grace is sufficient for you, for power is made perfect in weakness.' So I will boast all the more gladly of my weaknesses, so that the power of Christ may dwell in me. Therefore I am content with weaknesses, insults, hardships, persecutions and calamities for the sake of Christ; for whenever I am weak, then I am strong.
(2 Cor 12:8-10)

Summary

We are invited by God as our friend to accept his acceptance of our weakness and waywardness, the prodigal in each of us.

Questions for reflection

1) What words of scripture most help you to accept God's acceptance of you?
2) What is it about this feature that appeals to you?
3) As you contemplate this feature, do you notice any resistance in yourself to it?

One who, as a friend, wants the very best for us

> The best is yet to be,
> The last of life, for which the first was made;
> Our times are in His hand
> Who saith, 'A whole I planned, Youth shows but half;
> trust God: see all,
> Nor be afraid!
> (Robert Browning)

God deals with us 'face to face as with a friend.' (Ex 33:11) He not only rejoices in what we are but is intent on what we may be. He plans our welfare, the fullness of all good things he has destined for us, a future full of hope' (Jer 29:11).

This 'future full of hope' is realised in what Paul describes in his letter to the Ephesians as 'being filled with all the fullness of God.'

> For this reason I bow my knees before the Father ... that according to the riches of his glory he may grant you to be strengthened with might through his Spirit in the inner man, and that Christ may dwell in your hearts through faith; that you, being rooted and grounded in love, may have power to comprehend with all the saints what is the breadth and length and height and depth, and to know the love of Christ which surpasses knowledge, that you may be filled with all the fullness of God. (Eph 3:14-19)

God has a deep desire to quicken the dream within our languid minds.

> Softer than dew. But where the morning wind
> Blows down the world, O Spirit! show Thy Power:
> Quicken the dreams within the languid mind
> And bring Thy seed to flower.
> (E Underhill)

> And now I am about to go the way of all the earth, and you know in your hearts and souls, all of you, that not one thing has failed of all the good things that the Lord your God

promised concerning you; all have come to pass for you, not one of them has failed. (Jos 23:14)

In pursuing what is best for others, our energy is often drained by their lack of response. When others persistently fail to respond to our best efforts on their behalf, we tend to give up on them, to leave them to their own devices. God, we are assured, will seek with his steadfast love to 'bring his seed to flower.' He never cuts us off from his abundance, from 'the river of his delights.'

Your steadfast love, O Lord, extends to the heavens,
your faithfulness to the clouds.
Your goodness is like the mountains of God,
your judgments are like the great deep.
How precious is your steadfast love, O God!
The children of men take refuge
in the shadow of your wings.
They feast on the abundance of your house,
and you give them drink from the river of your
delights.
Yours is the fountain of life;
in your light do we see light. (Ps 36:5-9)

Let those who desire my vindication shout for joy and be glad and say evermore, 'Great is the Lord who delights in the welfare of his servant.' (Ps 35:27)

You might read again the piece on the diamond on page 148.

Summary

God plans our peace, that we should share in the fullness of life which he enjoys. He never gives up in his efforts to realise all the potential there is in us.

Questions for reflection

1) What would you include within the 'fullness of life' or happiness which God wants for you?
2) Do you find it hard to believe that God could be so intent on your happiness?
3) Have the words of Joshua a ring of truth for you?

One who wants our friendship

When someone really affirms us, it is a very moving experience. We feel we need to respond from the depths that have been touched in us. Being known and loved so intimately, so wholly and so deeply by God, calls out of us a need to know and love him in return. Our relationship tends to become a mutual knowing and loving.

> I know my own and my own know me as the Father knows me and I know the Father. (Jn 10:14-15)

In our response of knowing God, there is much more involved than an abstract knowledge, for it is much more like coming to know somebody in an intimate relationship. It means listening to him and responding to his revelation and gift of himself with a corresponding gift of ourselves. This is the heart of friendship, a gift of self in self-disclosure on both sides and a sharing in the happiness that this brings.

On his side, God sends Jesus who reveals to us 'everything he has heard from his Father' and in that way shares with us the happiness they enjoy.

> Greater love has no man than this, that a man lay down his life for his friends. You are my friends if you do what I command you. No longer do I call you servants, for the servant does not know what his master is doing; but I have called you friends, for all that I have heard from my Father I have made known to you. (Jn 15:13-15)

> I have told you these things that you might share my joy and that your happiness may be complete. (Jn 15:11)

The only adequate response to this is one made with all that is within us. Responding wholeheartedly with the gift of ourselves can appear very demanding, especially if we feel that God requires everything now.

> You shall love the Lord your God with all your heart and with all your soul and with all your strength and with all your mind and your neighbour as yourself. (Lk 10:27)

In fact, God is never demanding, even though he is always challenging us to take the step we are ready for, in the friendship to which he is always calling us.

When we are affirmed by God, and we gradually learn to believe that he really does like what he sees in us, there is a spontaneous desire to make our whole heart available to him.

> *I Have a Room, My Heart*
> Dear Lord, I'll fetch Thee hence, I have a room
> 'Tis poor, but 'tis my best if Thou wilt come
> Within so small a cell, where I would fain
> Mine and the world's Redeemer entertain,
> I mean my heart.
> (Anonymous)

What we have seen so far is that God reveals all that he has and is through Jesus and their Spirit. We are thereby invited to make our own of this revelation, to 'keep his commandments' (his word), and respond to it with our whole heart.

> As the Father has loved me, so have I loved you, abide in my love. If you keep my commandments, you will abide in my love, just as I keep my Father's commandments and abide in his love. These things I have spoken to you that my joy may be in you, and that your joy may be full. (Jn 15:8-11)

> My spirit cleaves to you
> and you hold me close to you. (Ps 63:9)

Summary

Friendship is a mutual gift. Being known and loved by God calls out of us the desire to know and love him in return. God's gift of himself in self-disclosure calls for our revelation of ourselves to him, by responding honestly to what he has revealed.

Questions for reflection

1) When it comes to the gift of yourself to God, do you hear a demand or an invitation? Is God pleased with the way you respond to him just now?
2) How essential is your response to the friendship with God to which you are called? Does it reveal something significant about God that he is interested in how you feel?

One who knows the value of genuine communication

> *Visitation*
> Love calls many times each day
> but finds me preoccupied,
> not able to make the time
> to be at home for her.
>
> I let the signs of her visitation
> Come and go unnoticed:
> And am not nourished
> by a love that is not recognised or named.
>
> So I continue to live in a world
> That deadens with its indifference:
> Alas, that I cannot be here when you call
> And have time to be at home together.

Making our own of the self-revelation of God, and responding to it, requires that we meet regularly to listen and talk with him. Without our listening, God's effort to reveal himself is frustrated, and without our speaking honestly to him in reply there is no sharing of ourselves with him. This 'combat of dialogue', symbolised by Jacob wrestling with God and thereby coming to see him face to face, is the price of friendship.

Like any relationship, our friendship with God will be as good as the quality of our conversation or sharing. Without this communication, the new covenant, in which we gradually come to 'know' God by listening to his word and responding to it, cannot develop. This is the price of the intimacy he offers us.

All this is expressed beautifully in a brief incident recorded in Luke's Gospel. In it Jesus says in effect that our intimacy with him is dependent on our ability to listen and respond adequately to his revelation of himself to us in his Word.

> Then his mother and his brothers came to him, but they could not reach him for the crowd. And he was told, 'Your mother and your brothers are standing outside, desiring to

see you.' But he said to them, 'My mother and my brothers are those who hear the word of God and do it.' (Lk 8:19-21)

The Gate of Heaven

There is a symbol in the book of Genesis of this dialogue with God which we call prayer. It is the ladder in Jacob's dream, stretching between heaven and earth. It represents God descending to us in his self-revelation and our ascent to him in response to this.

> ... he dreamed that there was a ladder set up on the earth, and the top of it reached to heaven; and behold, the angels of God were ascending and descending on it ... And he was afraid and said, 'How awesome is this place! This is none other than the house of God, and this is the gate of heaven. (Gen 28:12-17)

The only way we can come to know God, and be united with him in friendship, is through an on-going revelation of ourselves to him in the way he reveals himself to us. There is no doubt about God's desire for this kind of intense intimacy.

> I will betroth you to me in faithfulness and you shall know the Lord. (Hos 2:20)

> Behold, I stand at the door and knock; if any one hears my voice and opens the door, I will come in to him and eat, and he with me. (Rev 3:20)

In spite of our unworthiness, God bids us welcome to the banquet of his own company.

> Love bade me welcome; yet my soul drew back,
> Guiltie of dust and sinne.
> But quickey'd Love, observing me grow slack
> From my first entrance in,
> Drew nearer to me, sweetly questioning,
> If I lack'd any thing.

> A guest I answer'd, worthy to be here:
> Love said, you shall be he.
> I the unkinde, ungrateful? Ah my deare,
> I cannot look on thee.
> Love took my hand, and smiling did reply,
> Who made the eye but I?

Truth Lord, but I have marr'd them: let my shame
Go where it doth deserve.
And know you not, sayes Love, who bore the blame?
My deare, then I will serve.
You must sit down, says Love, and taste my meat;
So I did sit and eat.
(George Herbert)

This dialogue with God stretches us to our limits and it can be compared with Jacob's wrestling with God. At the end of his struggle however it says that he knew God, that he had 'seen him face to face.'

> And Jacob was left alone; and a man wrestled with him to the breaking of day ... Then Jacob asked him, 'Tell me your name.' But he answered, 'Why do you want to know my name?' Then he blessed Jacob who then said, 'I have seen God face to face and I am still alive.' So Jacob called the name of the place Peniel (i.e. The face of God), saying, 'I have seen God face to face.' (Gen 32:22-30)

Summary

Friendship with God involves an on-going dialogue in which we listen and respond honestly to what he reveals of himself. The quality of this communication will be a measure of our friendship. We have to wrestle, like Jacob did, with our weakness and infidelity, if we are to accept God's invitation to the banquet of intimacy with him.

Questions for reflection

1) Why is on-going dialogue so important in coming to see this Face of God?
2) Why is Jacob such a significant symbol of this element of friendship?
3) What does the poem Love Bade Me Welcome convey to you about God? Do you find yourself resisting what it says to you?

Endpiece

There is in friendship something of all relations,
and something above them all.
It is the golden thread
that ties the heart of all the world.
(John Evelyn)

This friendship of God, which emerges as we speak to him face to face, involves the growth of our experience of all the other faces. We see the life-giving God in the way he accepts and affirms us as friends. The life God gives is sustained by the affection of God, who has been, is and will always be working to bring his plans for us to full flower. There is no more personal way of doing this than in the way he speaks with us face to face as with a friend. It is in God's conversation too that we best come to the interior knowledge of his love and of the depth of his fidelity to us. It is in listening to his word and responding to it that we experience God's happiness, and the attractiveness through which he gradually wins our hearts and becomes our Lord.

The Divine Idea

Neglecting our gift
There is a term in the Enneagram called the Divine Idea, which is very relevant to what we have been contemplating in this book. Not much has been written on the Divine Idea so my reflections on it are very much my own. I am putting the material about it in this appendix as it may be of interest only to those who are familiar with the Enneagram and who would like to gain a greater understanding of one of its main aspects.

When we do the initial course in the Enneagram, most of our time is spent trying to find out our personality type. This is done through identifying our negative traits, our false images of self and the vices and compulsive behaviour that follow from these. This concentration on the negative aspects of our personality does not allow time to get to know much about what the Divine Ideas of the Enneagram can reveal to us.

The gift we are all invited to discover and to take possession of is the good News of God's love and providence. This Good News comes across to each of the nine types in the Enneagram in very different ways. Therefore, it is important for each of us to discover how we best take in this love of God, because how much of this love we believe in will determine the quality of our life and happiness.

To discover more about our gift we will begin by looking at how the Divine Ideas of the Enneagram have their source in the fact that we are each made in the image of God.

In the image of God
The Enneagram builds on the belief that there are nine aspects of God. I have called these the Nine Faces of God. Working on the belief that God is love, these Nine Faces reflect back to those who contemplate them the nine kinds of love we have examined in this book.

THE DIVINE IDEA   301

Now, since we are made in the likeness of God, each of us is made in the image of one of these Nine Faces. The basis of this likeness to God is the capacity we have for love, to receive as well as to give it. Being made in the image of God means that we each have a facility to be loved and to be loving in one of nine very distinct ways. In other words each of the nine types of people in the Enneagram have a distinct style of being loved and of loving.

It is through the Divine Ideas that we are able to find out what kind of love we have a facility to take in, the kind of love that we warm to. So, for example, if I am made in the image of the fourth Face of God, it means that I warm to being loved in a very personal way.

The creative power of the Divine Idea
The importance of the Divine Idea rests with:
1) the way it can reveal the kind of love we best respond to, and
2) the power of this love to create a true image of ourselves that can make and sustain us.

The Divine Idea reveals to us the kind of love that is most effective in making and sustaining us. It also helps us to discover the true image that this kind of love forms in us. There is an important connection here between the way we are loved and the image we form ourselves. This image is mediated to us through people like our parents. They reveal to us what we mean to them and thus gradually create an image of who we are for them. We see who we are, reflected back to us by our parents and other people who have had an important influence on our lives. We see ourselves and who we are in others' eyes.

The Divine Idea then, is an aspect of God's love that we warm to and that creates in us a true image of who we are in the eyes of God, the most significant person in our life.

Exploring our Divine Idea
As we contemplate these Nine Faces of God, we must learn to trust that God will reveal to us the kinds of love he especially wants us to take in and the image of ourselves which he wants us to accept. This does not mean that God wants to limit us to contemplating one of these Faces. It does mean that there are kinds of love that we are now ripe to receive, because of the kind of person we are and because of the present circumstances of our lives.

1) The first Divine Idea is Holy Perfection. The kind of love involved in this Divine Idea is one that wants us to be perfect in the sense of being whole or fully alive. This love, however, settles for the stage of growth we have already achieved. The love that the Ones warm to focuses more on what is already accomplished or perfect than on what is yet to be, or is imperfect. This kind of love is seen in the eyes of those who accept our limitations and appreciate all the potential we have already realised. This generates in Ones a true image of themselves as accepted and affirmed in a very life-giving way.

2) The Second Divine Idea is Holy Freedom. The kind of love involved in this Divine Idea is one that is a gift, a Grace, and has no strings attached. The kind of love that Twos warm to is seen in the eyes of those who love us with an affection such as we receive from parents or within our family. It has an unconditional quality that has not got to be earned. It creates a true image in the Twos of being loved for who they are, rather than for what they do.

3) The third Divine Idea is Holy Hope. The kind of love involved in this Divine Idea is one that gets us out on the road to the promised land and sustains us on our journey there. It is a love that is provident in that it has a plan for our 'peace' or fulfilment that is symbolised by the promised land. It goes to great rounds to bring this plan to full flower. The love that the Threes warm to is a very practical, concrete love like that of the Good Samaritan, and is expressed more in deeds than in words. Being loved in this way creates a true image in Threes of people who are loved and cared for in a very provident, all pervasive and practical way.

4) The fourth Divine Idea is Holy Originality. The kind of love involved in this Divine Idea is a very personal love. This is a response to the unique quality in themselves that Fours are very conscious of. The kind of love Fours warm to treats us in a personal way, calls us by name, and respects the unique road our life follows. It is a very sensitive love with a great range of feeling that identifies with anything we experience. This love, which a Four warms to, creates a true image of one who is special, chosen out from the crowd and called by name.

5) The fifth Divine Idea is Holy Wisdom. The kind of love involved in this Divine Idea is one that is filled with a sense of won-

der at the mystery of the simplest thing. The kind of love Fives warm to is the intimate knowledge that is born of loving another and of being deeply and wholly loved. It is experienced from those who respect the mystery that is each of us. We taste it in knowing and loving others and when they disclose themselves as love for us. This is an extraordinarily intimate knowledge which only God can give us in any full way. This love, which a Five warms to, creates a true image of one who is worthwhile knowing and loving deeply.

6) The sixth Divine Idea is Holy Faith. The kind of love involved in this Divine Idea is one that is anchored in the deep conviction of faith. This means becoming anchored in our belief in a love that never leaves us no matter how deviant we may become. The kind of love Sixes identify with is faithful, warm and devoted – it is a love that trusts in the convictions of faith and God's guidance. This love, which a Six warms to, creates a true image that is very positive and secure because it rests on the conviction of faith. It is an image of one loved faithfully no matter how deviant.

7) The seventh Divine Idea is Holy Work. The kind of love involved in this Divine Idea is one that is happy and wants to make others happy too. This happiness, Sevens have learned, is attained bit by bit and through hard work. The kind of love Sevens warm to is cheerful, optimistic and finds good in all. Their true image is of themselves as happy and as making others happy, not only in an emotional way, but as a result of the hard-won conviction of faith that they are loved. They see their happiness resting on convictions that they are willing to foster in a disciplined way.

8) The eighth Divine Idea is Holy Truth. The kind of love involved in this Divine Idea is one that seeks the truth and seeks justice too in living consistently with the truth. The kind of love Eights warm to is wholehearted, passionate and challenging. Their true image of themselves is of people who are loved and who love with intensity and energy. They see themselves as people who seek truth and justice in a generative way.

9) The ninth Divine Idea is Holy Love. The kind of love involved in this Divine Idea is that of friendship. A friend keeps in touch with our essential lovableness, when we tend to get preoccupied with the dark side of ourselves and with our poor self-image. Holy Love is poured into our hearts by the Spirit, (Rom 5:5) but

this gift has to be discovered and owned. Nines warm to the love of friends who put them in touch with their essential goodness. Being taught to listen to their essential worth in this way gives them energy to become active lovers. Nines develop a true image from this of their being essentially loved and lovable. They find themselves energised by discovering that they are essentially lovable people and respond by becoming loving in very active and practical ways.

The false image
If we remain unaware of our Divine Idea, and of the power of the love which it manifests to make and sustain us, we can easily slip into creating a false image or vision of what makes us worthwhile or significant.

We create this false image, because feeling insignificant is so essentially painful for us. In order to escape this pain we try to earn our worth by the misuse of our gift. Then what is meant to be a facility for receiving Grace or love is used primarily to make something of ourselves. According to the type we are in the Enneagram, we make a statement like the following about what we identify with: 'I am worthwhile if I am successful.'

The illusion of our insignificance is compounded by the added illusion that we can earn our worth. What worth we can earn for ourselves is very fragile and we experience a lot of negative feelings when people question our self-made worth in any way. These negative feelings feed the growth of the illusion of our poor self-image and this in turn causes the ultimate illusion of unbelief. Our poor self-image limits and even blocks the Good News of our worthwhileness in the eyes of the significant people in our lives.

If we put so much of our energy into creating this false image of ourselves, we will have little left over for the more important things of life. We will be so wrapped up in the concerns of our ego world that we will have little time or energy left over for the three great journeys of life. These are: to our inmost selves, to an intimate relationship with God and with others. We get cut off from what is essentially life-giving i.e. the care that makes and sustains us. Our life as a result becomes impoverished and dehumanised.

Repent and believe

The purpose of coming to know our false image, and the vices and compulsions it brings with it, is to become free to develop our gift, expressed in the Divine Idea. Seen in this way, the Enneagram is a very basic help to answering the essential call of Christ to repent and believe the good news. The discovery of our false image helps to pinpoint what areas in our life are most in need of repentance. The Divine Idea helps to clarify the style of being loved that we are particularly good at, how we best take in the good news.

WHAT YOU NEED FOR YOUR JOURNEY

This brief outline of what you need for your journey of faith will help as a reference for you as you begin to contemplate the Faces of God. More detailed background on each of the requirements is to be found in Chapter 4.

Making space for God
Always start by quietening yourself and then become aware of God's presence.

Exploring our own experience
The Key Experience which you find at the beginning of each Face is meant to help you to arouse areas of your experience that may lie dormant. This will make what you contemplate in each Face more tangible and real.

Take the time you need to make your own of the Key Experience, the ways you resist this and what is suggested to you in the exercises. Carry with you what you find helpful of this experience into your contemplation of the features of each Face. Keep adding to your experience what will make each Face of God more real for you.

Universal experience: traditional wisdom
The purpose of the Main Symbol, and of all the other symbolic material like stories and poems throughout these Faces, is to broaden out your own personal experience and get you more involved in it.

Read the story of the Main Symbol a few times in the light of the experience which you have so far surfaced. Ponder what it has to say to this experience. The story may take time to surrender its meaning, especially until you develop a facility for using stories to speak to your own experience.

Bible experience
What we have seen so far is an outline sketch of the Face of God which we are contemplating. We have now to fill in, one by one, each of the main features of this Face. The main place where God will reveal each of these features to you is in God's word. In order to bring what he reveals to life, it is vital that you contemplate it

against the background of all the experience you have so far accumulated.

Read a passage of scripture in the light of the feature you are contemplating. Beware of the tendency to get side-tracked from the feature that is meant to be the focus of your attention. Pause when some word or phrase of scripture says something to you about this feature. Ponder this word or phrase in the light of your experience so far.

Prayer: a conversation with God
The purpose of prayer here is to absorb what God has opened up about himself and his love for you, in whatever feature of this love you are focusing on. This will involve listening to what has struck you most forcefully about God's love for you. It will also involve responding, as honestly as you can, to the love he has expressed for you.

Listen to any aspect of God's love for you that has captured your attention. Let God say this to you in some simple and personal way. After some time this will give rise to certain feelings in you. Some of these feelings will be positive, but others will signify that you have difficulty taking in what God is saying to you. Become aware of both positive and negative feelings and, after you have found words for them, share how you feel, in as frank a way as you can, with God.

Reflection on our experience
The purpose of reflection is to become aware of the fact that God reveals himself to you in prayer. It is also meant to help you to become familiar with how God goes about this, by enlightening your mind and attracting your heart.

At the end of any period of prayer, spend time becoming aware of what struck you and what you felt attracted to stay with during your prayer. Record this, however briefly. Begin your next prayer period by reading what you have written. This will give continuity and lead to a build-up of what is being revealed to you. From this, a true vision of who God is, and who you are for God, will take shape. In this way you will be answering the essential Christian call to repent and believe the Gospel. (Mk 1:15)